WHEN BOYS BECOME BOYS

When Boys Become Boys

Development, Relationships, and Masculinity

Judy Y. Chu

WITH A FOREWORD BY CAROL GILLIGAN

NEW YORK UNIVERSITY PRESS
New York and London

NEW YORK UNIVERSITY PRESS
New York and London
www.nyupress.org

© 2014 by New York University
All rights reserved

References to Internet websites (URLs) were accurate at the time of writing.
Neither the author nor New York University Press is responsible for URLs that
may have expired or changed since the manuscript was prepared.

For Library of Congress Cataloging-in-Publication data,
please contact the Library of Congress.

ISBN: 978-0-8147-6468-8 (cloth)
ISBN: 978-0-8147-6480-0 (paper)

New York University Press books are printed on acid-free paper,
and their binding materials are chosen for strength and durability.
We strive to use environmentally responsible suppliers and materials
to the greatest extent possible in publishing our books.

Manufactured in the United States of America

10 9 8 7 6 5 4 3 2 1

Also available as an ebook

For Matthew, who makes everything possible,
and Xander, who makes everything worthwhile.

CONTENTS

CAROL GILLIGAN

In the epilogue to *Thirteen Ways of Looking at a Man,* the psychoanalyst Donald Moss tells the following story. When he was in first grade, they learned a new song every week and were told that at the end of the year, they would each have a chance to lead the class in singing their favorite, which they were to keep a secret. For Moss, the choice was clear: "The only song I loved was the lullaby 'When at night I go to sleep, thirteen angels watch do keep . . .' from *Hansel and Gretel.*" Every night he would sing it to himself, and as the song said, the angels came, saving him from his night terror and enabling him to fall asleep. It "was, and would always be, the most beautiful song I had ever heard."

The first-graders had learned the song in early autumn and in late spring when Moss's turn came, he stood at the front of the class. The teacher asked what song he had chosen. Moss remembers,

> I began to tell her, "It's the lullaby . . . " But immediately, out of the corner of my eye, I saw the reaction of the boys in the front row. Their faces were lighting up in shock . . . I knew, knew in a way that was immediate, clear and certain, that what I was about to do, the song I was about to choose, the declaration that I was about to make, represented an enormous, irrevocable error . . . What the boys were teaching me was that I was to know now, and to always have known, that "When at night I go to sleep" could not be my favorite song, that a lullaby had no place here, that something else was called for. In a flash, in an act of gratitude, not to my angels but to my boys, I changed my selection. I smiled at the teacher, told her I was just kidding, told her I would now lead the class in singing the "Marines' Hymn": "From the halls of Montezuma to the shore of Tripoli . . . "[1]

Thus Moss reminds us when looking at a man to think of the boy and to ask whether around the time of first grade, he may have learned not to reveal what he originally had loved unconditionally. He writes that his book "can be thought of as an extended effort to unpack that moment in front of the class and indirectly, to apologize to the angels for my treachery." He had been "unfaithful" to them, had "renounced them in public and continued to do so for decades." The residue was a melancholia, tied to the boy's awareness that

> what he is "really" doing in that fateful turning outward is simultane-
> ously preserving and betraying his original love of angels, affirming and
> denying his new love of boys; after all, now he and the boys are joined
> together in looking elsewhere for the angels they might have all once
> had.[2]

I read the epilogue to *Thirteen Ways of Looking at a Man* just after reading the manuscript of *When Boys Become Boys*, and I had the sensation of reading the same book twice. Chu observes what Moss remembers. The "Marines' Hymn" could well be the song of the Mean Team, formed by the four- and five-year-olds whom she studied. Their faces would also have registered shock if a boy chose a lullaby as his favorite song. They too learned a lesson taught by other boys: "to know now, and to always have known, that a lullaby had no place here, that something else was called for, had always been called for, would always be called for." With the internalization of this lesson, boys become "boys."

But the very fact that the word "boys" now is in quotation marks signifies that there is something uneasy or unreal, something inauthentic, about this masculinity that rests on betrayal. The price of becoming a "boy," as Moss attests, is an awareness that one is now looking elsewhere for the angels one might have once had, along with an ambivalence that does not resolve—or in Chu's terms, an inauthenticity that cannot be shaken because in becoming a "boy," a boy knows on some level that he has been unfaithful to a part of himself.

I remember the day when Chu told me the finding that crystallized after months of pouring over her data. We were having lunch at an Indian restaurant in Harvard Square, talking about her research, when suddenly she leaned across the table and said, "In—, they're becoming more in—." Over the two years of her study, as they moved from pre-Kindergarten through Kindergarten and into first grade, the boys who had been so attentive, so articulate, so authentic and direct in their relationships with one another and with her were becoming more inattentive, more inarticulate, more inauthentic and indirect with one another and with her. It was not simply that they were learning how to be "boys," internalizing a masculinity defined in opposition to anything considered "feminine." It was that they wanted something, wanted relationships with the other boys, and for the boys she was observing this meant becoming a member of the Mean Team—"a club created by the boys, for the boys, and for the stated purpose of acting against the girls" (chapter 4). The Mean Team established a masculinity defined both in opposition to and as the opposite of a femininity associated with being "good" and "nice." Thus the main activity of the Mean Team was to "bother people."

Once human qualities are bifurcated into masculine or feminine, everyone loses. Becoming a man or becoming a woman means burying or silencing parts of oneself. A key insight Chu came to in her research lay in her recognition that the relational capacities boys learn to abjure—the empathy and sensitivity that lead them to read the human world around them so accurately and astutely—are essential if they are to realize the closeness they seek with other boys. Yet in blunting or shielding their emotional sensitivity in order to be one of the boys, they render that closeness unattainable.

In a passage that resonates strongly with Moss's reflections, Chu writes,

> there was an unavoidable sense of loss as these boys—in their efforts to gain approval from the other boys and to protect themselves against rejection—became more guarded and selective regarding what they revealed about themselves and to whom. (Conclusion)

She goes on to give a precise and riveting description of what was lost and how and why:

> Whereas these boys had demonstrated a remarkable ability to be fully present and genuinely engaged in their relationships, they began to

nuance their behaviors and modify their styles of relating in ways that could feel contrived and made their relational capacities more difficult to detect. Although the boys were capable of being open and forthcoming in expressing their thoughts and opinions, they began to shield the qualities that had marked their full presence and genuine engagement in relationships. And as these boys became savvy about how they expressed themselves and strategic about how they related to others, their posturing and pretense gradually detracted from and overshadowed their presence, such that they began to appear disengaged, disinterested, or even defensive in their interactions. That is, they began to look more like stereotypical "boys," or how boys are often said to be. (Conclusion)

The cardinal discovery of Chu's research and the importance of this book lie in the demonstration that the relational insensitivity often associated with boys and men is not in fact part of their nature. It is the consequence of a renunciation they made in a desire to become one of the boys and the mark of a world in which the willingness to betray love is a proof of masculinity. Think of Abraham and Isaac, Agamemnon and Iphigenia, honor killings, fathers sending their sons to war.

Chu opens this book by writing about her son and the dilemma she and her husband faced in thinking about where to send him to school. A similar quandary came up when she and I met with the fathers of the boys in the study. At one of the meetings, I asked the fathers what they saw in their boys that led them to think "I hope he never loses that." They spoke of their sons' emotional openness, their "out-there quality," their "spunk," and their "real joy," the "delight he has in his friends"— qualities the fathers felt they had lost or muted on the road to manhood. Would their sons have to follow a similar path? The quandary was how to protect the vulnerability they saw without coming down hard on the openness they cherished. All of the fathers knew "the voice," the "Dad voice" as they described it. They knew how to do it: "lower your voice, speak loud . . . Clearly and loud. Forceful." They felt bad when they heard themselves using this voice with their sons, "ordering them around." They felt they had betrayed their love.[3]

Reading Moss's reflections on the moment in first grade when he betrayed his angels, I was struck by his awareness that in spite of his treachery, the angels "are still there." Like the honest voices girls silence in their desire to be loved and included, the relational capacities of boys are not lost. As sixteen-year-old Tanya, a participant in a study of girls' development, reflects: "the voice that stands up for what I believe in is buried deep inside me,"[4] so Chu observes: boys shelter their emotional sensitivity within themselves.

In *Deep Secrets: Boys' Friendships and the Crisis of Connection,* Niobe Way describes the reawakening in adolescence of boys' desire for intimacy and emotional closeness. They seek friendships in which they can share deep secrets, and their trust in their friends whom they know so deeply is not riddled by fears of betrayal. Their exuberance is unmistakable as they speak of their love for their best friends and their joy in their friendships. They know the value of these relationships. As George, a high school junior, explains, without a best friend to tell your secrets to, you would "go whacko."[5]

Yet in what amounts to a recapitulation of the process Chu witnessed, by the end of high school, most of the boys in Way's studies no longer had a best friend or shared their deep secrets. They had learned "how to be a man" in a world where being a man meant being emotionally stoic and independent. The very same boys who had spoken so openly about their love for their best friends now hedged any depiction of emotional intimacy with other boys with the phrase "no homo." As Way observes, relational capacities had taken on a gender (girly) and a sexuality (gay).

Like Way, Chu prompts us to listen more closely to the boys in our midst and to ask what our goals are as parents or teachers of boys. She does not mention the word "patriarchy," but the gender binary and hierarchy she describes are the building blocks of patriarchal institutions and cultures where being a man means not being a woman or like a woman and also being on top.

This book could not be more timely. As a society, we are in the throes of a conversation about masculinity and relationships. Are we independent or dependent? Are we on our own or in it together? For some, the question is: Are we like men, meaning "real men," or like women, meaning needy and dependent? The answer is we are humans, and as humans we are interdependent.

Chu's research brings new evidence to Erving Goffman's depiction of "the presentation of self in everyday life," to Judith Butler's discussion of gender as "performance," to David Richards's study of "disarming manhood," and to James Gilligan's analysis of the causes and prevention of violence. It complements Niobe Way's studies of adolescent boys and answers a question I raised at the end of my project on girls' development: Do boys between the ages of four and seven experience a process of initiation comparable to the one girls face as they enter adolescence?

The demand on boys to, in Moss's words, "Bury this. Silence this." was a demand I heard girls describe at a later time, using the same vocabulary.[6] They, too, felt the need to dissociate themselves from what had been a vital part of themselves in order to have the relationships they now desired. They also felt a sense of loss that was hard to shake, given their awareness that they were now looking elsewhere for what they might have once had. Through a process of initiation that mandates dissociation, they too had come, in the words of Anne Frank, to "have, as it were, a dual personality."[7]

In concluding this book, Chu addresses this split in the boys she studied, noting that

> the image of masculinity that boys learn to project also misrepresents boys because, despite learning to conceal qualities and behaviors that are deemed feminine, the boys did not necessarily lose these qualities (as popular discourse on boys suggests); nor did they feel less inclined towards these behaviors. Rather, boys' socialization towards cultural constructions of masculinity that are defined in opposition to femininity seems mainly to force a split between what boys know (e.g., about themselves, their relationships, and their world) and what boys show. (Conclusion)

An overriding contribution of Chu's research is that it allows us to see masculinity as the lynch-pin holding in place a process of initiation that begins with young boys and creates the splits that girls will internalize at adolescence, when the division between good and bad girls sets in. The effect of this initiation, which forces the internalization of gender binaries and hierarchies, is to naturalize patriarchy by leading it to appear not as imposed but as written into the psyche. By showing that at a very young age boys resist sacrificing their humanity, Chu reveals the capacity for resistance that is in fact built into our psyche.

It would be naïve to think that this resistance is not met with force. We can see this playing out in our politics, where efforts to effect a more complete realization of democratic ideals and values that rest on a premise of equality are met with attempts to reinforce hierarchies: men over women, masculine over feminine, "real men" over sissies and gays. It is not simply a question of competing visions and values. It is also a question of undoing dissociation. Moss adds a crucial piece to our understanding when he observes, almost in passing, that the lesson he learned from the other boys was that he was *to know now, and to always have known* what within himself he knew not to be true. The lullaby was his favorite, "was and would always be." Thus a falsification sets in and history is rewritten so that, at least on the surface, no gap appears between how things are and how they are said to be. Once internalized, the gender binary and hierarchy become something we know and always have known, seemingly part of our nature, rather than something imposed that leads us to conceal what we know, from others and also perhaps from ourselves.

Chu takes us to the place where all this begins. Her discoveries prompt us to ask the most immediate question: Can we avert these problems before they set in? What if boys, rather than becoming "boys," can be and become themselves? In a world grown increasingly interdependent, the future may hang on our ability to be attentive, articulate, authentic, and direct with one another and with ourselves. By highlighting these capacities in young boys and guiding us in distinguishing pretense from presence, Chu illuminates a way of looking at men that encompasses their humanity.

Introduction

Even before our son Xander turned five, my husband and I fretted about finding a good school for him. Our concerns extended beyond the fact that good schools are few and hard to get into in San Francisco, where we live. Our main concern was about whether we would be able to find a school that was a good fit for him, given that he is both particularly sensitive and exceptionally bright.

In pre-school, because he preferred calm, quiet activities and could feel shy at times, Xander tended to play alone. As he generally kept to himself and was rarely if ever disruptive, he was easily overlooked by his teachers, who needed to focus on kids who required more attention. But it wasn't until our "sensitive boy" was ready for elementary school that our troubles really began.

We tried a public school for one year, starting when Xander turned five. Although he had a good teacher and the school did the best it could with what resources it had, the curriculum was not challenging enough for Xander, who was an early reader and excels in math and science.

Next, we tried a private school for one year, when Xander turned six. After three months, we were asked to leave the school upon completing the school year. We were informed that our son was "not a good fit" for this school. When we inquired further, we were told that his shyness was problematic. Offering an example, the teacher remarked that Xander rarely played with the other boys during recess. Instead, he often chose to sit and watch as the other boys ran around and chased each other (and occasionally he played with girls). When we asked Xander whether he wanted to join in the boys' activities but felt like he couldn't, he said he just preferred to sit and watch, and explained that, "some of the kids play too rough."

My husband and I could understand our son's decision. He had never been interested in boys' (or girls') rowdy and rambunctious play. Although he liked his classmates and was less reserved when interacting with them one on one, he tended to be cautious in social situations, especially with the more aggressive kids, and he generally preferred (and could be quite active and gregarious in) the company of adults, to whom he could relate more easily. Moreover, Xander was comfortable playing on his own and didn't feel compelled to do whatever the other kids were doing. One time when a boy from his class approached Xander on the playground at school, punched him playfully on the arm, and invited him to "chase me," Xander responded by smiling and saying simply, "Uh, no."

When we relayed Xander's preference to the teacher, she indicated that this was precisely the reason for her concern: He didn't *want* to join in the boys' activities. And so it seemed our son's "problem" was not merely his shyness but that he didn't behave like a typical boy or conform to the teacher's notions about how boys ought to act. When we told the teacher that we were fine with Xander's decision to opt out of the boys' rough-and-tumble play, his teacher seemed exasperated: "Well, I just don't know what to do with him."

Sadly, Xander knew that this teacher didn't like him. Her disapproval was evident in the way she looked at and spoke to him (and us). As Xander observed, "She never smiles." And it was heartbreaking to take him to school every day knowing that he was misunderstood, devalued, and even resented there.

At times, we felt as though this teacher would have preferred for Xander to misbehave or act out. Then, at least, she would have a ready response or some ideas about how she should deal with him. But Xander's mild manner did not match her expectations for boys, and this seemed to make her uncomfortable. Rather than question her own assumptions about what boys could and should be like, this teacher decided there was something wrong with Xander. Her negative assessment was especially apparent when, later in the year, she reported to us that Xander had "gotten better," citing, for example, how she had caught him and another boy peeking into the lost-and-found box (something the students are forbidden to do). With a nudge and a wink, she added proudly that she had allowed this trespass because she was so happy to see Xander "branching out."

As we did not want simply to ignore or dismiss this teacher's view, my husband and I consulted a range of specialists—including a pediatrician, a pediatric neurologist, a developmental psychologist, and an occupational therapist—over the course of the school year. Each of these specialists concluded that Xander is a "fully normal child" who is "very bright and cooperative" and "very sensitive" with no symptoms of pathology, either social or psychological. And so we had to reconcile the teacher's perception that our son's conduct was worrisome with our sense that the qualities that seemed to distinguish him from the other boys were, in fact, within the range of normal.

* * *

The issues my husband and I were confronting in our son's education brought me back to my studies with Carol Gilligan, whose groundbreaking research with girls has inspired and informed worldwide efforts to support girls' healthy psychological development and whose book *The Birth of Pleasure*[1] makes the link between girls' gender socialization at adolescence and boys' gender socialization at early childhood. Drawing on her work, I undertook the first research study to apply a relational framework and use relational methods to examine boys' socialization experiences and development during early childhood.[2]

The importance of relationships, particularly as a context for development,[3] has been widely recognized in most developmental and psychological theories.[4] What distinguishes relational theory is that it starts from the premise that our perceptions of, and subsequently our knowledge about, our selves and our world are inextricably embedded within and influenced by our interpersonal relationships as well as our social and cultural contexts.[5] That is, relational theories of human development and psychology emphasize the centrality of relationships in people's lives.[6] From this perspective, human development occurs not in isolation (with the *option* of having relationships), but through and within relationships with other people. More than a context for our development, our relationship experiences—including how we experience our selves in relationships—are a primary means by which we develop our self-image and learn how it is possible for us to express ourselves and engage with others.

A relational approach to psychological inquiry reframes the study of psychology as a practice of relationships and emphasizes the need for researchers to account for the fact that the quality of collected data depends in part on qualities of the researcher-participant relationship.[7] In other words, relational methods center on the understanding that the stories people tell us, or what people are willing to share with us about their experiences and their lives, are partly determined by how they view us and our intentions, and whether they trust us. In my study, I used a voice-centered relational method that involved attuning myself to what the boys said and how they said it, and also reflecting on how the boys responded to me and how I responded to them in our interactions.

Revisiting Boys' Development

In the autumn of 1997, Carol Gilligan and I went to the Friends School[8]—an independent primary school (pre-Kindergarten through grade six) in New England—to study the boys in the pre-Kindergarten class. Carol had studied sixth-grade girls at this school[9] with her colleagues from the Harvard Project on Women's Psychology and Girls' Development,[10] and their research had revealed ways in which heightened pressures at adolescence—to conform to conventions of femininity, or notions about what qualities and behaviors are appropriate and desirable for girls—could constrain girls' expression of a full range of thoughts, feelings, and desires, and thereby hinder their relationships.[11] In this work, Carol had been particularly impressed by the girls' knowledge about the relational world (including their attunement to interpersonal dynamics, their ability to reflect critically on gendered norms of behavior, and their ability to distinguish between appearances and reality), the girls' resistance to giving up their voices (including their struggles to remain open and honest within their relationships), and the girls' ability to articulate both their knowledge and their resistance.[12]

Based on the research with girls, Carol introduced the concept of resistance as a way of capturing what she had come to see as "a tension between psychological development or well-being and an adaptation that was both culturally scripted and socially enforced (i.e., an initiation into gender binaries and hierarchies that divide human qualities into 'masculine' and 'feminine' and privilege the masculine while at once idealizing and denigrating the feminine)."[13] Carol had observed girls resisting this initiation and described "the paradox girls face when pressed to silence an honest voice in order to have 'relationships' that girls recognized were not relationships in any meaningful sense of the word."[14] The significance of this work is its emphasis that, as individuals, "we have a voice and, with it, a capacity for resistance."[15] Subsequently, Carol asked whether boys also know about the relational world and show a similar resistance (e.g., against compromising their sense of agency and choice) when faced with pressures to align with conventions of masculinity that—despite the social advantages of being male and acting masculine—may be detrimental to boys' psychological health and jeopardize boys' relationships. It was this question that led to my study with four- and five-year-old boys.

I was interested in learning how boys at early childhood experience and respond to their gender socialization, and specifically how boys negotiate their self-image, behaviors, and styles of relating to others in light of cultural constructions of masculinity that manifest in their everyday interactions with peers and adults at school. I had spent the previous two years studying adolescent boys and found that most of the boys had already resolved any conflicts they may have experienced regarding their gender socialization. For instance, many of the adolescent boys in my studies had come to accept any gaps between *the way they experience themselves to be* (e.g., their self-knowledge) and *the way they are said to be* (e.g., societal norms and expectations for boys) as being *the way things are*.[16] With Carol's encouragement, I decided to study younger boys in hopes of gaining insight into how they reconcile any tensions or contradictions between their self-image and prevailing assumptions regarding what makes a boy a "real boy," at a moment in boys' development when they are increasingly exposed to cultural messages and societal pressures pertaining to gender and when they are in the process of figuring out how they can act and be with others.

I was also interested to learn what young boys are capable of knowing (about themselves and others) and doing (in terms of expressing themselves and engaging others) and how these capacities evolve through and are influenced by their socialization and development. As every human is born into relationships with other people (otherwise one could not survive), we all begin with an original sense of relational connection.[17] Studies of infants have shown that both boys and girls are also born with a fundamental capacity and primary desire for close, mutual, responsive relationships with other people.[18] Thus, boys are not inherently less capable than girls of being attuned to emotions (their own and others') and responsive within their relationships.[19] Moreover, studies indicate that boys[20] as well as girls[21] seek to cultivate and sustain close interpersonal relationships throughout their lives. Yet, older boys[22] and adult men[23] report having fewer close relationships and lower levels of intimacy within the relationships they do have. This discrepancy between infancy and adulthood suggests that boys' development is somehow associated with a move out of or away from relationships. However, few empirical studies have examined boys' relational development—that is, boys' development as a process wherein relationships play a central and critical role, and boys' development of certain styles of relating to other people—much less from boys' perspectives.

Popular Discourse on Boys

I conducted my study against a backdrop of literature that highlighted ways in which pressures for boys to conform to conventions of masculinity could negatively impact boys' development. Research on girls' development conducted by the Harvard Project on Women's Psychology and Girls' Development during the 1980s and early 1990s had inspired a resurgence of interest in boys' development during the late 1990s. Specifically, revelations regarding the centrality of relationships in girls' lives and the relational nature of girls' development called into question traditional models of human development that promote individuation and separation in the name of growth, health, and, for boys, manhood.[24] Following the studies of girls, a number of books focused on how boys' socialization—towards masculine ideals that emphasize, for example, physical toughness, emotional stoicism, and projected self-sufficiency—may lead boys to devalue and disconnect from their emotions and relationships.[25]

While this popular discourse on boys has been helpful in drawing attention to possible problems pertaining to boys' gender socialization, it has been limited by its tendency to pathologize boys and problematize boys' development. For example, most of these books are based on clinical populations of boys and adopt a diagnostic approach to understanding boys' development. Starting from the assumption that there is something wrong with boys, these books emphasize their alleged emotional and relational deficiencies (as compared to girls) and aim to identify what is wrong and who or what is to blame. Boys' emotional capacities and relational strengths are rarely mentioned, much less addressed. Furthermore, these books do not account for group and individual differences in boys' socialization experiences and outcomes, including how some boys manage to thrive, and not merely survive, within the same contexts that can be debilitating for other boys.

There is also a tendency in much of the literature on boys to conceptualize boys' gender socialization in terms of a linear model of cause-and-effect wherein cultural messages about masculinity and societal pressures to conform to group norms manifest in boys' everyday lives and subsequently affect their attitudes and behaviors. In depicting boys as passive recipients of culture and helpless victims of their socialization, this approach tends both to objectify boys and to discount their ability to influence their developmental outcomes. Seldom considered are ways in which boys—as active participants in their learning and development[26]—can mediate the effects of their gender socialization, for instance through ways in which they make meaning of cultural messages and respond to societal pressures.[27]

A more balanced depiction of boys' agency and awareness appears in Niobe Way's and Carlos Santos's research on adolescent boys. In her studies of boys' friendships, Way acknowledges the obstacles that boys commonly encounter in their efforts to develop close friendships, including issues of trust and cultural stereotypes that denigrate emotional intimacy as feminine. However, Way also underscores the intense emotional intimacy in boys' close friendships, especially during early and middle adolescence, and she emphasizes how boys value and fight to maintain (but often end up losing) their emotional connections to others. The core finding of Way's *Deep Secrets* is that boys resist as well as adhere to norms of masculine behavior. She also indicates that a boy's refusal to buy into masculine ideals is ultimately beneficial to his psychological health.[28] Building upon Way's work, Santos's longitudinal survey study with middle-school boys similarly emphasizes boys' resistance against societal pressures to align with masculine norms, and shows this resistance to be linked to higher levels of academic engagement,[29] as well as to higher self-esteem and lower levels of depression.[30] These studies add depth to the discourse on boys by highlighting boys' resistance to gendered norms and expectations that constrain their self-expression and hinder their relationships, and by demonstrating that this form of resistance—which emerged and gained prominence primarily through research with adolescent girls[31]—is also vital to boys' development and important for boys' well-being.[32] Moreover, these studies suggest the need to examine patterns of resistance in boys' development prior to adolescence, in order to understand how and why, in the course of their socialization and relationship experiences, boys' healthy resistance to gendered stereotypes might eventually give way to accommodation.

Importance of Early Childhood

Developmental theorists have identified early childhood as an important time of change, particularly for boys.[33] Jean Piaget referred to early childhood as the time when gender bifurcated schemas that shape human behaviors and experiences are constructed and reinforced.[34] Lawrence Kohlberg concluded that children acquire their gender lens by age six.[35] Erik Erikson observed that, from this age on, "Conscience . . . forever divides the child within himself by establishing an inner voice of self-observation, self-guidance, and self-punishment,"[36] as children learn to reconcile their desire to act on their impulses with their desire to avoid the disapproval and rejection that can result from behaving inappropriately. And Sigmund Freud described early childhood as a pivotal moment in boys' initiation into manhood—a moment when boys establish their masculine identities by separating from women and girls and aligning with men and boys.[37]

Although ideas about gender and gender-appropriate behavior may be introduced as early as infancy (e.g., through adults' differential treatment of and responses to boys and girls[38]), it is during early childhood that boys (and girls) begin to understand how these ideas may have implications for how other people view them and also for how they can be with others and in the world. Moreover, studies have found in boys a marked increase both in symptoms of psychological distress[39]—including depression, learning and speech disorders, attention deficits, and hyperactive or out-of-control behaviors—and in the use of Ritalin at this age.[40] Yet, little research has been conducted to explore how boys experience their socialization during early childhood and how these experiences may have implications for their connections to their selves (e.g., self-acceptance, self-esteem) and to others (e.g., relationships).

The growing realization that pressures for boys to conform to masculine norms may negatively impact their development—coupled with concerns about young boys' susceptibility to behavioral and learning problems—suggest our need and readiness for a new way of looking at boys and thinking about their development that both emphasizes their agency and awareness and considers what factors influence and motivate individual boys as they respond to their gender socialization. This book contributes to this emerging conversation by focusing on boys' experiences at the time in their development when they are said to disconnect from their emotional lives and their relationships.[41] Its centerpiece is an intensive two-year study of four- and five-year-old boys, and it is through their eyes and in their voices that we enter their world. The overarching argument is that boys have certain relational capabilities that are important to their health and happiness but are often overlooked or underestimated (e.g., in the literature on boys and in boys' everyday lives) and may be at risk as boys adapt to dominant norms of masculinity that manifest, for instance, in their school and peer group cultures. Through documenting the pressures young boys face as they come up against gendered norms and expectations, and also highlighting ways in which boys can resist the loss of vital human capacities, this book brings research evidence to bear on current concerns about boys and boys' development, and suggests ways in which parents, teachers, and others who have boys' well-being at heart can join this healthy resistance in boys.

1

Entering Boys' World

With the goal of learning about boys' experiences from their perspectives, in their words, and on their terms, I adapted a relational approach to psychological inquiry that focused on developing comfortable relationships with the boys, earning their trust over time, and observing them as they interacted with each other and with me. In many regards, my study started from a place of not knowing. I explained to the boys that, because I am a woman (who was once a girl), I do not know what it is like to be a boy and therefore I would be looking to them as my teachers and relying on them to help me understand their experiences.

A Hierarchy of Boys

The participants in my study were all six boys in the pre-Kindergarten class at the Friends School, an independent primary school in New England whose stated mission is:

- to encourage children to wonder, explore, invent, imagine, develop skills, and persevere at challenging work,
- to be a varied and vibrant community of teachers and families, where in-depth learning is shaped by the needs, the joys, and the interests of growing children,
- to guide children to value the differences and similarities that define them as individuals, and to be respectful, contributing members of the larger world.

All of the boys were four years old at the start of my study and lived in middle-class, suburban communities. Their parents were construction site managers, engineers, homemakers, music teachers, schoolteachers, therapists, and university professors.

A hierarchy among the boys was apparent as early as the third week of the new school year. This hierarchy seemed to reflect each boy's relative popularity and power, or ability to influence his peers, and could be regarded as a precursor to the competitive framework that often characterizes the social and cultural contexts of older boys and adult men.

At the top of the hierarchy was Mike, a Caucasian boy with short dark brown hair who lived with his mother and older sister (by two years). Mike's parents had recently separated but he still saw his father regularly. Mike was the oldest, tallest, and most domineering of the boys in this class. When interacting with his peers, Mike typically adopted a tough guy persona and projected an image of strength and superiority that allowed him to appear both intimidating and impressive. In seeking his peers' respect and admiration (and because he felt vulnerable to their rejection), Mike tended to be assertive, controlling, and at times forceful. In his interactions with adults, Mike was more tentative and took care to adjust his behaviors to avoid drawing negative attention to himself.

Next in the boys' hierarchy was Min-Haeng, a Korean American boy with very short black hair who lived with his mother, father, and extended family members, including two sets of grandparents, an aunt, and five older cousins (three girls and two boys) who would sometimes tease him about being the baby of the family. Despite being the shortest boy in class, Min-Haeng exuded an air of confidence and poise in his interactions with adults and peers. Even when playing (e.g., drawing, building with blocks), Min-Haeng usually was very focused, had a specific vision for how he wanted things to be, and worked meticulously towards his goal. If anyone questioned or deviated too much from his plans, Min-Haeng did not hesitate to assert himself and defend his preferences. Although Min-Haeng got along well with the other boys, he was also content to play on his own and would occasionally (and amicably) disengage from the group in order to pursue his own interests.

In the middle of the boys' hierarchy were Rob and Jake, who tended to be less likely (as compared with Mike and Min-Haeng) to expect and urge others to comply with their wishes.

Rob is Caucasian, had platinum blond hair that hit just below his ears, and lived with his mom, dad, an older brother (by two years), and a younger brother (by four years). In his interactions with adults as well as peers, Rob tended to have a quiet and unassuming manner. As one of his teachers put it, "Rob just melts with you," which I think perfectly describes the way in which Rob's presence tended to feel unforced and unrushed. Although Rob could express his thoughts and feelings openly with his peers, he usually chose to listen. Preferring to avoid conflict, Rob tried to be considerate and cooperative and rarely insisted on getting his way.

Jake is Caucasian, had short sandy blond hair, and lived with his mother, father, and older brother (by four years). Jake had a ready smile and an easy-going attitude and seemed comfortable and confident in his interactions with both adults and peers. Jake seemed to delight in his friendships and showed his support for his peers by taking an interest in what they were doing, responding sincerely to their concerns, and making an effort to include everybody. Jake also tended to be generous with his peers, even though the other boys didn't always reciprocate and sometimes took Jake's support for granted. Although I found Jake's exuberance and enthusiasm (e.g., for things, people, and the things he did with people) to be very appealing, these qualities could sometimes get him into trouble with his teachers at school.

Finally, Dan and Tony were at the lower end of the boys' hierarchy. In contrast to Mike and Min-Haeng (higher status), who knew what they wanted and actively pursued their goals, Dan and Tony tended to be less focused and less ambitious. Like Rob and Jake (middle status), Dan and Tony seemed more interested in being a part of the group (or a part of *a* group), and being involved with their peers. However, whereas Rob and Jake knew what they wanted but were willing to compromise in order to preserve peace and order within their relationships, Dan and Tony seemed less clear (or less specific) about what they wanted and may have therefore found it easier, or less of a compromise, to go along with other people's plans or views. Dan and Tony also seemed less concerned about displaying gender-appropriate behavior and deviating from gendered norms and could be found, for example, playing with the girls or with "girls' toys."

Dan is Caucasian, had curly strawberry blond hair, and lived with his mother and older brother (by four years). Dan's parents were separated, and he saw his father only occasionally. Dan had a bubbly personality and a fondness for fantasy play. For Dan, having lower status within the boys' hierarchy resulted in part from choices that he made. For example, in his quest for fun and excitement, Dan was undiscriminating in choosing his play companions. Whereas the other boys tended to play mainly with the boys, Dan seemed as happy and comfortable playing with the girls and engaging in the girls' activities as he was playing with the boys and engaging in the boys' activities. If his affiliation with the girls made him different from or undermined his status among the boys, Dan either didn't notice or didn't care. Rather, Dan delighted in every opportunity to play and seemed unabashed about his choices, even when they set him apart from the other boys.

At the bottom of the boys' hierarchy was Tony, an African American boy with very short, curly black hair, and big brown eyes, who lived with his mom, stepdad, and three stepsisters (twins who were four years older and one who was the same age and in this class). At the time of my study, Tony's mom was recently remarried, pregnant, and a teacher at this school, so Tony was learning to share his mom not only with his new family but also with his mom's students. With peers and adults at school, Tony often seemed uncertain about how to engage with others and would fluctuate between being bashful and being impetuous. With his mom's classroom being just across the hall, Tony could (and did) seek her assistance and visit her throughout the day. As a result of his insecurities and frequent departures from class, Tony often struggled, even though he seemed eager, to be included by the boys.

The Girls

Whereas the boys' hierarchy was obvious, a social hierarchy based on popularity and power did not appear to exist among the girls at this age. Unlike the boys, the girls did not seem to identify strongly as a group (e.g., as being one of the girls). Rather, the girls began to distinguish and separate themselves from the boys only after the boys collectively defined themselves in opposition to the girls. Perhaps as a result, the girls seemed more able to act and view themselves as individuals, for example by making their own decisions and doing as they pleased.

There was Gabriella, an African American girl with curly black hair that she wore in braided ponytails. She is Tony's stepsister and was living with her father, stepmother (Tony's mom), twin older sisters (by four years), and Tony (who is the same age). Playful and outgoing, Gabriella engaged comfortably with adults as well as peers, and boys as well as girls. Gabriella especially enjoyed assisting the teachers with their tasks (e.g., setting up activities, preparing snacks) and delighted in being praised for her helpfulness.

There was Tatiana, a Caucasian girl with long sandy blond hair, who lived with her mother and grandfather. Despite being the youngest of the girls, Tatiana was exceptionally perceptive, sensible, and self-assured. She had a warm and friendly manner and a very agreeable attitude, which enabled her to engage amiably and effortlessly with both adults and peers. Tatiana was also able to keep herself happily entertained and could enjoy playing alone as well as playing with others.

There was Nicole, a Caucasian girl with short brown hair who lived with her mother, father, and older brothers. Nicole played mostly with other girls (usually in pairs) and tended to go along with whatever her playmate(s) wanted to do. When conflicts arose among the girls, Nicole tended to look to adults to intervene and mediate.

Finally, there was Miranda, a Caucasian girl who had shoulder-length brown hair, wore glasses, and lived with her mother and father. Miranda was a straightforward, no-nonsense tomboy who did not hesitate to say what she thought. For instance, one time when Tony grabbed Gabriella roughly and put her in a headlock, Miranda immediately came to Gabriella's defense, telling Tony firmly, "Don't," and making sure that Tony complied with her command. Miranda was similarly confident in her interactions with adults and seemed to expect that people would be interested in what she had to say.

The Teachers, Classroom, and School

The teachers in this pre-Kindergarten class were Lucia, who was older and more experienced, and Jen, who was younger and relatively new to teaching. The physical space of the classroom was divided into separate areas through the strategic arrangement of several short, wooden bookshelves. Near the front entrance to the room was the work area, which included a long rectangular table, a smaller rectangular table, and two circular tables. At the start of each school day, the teachers would set out a variety of materials for arts and crafts (e.g., clay, paints, construction paper) in the work area for the students to use as they arrived at class. Adjacent to the work area was the house area, which contained clothes for dressing up and toys resembling various foods and house wares. Adjacent to the house area was the block corner, which contained wooden blocks of various sizes, jigsaw puzzles, and plastic bins containing Duplo blocks. Next to the block corner was the reading corner, which had a futon, several cushions for sitting, and several books on display. The remaining space (between the reading corner and the work area) was the meeting area, where the kids gathered during circle time for lessons, story time, and group activities.

The entrance to the pre-Kindergarten classroom was located at one end of a long, carpeted hallway lined with students' lockers and doors to other classrooms, a library, and the director's office. At the opposite end of the hallway was an exit to the playground—a vast space that included two sand boxes, a jungle gym, a swing set, a tire swing, and a large field of grass framed by trees, bushes, and wire fencing that separated the school grounds from the surrounding residential neighborhood. The closer end of the hallway opened onto an auditorium/gymnasium, which served as a passageway to administrative offices and the main entrance to the school. The school was housed in a two-story, red brick building with a large parking lot that separated it from the traffic of a suburban street.

An Exploratory Study

During the first weeks of the study, Carol and I met with the teachers and did some observations together. Then I continued to observe (and eventually interviewed) the boys over a two-year period—following them from pre-Kindergarten through Kindergarten and into first grade—with Carol supervising my research.

My observations of the boys in their school setting took place during weekly visits and lasted about two hours, usually in the morning. On a typical day, I observed structured activities such as lessons, clean up, and story time, and unstructured activities including the boys' arrivals in the morning with their parents, free play, and snack time. I also observed the boys outside of class during recess and on local field trips (e.g., to a nearby park). For the most part, I was able to distinguish myself from the boys' teachers and parents by observing but not monitoring or correcting the kids' behaviors, unless they were in danger of hurting themselves or others. For example, when I happened upon activities that I knew were forbidden by other adults, I tried not to seem judgmental and made a point of showing the boys that I would not tell on them. I also refrained from intervening in their conflicts and instead allowed the boys to work things out on their own. Most importantly, these observations provided time and space for the boys and me to build rapport and become comfortable with each other, which proved to be crucial when I began to interview them in the spring.

My interviews with the boys were informal meetings during which I observed and interacted with them and asked them questions. I met with the boys individually and in groups, depending on their stated preference, to inquire about the meanings of their activities, the motives for their behaviors, and their views on and opinions about their social interactions and relationships at school. I very quickly realized that a structured question-and-answer format aimed at eliciting personal narratives was not going to work with boys this age. Instead, I started bringing Playmobil toys, which were very popular among these boys at the time, to our meetings and asked questions intermittently while the boys played. Whenever I brought out the toys during our meetings, the boys would immediately begin to talk excitedly with each other about which characters they wanted to be and what storylines they wanted their characters to enact. The toys also helped to facilitate the boys' interactions with me by giving us something to talk about that the boys were interested in discussing. Over time, as the boys understood that the purpose of our meetings was simply to play and talk, they became more at ease during the meetings and even made requests to meet with me.

Getting Acquainted

My first few visits to this class were focused on getting to know these kids and allowing them to get to know me. As I was a stranger to them, I knew it might take some time before they came to trust me. As I did not want any of the kids to feel singled out or cornered, I did not attempt to engage them at this point. Instead, I began by simply observing them from a distance and waiting for them to engage me when they felt ready.[1]

During my first visit to this class, I arrive with Carol before the start of the school day to meet the two pre-Kindergarten teachers, Lucia and Jen. We introduce ourselves, briefly describe our intentions, and invite Lucia and Jen to share with us—at any time during the study—their insights regarding boys' experiences at this age. When the children begin to arrive, Lucia and Jen get up to prepare for the day while Carol and I remain seated at the round table in the work area. Most of the boys (and girls) instantly become shy when they first notice Carol and me in their classroom, which is understandable given that they have never seen us before and no one really introduces us or explains why we are there.

Tony and his stepsister Gabriella are the first to arrive. They are chatting animatedly with each other as they enter the room and fall silent when they see Carol and me. Gabriella quickly scans the room and when she spots Jen, walks over to greet her. Left on his own, Tony avoids our gaze and heads directly to the block corner at the opposite end of the room, where he peeks at us cautiously while hiding just out of our view.

As Rob enters the classroom, he also notices our unfamiliar faces and immediately hides behind his dad, burying his face against his dad's thigh and wedging his body between his dad's legs. When Rob's dad slowly cranes his neck and turns around to look at Rob, Rob adjusts himself to ensure that his dad's body continues to block our view of him and his view of us. I look away for the moment to give him some space. Eventually, Rob emerges from hiding behind his dad, and they head over to the meeting area, take out the classroom set of Playmobil toys, and sort through the pieces together. While Rob's dad sits on the floor with his legs folded like a pretzel, Rob climbs into his dad's lap and snuggles up close so that he seems completely immersed within his dad's encompassing embrace. As Rob's dad talks to him softly, Rob leans back, rests the back of his head against his dad's chest, reaches up with one hand and gently touches his dad's face with his fingertips, then rests his hand at the nape of his dad's neck. In response to Rob's touch, Rob's dad leans forward and lowers his head slightly. They continue to engage each other quietly and tenderly for the duration of their interaction. When Jen eventually comes and joins them, Rob's dad gently says goodbye to Rob, who simply watches (and does not struggle or protest) as his dad leaves.

Jake is the next boy to arrive, and when he first notices Carol and me, he pauses momentarily and moves slightly closer to his dad. However, Jake soon forgets about us when he and his dad decide to head to the block corner. When Jen and Rob join them, Jake's dad gets down on his hands and knees and crawls over to talk to Jen. Seizing this opportunity, Jake climbs excitedly onto his dad's back, loops his arms around his dad's neck, rests his cheek between his dad's shoulder blades, and calls out happily to the other kids, "Look at me!" Moments later, as Jake is sitting next to his dad on the floor, Jake delivers several kisses and hugs, to which his dad responds lovingly and joyfully. When it comes time for his dad to leave, Jake gives his dad a final kiss and hug and says good-bye without any complications.

A couple of the boys did not seem to notice Carol and me, or, if they did, they didn't dwell on it. Upon arriving at class, Min-Haeng immediately leaves his mom's side and heads straight to the block corner while his mom remains in the work area (near Carol and me). Min-Haeng doesn't look back at his mom, and she doesn't seem inclined to follow him. Mike, who arrives moments later, is also quick to leave his mom's side and makes his way directly to the block corner to join Min-Haeng. As Mike and Min-Haeng use the Duplo blocks to construct their projects, they pay little if any attention to their moms, to us, or to anyone else for that matter. They appear to be completely absorbed in their play. When Min-Haeng's mom goes over to say goodbye, Min-Haeng stays focused on his task and barely acknowledges her.

Meeting and Exceeding Expectations

As it happened, it was a girl who first approached and engaged me. Upon entering the classroom, Tatiana and her mom walk towards Carol and me (as though they were expecting to see us) and join us at the table where we are sitting. As they sit down and begin to play a board game, Tatiana's mom introduces herself to us. While her mom talks with us, Tatiana keeps herself occupied by looking at the game board and examining the game pieces. She doesn't cling to her mom or seek her mom's attention. Rather, Tatiana seems content and comfortable. Later on, after her mom leaves, Tatiana approaches me as I am sitting on the floor and observing the other kids during free play. She smiles, introduces herself, and sits down to join me. When she tells me her name, I fail to hear her correctly the first three times, and she patiently corrects me until I finally get it right. Tatiana tells me that she has lots of energy, that she can jump on one foot, that she can howl like a wolf, and that she can roll on the ground and tumble across the floor—all of which she demonstrates. Tatiana then invites me to work on some puzzles with her, and when I accept her invitation, leads me to the block corner, where the puzzles are stored.

Tatiana was not the only one to approach me during this visit, however. After overcoming his initial shyness, Tony also takes an interest in me and engages me in a warm and friendly manner. As Tatiana and I work on a puzzle together in the block corner, Tony gradually makes his way over to where we are sitting. When I greet Tony, he seems pleased by the fact that I know his name (from hearing Lucia greet him earlier), and decides to join us.

After completing the puzzle together, Tony, Tatiana, and I move to the work area and make "pictures" by inserting colorful pegs into wooden boards riddled with holes and using rubber bands to "draw" lines between the pegs. When Jen holds up a rain stick, Tatiana explains to me that the rain stick means, "Look up and listen," which she does immediately. After Jen announces that it is time to clean up, Tatiana explains that later on the rain stick will signal naptime. Tatiana also points out that the two girls who are running around and giggling are named Nicole and Miranda. Tatiana is effortlessly and impressively thoughtful as she considers my perspective as a newcomer to this class and teaches me what I need to know about its rules and members.

After clean up, everyone gathers on the floor in the meeting area for circle time. Tony sits calmly in my lap and Tatiana sits next to me and leans against my arm. Today's lesson is about fruits and seeds, and Lucia has brought a few examples to show the kids. When Lucia picks up a pomegranate and asks whether anyone has ever eaten this fruit, Tony turns to me and quietly asks if I have. When I tell him, "Yes," he helps to ensure my participation in the discussion by gently lifting my arm and encouraging me, "Then raise your hand."

As I had been feeling anxious about my first visit to this class and unsure about how to approach kids this age, I was grateful for Tatiana's overture and Tony's efforts to include me. Whereas Tatiana's friendliness and warmth were consistent with my expectations (based on gendered stereotypes that depict girls as nurturing), Tony's attentiveness and responsiveness exceeded my expectations (based on gender stereotypes that depict boys as being more self-centered). In the course of my study, I would come to see that the other boys in this class also possessed certain relational capabilities and that the boys as well as the girls seemed to understand that a good way to elicit other people's attention and interest is by being attentive to and interested in other people.

I would also learn that Tony's desire for close, personal attention in his relationships was especially intense, as compared to the other boys and also the girls. For instance, at the end of my first visit, Tony gets upset because I will not play with him exclusively. After circle time, the kids head out to recess, return to class for story time, and then have free play. During free play, Tony and Tatiana join me in the block corner and ask me to work on puzzles with them. Gabriella (Tony's stepsister) also joins us. When Tony asks me to work on a puzzle with him only, without Tatiana and Gabriella, I suggest that we work—along with the girls—on the puzzle that he has chosen. Tony repeats his request but I tell him that the girls can help, if they want. Upon being refused, Tony becomes disgruntled and agitated, and when he subsequently struggles to place one of his puzzle pieces, he makes a big fuss about giving up on his puzzle. Although Tony may be frustrated by the challenge of completing the puzzle, he seems mainly irritated by my unwillingness to give him my undivided attention. Tony then disengages from the interaction by heading to another part of the room (and he doesn't really engage me or seek my company again until months later on my twenty-second visit).

Boys Being "Boys"

Except for Tony, the other boys generally kept their distance and focused on their own activities during my first visit. When they did engage me, it was mostly through physical contact and to "attack" me. For instance, as the kids line up in the hallway for recess, Min-Haeng and Dan make a game of crawling through my legs while I am standing. The two boys giggle the whole time and occasionally bump into me, but they do not speak to me at all. During recess, Rob and Min-Haeng chase me, Jake pretends to beat me up by throwing punches and kicks in my direction while standing a few feet away from me, and Min-Haeng captures me and holds me as his prisoner. In this sense, the boys did display qualities and behaviors that are consistent with masculine stereotypes.

During these early interactions with the boys, I didn't know what to make of the boys' rowdy, rambunctious, and seemingly aggressive behaviors. On my second visit, Min-Haeng arrives at class with his mom, who greets Carol and me in a warm and friendly manner. As his mom talks with Carol, Min-Haeng heads over to the reading corner, where Jen takes him onto her lap and reads to him. When I look in his direction, Min-Haeng makes a gun with his hand and "shoots" me. Unsure how to respond (and keeping in mind that these kids are trying to get a sense of what I am like), I neither encourage nor discourage him and simply look away.

I eventually realized (and was relieved to find) that the boys' "attacks" didn't necessarily reflect hostile feelings towards me. For the most part, the boys seemed mainly to be looking for a lively response. During my fifth visit while the kids are finger-painting in class, Min-Haeng runs toward me with his hands covered in paint and a mischievous smile on his face. Min-Haeng threatens in a singsong tone, "I'm going to wipe my hands on you," and giggles excitedly when I react with alarm and place my hand on his chest to keep him at arm's length. Later that day, Min-Haeng approaches me as I am sitting in the reading corner with Tatiana on my lap and once again "shoots" me using his hand positioned like a gun. This time, I respond by smiling and shooting him back, which prompts Min-Haeng to explain that when he shoots me, I'm supposed to fall backwards. He then tries again and looks pleased when I comply with his instructions.

There was no question that these boys could be full of energy and that they enjoyed their rough-and-tumble play. However, it is worth noting that the girls also engaged me through physical contact and could be boisterous in their play. For instance, during my fifth visit as I am sitting on the floor in the meeting area and watching the boys play in the block corner, all four of the girls approach and decide to climb on me. When they cause me to topple over, the girls giggle and shriek with delight, and soon the boys come to join in the fun. When I sit up with my feet flat on the ground and my knees bent towards the ceiling, Rob climbs under my legs, and Jake and Min-Haeng pile on top of him. When I manage to extract myself and stand up, Dan suggests excitedly, "Let's knock her down!" Luckily for me, Lucia calls the kids to circle time, and I am able to escape.

As we became more familiar with each other, the boys continued to engage me through physical contact, but they began to engage me in other ways as well, especially when they approached me individually. For instance, moments after mischievously threatening to wipe his paint-covered hands on me during my fifth visit, Min-Haeng asks to sit in my lap during story time, nestles himself in my embrace, and comments softly as he listens to the story. And during my ninth visit, Jake playfully engages me in a game of peek-a-boo while standing behind a full-length dressing mirror in the house area. Jake initiates the interaction and elicits my attention by stealing glimpses at me and then hiding and giggling when I look in his direction. We do this back and forth until Jake stumbles backwards and bumps his head, at which point he emerges from his hiding place and walks towards me while rubbing his head. I ask if he's all right, trying not to sound overly concerned (as I have noticed that some of the boys get defensive if they think they are being coddled). As Jake continues to rub his head, he nods, smiles, and says cheerfully, "It warmed my head at least."

Gaining Access

During these initial visits, the boys would occasionally remind me of my outsider status. For instance, during my fifth visit, when I approach the boys while they are playing in the block corner, Min-Haeng tells me, "No grown-ups allowed." For the most part, however, the boys gradually became less self-conscious around me. They still noticed me (of course), but they paid less attention to me and could focus instead on whatever they were doing. As a result, I was able to sit amongst the boys as I observed them, whereas I had previously positioned myself to observe them from the periphery of their interactions. Over time, the boys also seemed more comfortable when engaging me, and they increasingly addressed and included me in their conversations.

Through this closer proximity to the boys (and the boys' realization that I was not going to tell on them), I was even permitted access to "illicit" activities that the boys generally hid from their teachers and parents. During my ninth visit, Rob and Jake are constructing toy weapons in the block corner when I head over to observe. Rob is making a sword, and Jake is making a dagger. The boys know (and they know that I know) that weapons are not allowed in class. Without my asking, Rob tells me that "like in fencing," he put "a little piece," which he calls "the safety," on the end of his sword "so no one will get hurt." Rob also explains that he can take the piece off "when it's time to kill." Rob and Jake then begin a game of knights and castles. In a deep voice, Rob commands Jake, "Get your dagger out. Stab it in the neck. Just kill our prey." Although Rob makes a point of explaining how he has made his weapon safe, he does not hide or disguise the violent language and themes of his play. And when I ask about their play, both boys happily show me their weapons and excitedly point out the special features on each.

Gradually, my observations of the boys' behaviors included not only their physicality and "aggression" (i.e., behaviors that reflected masculine stereotypes) but also their thoughtfulness and equanimity. At the end of my ninth visit as I am taking notes at one of the tables, Rob comes to sit next to me and is so calm and quiet that I don't even notice him at first. When I see him and say that I had thought he was on the other side of the room, he looks at me with a steady gaze and a small smile. Rob's demeanor is composed and assured. He does not seem compelled to fill the silence, so to speak, with superfluous words or extraneous activity. He simply sits with me and watches patiently as I write in my notebook. As I put away my notebook and prepare to leave, Rob mentions that he knows "a lot of knight scenes that are real" and, when I respond with interest, "Oh, yeah?" he offers to tell me about them during my next visit.

Developing Trust

As I became a regular presence in their classroom, the boys became more accustomed to having me around but they still did not know exactly why I was there and what I was doing in their class. I had not meant to be surreptitious about my intentions and was happy to answer any of their questions. From what the boys told me, I gathered that their parents or teachers had mentioned that I was studying the boys. The boys were not sure, however, about the specifics and finally asked me about my study in March, after I had been observing them for six months.

During my eleventh visit, I arrive at the school to find that the auditorium has been transformed into a marketplace for El Mercado. It looks as though almost everyone (teachers, parents, kids) is in the auditorium, where tables have been set up to display students' art and homemade food for sale. When I enter the classroom, Dan is the only one there. I join Dan at the table where he is sitting and playing with some toys. We greet each other and he shows me what he purchased at El Mercado. When I begin to take notes, Dan asks me why I'm always writing things down. I tell him it's so I can remember what happens. I then give an example by reading back what he told me about his toys. When Dan asks if I'm writing stuff only about him, I flip through my notebook and read a description of something Mike said and did during a previous visit. Dan seems satisfied and asks if I have also written about Min-Haeng. I turn to another page in my notebook and read a story that Min-Haeng told me, which makes Dan smile and laugh.

Like Dan, some of the other boys were still uncertain about my intentions and remained cautious about what they allowed me to observe of their behaviors and interactions. After the rest of the kids return to class from El Mercado, I join Rob, Jake, and Mike in the block corner where, as usual, something elaborate is in the works. When I peek in, Rob and Jake seem unfazed and continue with what they are doing. Mike, however, seems eager to avoid my gaze and eventually goes to crouch in a small space in the corner, which I later learn is his favorite hiding place when he doesn't want to be noticed. Mike is still suspicious of me and is careful about what he says and does when I am around. As Mike gives orders to Rob and Jake from his "protected" position in the corner, Mike and I happen to make eye contact and he tells me hastily, "I'm resting." Having overheard the boys' plans, I try to show Mike that I know what he is doing and I am not going to get him in trouble. Using the boys' words, I express interest in the boys' play and encourage Mike to tell me more: "How about the bad guys? Are you planning a defense?" As Mike nods warily, Rob, who overhears my questions, nods heartily in agreement and cheerfully elaborates on Mike's behalf. A moment later, Mike notices that I am looking at a construction that he made and again seems compelled to explain himself. He begins, "It's a special . . . " and then pauses to think of something appropriate. Sensing his hesitation, I try to encourage him by asking gently and with a smile, "Is it a weapon?" In response, Mike sighs heavily and tells me, "It's a cannon . . . It's a bomb." However, Mike immediately seems uncomfortable with this admission, quickly turns away from me, and urgently engages Rob: "I have to tell you something funny. My grandpa, he builded bombs when he was only eight." Mike then returns to his hiding place and watches the action from there. In the meantime, Jake comes to show me his two weapons and explains happily that they are exactly the same so it doesn't matter if he mixes up the right and left ones.

Eventually, the other boys also began to ask me about my intentions. On my twelfth visit, I bring a tape recorder (a small hand-held device) to class for the first time, and it catches the boys' attention. During free play, I join the boys in the block corner where Rob, Min-Haeng, and Jake are using Duplo blocks to construct guns and other weapons, and Dan and Mike are preparing to enact scenes from the movie *Star Wars*. As Mike gathers props for their play, he pauses in front of me and asks about my tape recorder, "Why do you have that thing?" I explain that it is a tape recorder and that it is used to listen to music and to record things. Although I (unintentionally) do a poor job of answering his question, Mike simply says, "Oh," and returns to playing, albeit tentatively. Eager to begin their fantasy play and unwilling to sacrifice any more precious play time, Dan notices Mike's lingering discomfort and tries to remedy the situation by walking over to me, gently placing a white lace shawl (that he retrieved from the house area) over my head, and casually informing me, "We're just going to pretend you're not here." Dan then takes the lead as the boys proceed to construct a narrative for their fantasy play. A minute later, once the boys are absorbed in their play, I remove the lace shawl and begin to take notes. For the most part, the boys continue to ignore me and do their own thing.

Although Mike seemed encouraged by his peers' willingness to trust me and by the fact that I did not report the boys' weapons play or other "illicit" activities to the teachers, he continued to be somewhat guarded in his interactions with me. During my fourteenth visit, Mike struts by me wearing a black eye patch and shows me his pirate impersonation: "Arg." When I compliment his eye patch, Mike responds in a friendly manner: "Thanks." However, when I approach him later that day and try to engage him in conversation, he resists my questions by answering curtly, changing the topic, or ignoring me altogether. As I do not want to pressure him or put him on the spot, I offer to leave him alone when I notice his discomfort, which he seems to appreciate.

Throughout the development of our relationships, I found the boys to be honest and upfront in our interactions in the sense that their conduct seemed consistent with their thoughts and feelings—including their wariness and hesitancy to trust me—at the time. For instance, during my fifteenth visit, the boys are articulate and direct as they let me know that they are not yet ready to let down their guard completely. While Jake, Mike, and Rob are playing quietly in the block corner, I move to sit closer to them on the floor. The boys don't seem to mind me at first. However, I become suspect when Gabriella approaches me and asks what I'm doing. Upon hearing Gabriella's question, the boys immediately tune in. When I explain that I am trying to learn about the boys, Jake asks, "What *exactly* do you want to learn?" When I tell Jake that I want to learn what it's like to be a boy, Jake turns to consult Mike, who asks, "Do you think we should trust her?" Jake glances in my direction, then turns to face Mike and, with a smile on his face, shakes his head slowly from side to side to indicate no. I appreciated that these boys engaged me only when they felt ready and only in ways that felt comfortable for them. Given my goal to learn about boys' experiences from boys' perspectives, I was grateful that these boys would communicate through their words and behaviors exactly what they were thinking and feeling. In fact, it was because the boys were honest and upfront in expressing their doubts and concerns that I felt I could believe them when they did eventually come to trust me and to show and tell me things.

Coming into Relationship

As I was able to prove my interest and loyalty over time, even Mike—who had been especially cautious around and suspicious of me—felt comfortable enough to reveal vulnerable details about his home life, which he tended not to discuss at school. For instance, in a meeting with Mike on my eighteenth visit, Mike tells me about his parents' separation. This is my first time meeting with Mike one on one, and I am surprised when he seems eager to meet with me, given that he generally has been inclined to avoid me. When I motion for him to come with me, he gets up, wide-eyed and smiling, and rushes to my side. Although I give Mike the option to bring one of his buddies, he chooses to meet with me on his own.

Our first task is to find a meeting space. As we search together for a room, Mike casually strikes up conversation, asking me which football teams I like. He engages me charismatically and seems pleased when I am able to speak to this topic. As we wander through the hallways together, we find that most of the classrooms and offices are occupied today. After we have searched for a while, a teacher suggests that we use one of the classrooms in the basement. She says that students usually are not allowed to go down there but it might be all right in this case. With this permission, Mike and I head down to the basement, where neither of us has been before. I didn't even know the school had a basement. Like the main and upper levels of the school, there's a hallway with doors on both sides that lead to classrooms. However, in contrast to the brightness and warmth upstairs, the basement is dim and cold. The electricity does not appear to be working down here, and the only light is that which comes in through the classroom windows. As the weather outside is gray and overcast, the space feels somewhat dark and eerie. Mike and I walk slowly through the hallway looking for a room we can use. All of these class-rooms look as though they have been out of use for some time. A few of the rooms have bits of construction strewn on the floor. We settle for a room that contains a rectangular table and a few chairs.

We are both somewhat timid as we sit down together and try to make ourselves comfortable in this unfamiliar place. In contrast to the tough guy persona that Mike often projects among his peers, he seems small and vulnerable here in this setting, and I suddenly see him as the five-year-old boy that he is. So, when I notice that he is shivering, I feel free to express my concern and try to take care of him.

> JUDY: Are you cold?
> MIKE (*AUTOMATICALLY*): Not really.
> JUDY: O.K.
> MIKE: Are you cold?
> JUDY (*HESITATING*): A little bit. Are you?
> MIKE: Yeah, a little bit.

Like Mike, my first inclination is to deny that I am cold, even though I am. Maybe I think he might consequently feel obligated to do something to alleviate my discomfort, and I don't want to burden him. Regardless, I end up admitting that I am cold, and my willingness to reveal this vul-nerability seems to enable Mike to do the same and admit that he is also "a little bit" cold. I consider going upstairs to get something warm for Mike to wear but decide against it and instead offer him my flannel shirt (which I am wearing over another shirt), which he accepts.

> JUDY: Want me to run up and get, well actually, I can't leave you. You want
>   to wear my shirt?
> MIKE (*IN A BABY VOICE*): Um, hey, I remember these. (*He points to my
>   Playmobil toys.*)
> JUDY: Yeah? Here, why don't you put my shirt on so that you don't get
>   freezing in here? It'll be a little bit big. What do you think?
> MIKE (*IN A BABY VOICE*): I think it will be big.

Whereas Mike usually assumes a dominant stance, particularly when among his peers, he uses a baby voice as he accepts my assistance and allows himself to be comforted. It is while assuming this vulnerable stance that Mike tells me about his parents' separation.

> JUDY: Have you ever gone to [work] with your dad?
>
> MIKE: No. Not exactly.
>
> JUDY: But you've been [to his work place]?
>
> MIKE: I've been to his apartment, but he doesn't work there.
>
> JUDY: Oh.
>
> MIKE (*IN A SOMBER VOICE, WITH HIS HEAD LOWERED, HIS EYES CAST DOWNWARDS, AND HIS CHIN TUCKED TOWARDS HIS CHEST*): He separated from my mom.
>
> JUDY (*GENTLY*): Oh really? What that's like for you?
>
> MIKE (*HESITATING*): I think they're going to get back together in a month.
>
> JUDY (*GENTLY*): Oh, they are? What makes you think that?
>
> MIKE (*SIGHING*): I don't know. (*He turns his attention back to the toys and asks me about a particular piece.*) Does this go . . . ?
>
> JUDY (*GENTLY*): What happened? How come they got separated?
>
> MIKE: Sometimes my dad is rushed. He rushes. Just rushy.
>
> JUDY: He's rushy?
>
> MIKE: Uh-huh. What do you expect him to be?
>
> JUDY: Do you wish your dad would move back in?
>
> MIKE (*INSTANTLY*): Uh-huh.
>
> JUDY: Yeah? It must be kind of difficult with him not being around.
>
> MIKE (*SIGHING*): Yeah, very difficult.
>
> JUDY: Very?
>
> MIKE: Very.

Mike then returns to playing with the toys. Although Mike no longer wants to talk about his parents' separation, he continues during the remainder of our meeting to engage me in a way that feels very grounded and forthright. He looks me in the eyes as we talk. He pays attention to what I say. He responds thoughtfully to my questions. For example, when I ask him about the biggest difference between a boy and a girl, he begins by saying, "Um, long hair, short hair," but then pauses as he thinks of exceptions, "Some women [have short hair]," and finally decides, "I don't know the difference." He also responds plainly to my questions, as when I ask him what kinds of things make him feel happy, and he replies instantly, "When I have bubble gum." And when he tires of my questions, he lets me know, first by rolling his eyes, slumping his body, and responding in an annoyed and drawn out voice, "I don't know," and then, when I laugh and ask, "Are you tired of my questions?" by telling me straight out, "Yeah."

In contrast to his avoidant and suspicious manner when interacting with me on previous occasions, Mike is noticeably more at ease and even seems to enjoy this meeting. Whereas he had been the one to cut short our interactions (e.g., when I tried to engage him in class), Mike prolongs our conversation (possibly to postpone his return to class) by broaching new topics after I offer to bring our meeting to a close. For example, Mike asks whether I have seen *The Magic Flute* (an opera that was recently performed at school). When I say that I have and ask what he liked about the opera, Mike livens up and enthusiastically re-enacts his favorite scenes, including one in which the characters fight with swords. Mike also tells me about his plans to see a favorite movie of his and is encouraged when he discovers that I know it as well.

MIKE: Did you know that I, there's this video called *Ace [Ventura] Pet Detective*?

JUDY (*NODDING IN RECOGNITION*): Uh-huh, uh-huh.

MIKE (*SURPRISED*): Um, you know?

JUDY: Yeah, I saw it.

MIKE (*SURPRISED*): You saw it?

JUDY: Yeah.

MIKE (*LIVELY*): I really liked the part where he, like, he comes out of the bathroom and he's like, "Do *not* go in there!" (*We both laugh.*) My babysitter has that. I'm going to her house today, and I'm going to watch it.

JUDY: Oh.

MIKE (*GETTING EXCITED, GIGGLING*): I saw it, I've seen it two times. I've seen part of it, I sneaked in and I watched part of it and then my babysitter said (*mimicking his babysitter in a singsong tone*), "Mikey, could you *please* get out of here?" (*We laugh.*) Because I saw it, this will be the third time I'm seeing it. (*He sighs with pleasure.*) And I can't wait.

Mike's presence during this meeting feels authentic, not only because he expresses himself openly and engages me freely but also because his manner changes to reflect his mood as we encounter new circumstances and discuss different topics. He chats with me casually and charismatically as we search together for a place to meet. He becomes timid as we settle into the cold and eerie classroom in the basement. He becomes thoughtful while responding to my questions. He becomes sullen when he tells me about his parents' separation, but livens up as he re-enacts his favorite scenes from an opera he saw recently. And he lets me know when he has had enough of my questions. While none of these behaviors may seem extraordinary, Mike's ability to say whatever is on his mind, to act on his instincts, and to be in the moment, so to speak, is remarkable. Mike's example demonstrates how the boys' ability to be genuinely engaged in their relationships did not hinge on whether they disclosed their innermost thoughts, feelings, and desires, or the frequency or extent to which they did so. Rather, it depended on their ability to express themselves and engage others in ways that reflected their meanings and intentions. For this reason, Mike's ability to be fully present in relationships was exemplified as much by his initial hesitation to engage me as by his willingness during this meeting to talk and be with me.

After this meeting, Mike was no longer wary of me and he even initiated contact with me. For example, after we return to class from our meeting, Mike approaches to engage me (something he had never done before) as I fumble around with my tape recorder. When Mike notices the bag in which I keep my tape recorder (a blue cloth bag bearing an image of a cartoon duck), he remarks enthusiastically, "I love that!" Mike then sits down across from me and asks how old I am. He guesses that I'm twenty. When I tell him that I'm twenty-five, Mike reassures me, "That's all right because Lucia is older than that." Mike then walks over to ask Lucia how old she is. Mike also approaches me upon arriving at class with his mom on the following day (my nineteenth visit). When Mike enters the classroom, he walks directly towards me, looking as though he has something he wants to tell me. However, as he gets closer, he becomes a little shy and hesitates slightly. He then greets me with a nervous smile, "Hi." I return the greeting, pleased that he makes an effort to engage me. Mike and I are both somewhat self-conscious during this exchange, as we can see that his mom (who seems surprised by and curious about his sudden interest in me) is watching us intently. We struggle to think of something to say, and Mike finally asks, "How are you?" I tell him, "I'm good," and ask how he is. "Good." After a few more seconds of awkward silence, Mike turns and heads over to another part of the room. By my twentieth visit, Mike and I are on friendly terms. He introduces me to his beloved plush dog, Bobo. He includes me in everyday conversations, as when he tells Rob, "You're the blond-haired one. I'm the brown-haired one," and, turning to me, adds, "You're the black-haired one." He engages me outright, as when he announces, "I want to tell you a rhyme," and then proceeds to do so: "Tarzan, Tarzan in the air . . . " He even asks me how to spell the "A-word," whereas he had been careful during my earlier visits not to reveal to me his knowledge of profanity.

* * *

Altogether, the examples presented in this chapter illustrate how my use of a relational method—one that centered on developing comfortable, trusting relationships with these boys—influenced what they allowed me to see and hear (e.g., of their activities and interactions) and thereby what I was able to learn from them. In the beginning when we were getting acquainted, the boys tended to keep their distance and engaged me mainly through physical contact (usually to "attack" or "capture" me). In retrospect, I can see that, had I limited my study to these earlier visits, I would have come away with a very different impression of these boys—one similar to gender stereotypes that depict young boys as boisterous and easier to engage through rough-and-tumble play than through calmer and quieter means. However, as the boys and I became more familiar with each other over time, I was able to observe and experience a broader range of the boys' relational capabilities and styles. I saw how they could be honest and upfront with me, whether they chose to show and tell me things or to express their reservations. I also saw how, once I had earned their trust, they could feel confident enough to be vulnerable with me. That is, it was mainly because of my relationships with these boys that I was able to gain deeper insight into and appreciate more fully what boys at this age are capable of knowing and doing in their relationships.

2

Boys' Relational Capabilities

Through developing relationships with four- and five-year-old boys and working closely with them over time, I observed these young boys to have the cognitive and emotional capacity to exhibit qualities and skills that challenge how boys are commonly thought of and spoken about in the literature on boys' development and in our everyday lives. These boys' relational capabilities included, for example, the ability to be:

1. attentive, in the sense that they could listen carefully and respond thoughtfully as they engaged in their interactions with others;
2. articulate, in the sense that they could describe their perceptions and experiences in a clear and coherent manner;
3. authentic, in the sense that they could conduct themselves in ways that reflected their thoughts, feelings, and desires at a given moment; and
4. direct, in the sense that they could be forthright and straightforward in expressing their meanings and intentions.

In contrast to depictions of boys as being insensitive to emotions and incapable of or uninterested in developing close relationships, the boys in my study demonstrated a remarkable ability to be astute observers of their own and other people's emotions, sensitive to the dynamics and innuendos within their relationships, and keenly attuned to norms and patterns within their social interactions and cultural contexts. Regardless of their individual temperaments (e.g., being introverted or extroverted, reserved or outgoing), all of these boys sought to establish and sustain meaningful connections with others. Thus, the capacity and desire for close, mutual, responsive relationships that researchers have observed in infants are evident during early childhood as well.

Within the context of their school setting, the boys' capacity and desire to be emotionally and physically close with others were especially apparent in their interactions with their fathers. The boys clearly derived a sense of security, support, and pleasure from these relationships, which could enable them to face each day with confidence, courage, and gusto. For example, on days when Rob arrived at school with his dad, the two of them would sit and play together quietly until Rob seemed comfortably settled in. Like Rob, Rob's dad also had a quiet and gentle manner. Although they usually didn't say much as they played together, their actions nevertheless seemed coordinated and complementary. When they did talk, they spoke in soft tones, just loudly enough for each other to hear. Even though they were not effusively affectionate (e.g., giving lots of hugs and kisses), their interactions were unmistakably warm and loving as they focused completely on each other and managed to establish and maintain a private intimacy within this public setting.

Jake and his dad were also tender and affectionate with each other. However, consistent with their gregarious and ebullient personalities, they were more open and exuberant in expressing their feelings for each other. During my eighth visit, Jake and his dad are sitting on the floor in the block corner when Jake's dad prepares for his departure by crawling over to Jake and saying that it's time for him to leave. When he asks Jake for a big hug, Jake responds by enthusiastically flinging his arms around his dad's neck, adding cheerfully, "And kiss!" and giving his dad a kiss on the cheek. As his dad walks out the door, Jake springs to his feet and runs after him joyfully. In the hallway, Jake gives his dad another big hug and then skips back into the room with a big smile on his face.

Even Mike, who typically projected a tough guy image while at school, occasionally lowered his guard to engage tenderly and affectionately with his dad. During my seventeenth visit, instead of heading directly to join the other boys upon arriving at class (as he usually does), Mike stays with his dad and follows him to the reading corner. After they look through a book together, Mike's dad prepares to leave by asking Mike for a hug and kiss goodbye. Although Mike typically refuses to comply (or complies reluctantly) with such requests, today he relents and responds wholeheartedly—closing his eyes tightly, smiling broadly, and patting his dad affectionately on the back—as he delivers a big hug. As Mike and his dad begin to pull away from their mutual embrace, they pause for a bit, looking at each other and enjoying the moment. After they separate, Mike playfully taunts his dad and reacts with glee when his dad lunges forward and tries to grab him. When his dad leaves, Mike returns to the reading corner by himself and sings happily as he sits down and looks through a book.

The boys also engaged in displays of tenderness and affection with each other. During my nineteenth visit, as the kids gather on the floor for circle time, Mike sits behind Min-Haeng and extends his legs on each side of Min-Haeng's body so that it looks as though Mike is holding Min-Haeng on his lap. As they sit facing Lucia (their teacher), Min-Haeng leans back and rests the back of his head against Mike's chest. When Mike puts his arms loosely and protectively around Min-Haeng, Min-Haeng turns around while remaining seated and delivers an affectionate hug in return. Both boys then return their attention to Lucia, and Mike gently strokes Min-Haeng's hair as they listen to what she has to say. And during my twenty-first visit, Min-Haeng, Tony, and Rob share a quiet moment together when Min-Haeng and Tony join Rob as he is sitting on a child-sized rocking chair, rocking gently and contentedly back and forth. Min-Haeng arrives first and sits on Rob's lap, followed by Tony, who sits on Min-Haeng's lap. Rob then hums a lullaby while the three boys rock together slowly. When Rob has had enough, he says casually, "Now get off of me," at which point Tony and Min-Haeng immediately stand up. Of course, the boys' relational capabilities were not limited to their capacity for tenderness and affection, but these examples help to show that the boys' relational repertoire, or how they could conduct themselves and engage with others within their social interactions and relationships, extended beyond typical (and stereotypical) depictions of boys.

A Shift in Boys' Relational Presence

In addition to observing the boys' relational capabilities, I also noticed a striking shift in their relational presence, or how they presented and represented themselves in their relationships.[1] The shift seemed to occur about halfway through during their pre-Kindergarten year. Whereas these boys had demonstrated the ability to be attentive, articulate, authentic, and direct, they began to show signs of becoming:

1. inattentive, as they learned to focus more on impressing people than on engaging people (e.g., in their efforts to connect with others);
2. inarticulate, as they learned to withhold their personal insights and opinions (e.g., for the sake of preserving their group affiliation and peer relationships);
3. inauthentic, as they learned to display attitudes and behaviors that did not necessarily reflect their own interests, preferences, and beliefs (e.g., in order to accommodate to other people's expectations);
4. indirect, as they learned to obfuscate their meanings and intentions (e.g., in their attempts to avoid causing or getting into trouble).

That is, the boys' relational capabilities became less apparent as they became more focused on gaining other people's approval and acceptance and, to that end, learned to align their behaviors with group and cultural norms.

This shift in the boys' relational presence was not merely a matter of displaying behaviors that are consistent with conventions of masculinity; the boys did that all along. For instance, the kinds of physical, high-energy, and occasionally raucous behaviors that commonly prompt adults to remark or conclude that "Boys will be boys" were evident as early as my first visit to this class. During recess, the boys pick up dirt from the ground and throw it into the air, calling it "potion." They run, hide, and pretend to hunt. They taunt Mike's older sister and her friends and urge them to "Chase us." They seem inclined to move around as one large group, whereas the girls tend to play individually or in pairs. Similarly, during my fifth visit, the boys gather in the house area and pretend to eat plastic toy vegetables before tossing them frivolously into the block corner. Their play is rambunctious without being rowdy, and the boys seem to be enjoying themselves thoroughly. When I ask the boys what's going on, Rob smiles broadly and says, "We're messy eaters." Although the boys' boisterous behaviors in these examples are stereotypically masculine, the boys are nonetheless attentive, articulate, authentic, and direct at these moments. Therefore, their ability to be fully present and genuinely engaged in their relationships did not necessarily preclude their acting like "boys." Rather, the shift that I observed had more to do with the quality of the boys' relational presence, which appeared to be gradually overshadowed by pretense as the boys' behaviors and styles of engaging with others increasingly involved some degree of posturing and began to feel somewhat contrived.

From Presence to Pretense via Posturing

Most commonly, the boys' posturing involved mimicking things they had heard or seen, usually in the media. For instance, Mike tended to adopt mannerisms and expressions that could make him appear tough and confident (or tougher and more confident). On my twenty-first visit, Mike is feeling left out (having arrived at school to find that Jake, Rob, and Tony were meeting with me without him), and when I ask him about the incident, he responds by using clichés and singing lyrics to a highly masculine song.

> JUDY (*GENTLY*): Mikey, what were you upset about earlier, with Jake?
> MIKE (*SOFTLY*): Nothing. (*Decidedly*) None of your business.
> JUDY: Oh, sorry. Are you feeling better now?
> MIKE: Yeah. (*Singing a verse from a popular song on the radio*) I get
> knocked down, but I get up again, you ain't ever gonna keep me
> down . . .

As Mike does not want to talk about his feelings, at least not with me, his posturing allows him to sidestep my questions and shield himself from my intrusion on his privacy.

The boys' posturing could also involve more elaborate role-playing, as when Mike adopts a menacing tone and rough manner to accuse Rob of hoarding a popular toy figure during my fourteenth visit. In this exchange, Mike joins Rob and Jake while they are playing with the classroom set of Playmobil toys. Soon after arriving on the scene, Mike makes an accusation: "Rob, you always got to have [the king]." In response, Rob tries to defend himself by claiming that he has had the king only a few times. Eager to avoid being similarly accused, Jake immediately assures Mike that he has not played too many times with his toy figure, "I only got to have [the knight] once." Just then, Mike notices Miranda walking by, suddenly drops his pretense, and remarks enthusiastically, "You got a suntan, Miranda! A *real* suntan!" before returning his attention to Rob, resuming his authoritarian stance, and continuing with his tirade.

MIKE (*STERNLY*): You got to get [the king] a hundred times.

ROB (*NERVOUSLY*): Well, I'm gonna let Jake get him. I'm gonna let Jake
    have him. And then tomorrow, I'm gonna let you have him. (*Rob
    hands the king to Jake. Jake hands the knight to Rob.*)

MIKE (*UNSATISFIED*): You got [the knight] before.

ROB (*DEFENSIVELY*): Not [the knight].

MIKE (*STERNLY*): Guess what? I'm never gonna play with you ever again.

ROB (*PLEADING*): I'll let you have him tomorrow.

MIKE (*STERNLY*): That's not good enough. I want you to pay me $10,000,
    all in advance.

ROB (*DESPERATELY*): Let me tell you, Jake came over and he took out [the
    knight] first. He was the first one today to get [the knight]. I didn't
    take [the knight] out.

MIKE (*STERNLY*): If you get [the knight], if you get that guy, you pay me,
    I'll tell you what, $10,000.

ROB (*DESPERATELY*): I don't have any money. Only my one-dollar bill is all
    I have.

MIKE (*THREATENING*): Well, guess what?

Mike then pushes Rob in the chest, leans in so that his scowling face is
just inches from Rob's, gets up, and walks away in a huff.

Although Mike may actually be angry with Rob, Mike's language ("I
want you to pay me $10,000, all in advance"), gestures (pushing Rob in
the chest, getting in his face, storming off), and the fact that he drops his
menacing tone momentarily to comment on Miranda's suntan, suggest
that Mike is also enacting a role, or posturing. Instead of simply saying
what he thinks or wants in his own words and using his regular speaking
voice, Mike adopts a tough guy persona—probably something he saw on
television or in a movie—to make his point. Mike becomes so absorbed
in enacting this role that it becomes unclear what he wants exactly, or
what Rob could do to appease him, and the interaction becomes focused
more on Mike's performance than on reaching a resolution. If at some
point Mike had wanted the king that he originally accused Rob of hoarding, he seems to lose sight of that goal, and this exchange becomes just
another example of Mike's tendency to dominate his peers.

In addition to appearing tough, the boys' posturing could also make
them appear (and maybe feel) more powerful and in control, particularly

in situations where they might feel vulnerable. For instance, during a meeting with Mike, Jake, and Rob on my fifteenth visit, Mike adopts an authoritative tone and a pedagogical manner to deal with me on the boys' behalf when I inadvertently corner them with my abstract questions. This is my first time meeting with the boys outside of class, and they are understandably reserved and wary. We are in a school administrator's office that we were given permission to use. The office is small, with a couch on one side and a desk and bookshelves on the other side. I sit on the floor in the center of the room and face the boys, who are sitting together on the couch. The boys anxiously look around the small room and seem eager to avoid being singled out by me. I begin by thanking them for their help and explain that I am interested in learning about what boys think and what boys do. I then ask if they can—because they are boys—tell me what it's like to be a boy. Rob and Jake look to Mike expectantly, who thinks for a moment and tries to respond but shrugs his shoulders and gives up.

JUDY (*TO MIKE, GENTLY*): You don't know what it's like to be a boy?

JAKE (*IMMEDIATELY*): I don't either.

JUDY: How about when you guys grow up? What's that going to be like?

MIKE (*CONFIDENTLY*): I'm going to fight criminals.

JUDY (*INTERESTED*): You are?

JAKE (*BRIGHTLY*): [Mike's] going to be a policeman, and I'm going to be an inventor.

MIKE (*CONFIDENTLY*): Actually, I'm not going to be a policeman. I'm going to be a revolutionary spy. Besides, I am a revolutionary spy.

JUDY (*INTERESTED*): You are?

ROB (*SOFTLY*): I'm going to be in the army.

JUDY (*INTERESTED*): You are?

MIKE (*CAUTIONING*): Then you'll get killed.

ROB (*UNCONVINCINGLY*): I don't care.

JAKE (*EMPHATICALLY*): Yeah, I don't care. That's what I want.

JUDY (*TO JAKE*): You want to be in the army?

JAKE: Yeah, and I want to get killed.

Amidst Rob and Jake's macho posturing ("I don't care," "I want to get killed"), Mike gets up from his seat, straightens his posture, and begins to report in a formal tone, "Excuse me; it's something about military, other world (*Jake giggles*), other word for revolutionary. No. Revolutionary spies, steal plans. So, um, there were . . . " As Mike speaks, he paces back and forth with his hands clasped behind his back. His conduct resembles that of someone giving a lecture, and I wonder if he is imitating his dad, who is a professor.

Mike's lecture continues for several minutes. Despite constant interruptions by Rob, Jake, and me, Mike manages to stay impressively on task and in character for the most part. Whenever he is interrupted, Mike returns to his point as though he were reading from a prepared script. For example, when Jake removes a small ceramic pot from one of the bookshelves and causes some paper bookmarkers to fall onto the floor, Mike pauses to help remedy the situation and then brings us back to his line of thinking.

> JAKE (*WATCHING THE BOOKMARKERS FLUTTER DOWN*): Ooh! Wow!
> JUDY (*TO MIKE*): How about the good guys and the bad guys?
> ROB (*TO JAKE, CONCERNED ABOUT THE MESS*): Don't.
> JUDY (*PICKING UP MOST OF THE BOOKMARKERS*): Uh-oh. Be careful. That's somebody else's stuff. (*To Mike, who is looking at one of the fallen bookmarkers*) Why don't you pick it back up, put it back on the shelf?
> ROB (*URGENTLY*): Put it back on the shelf!
> MIKE (*WALKING TOWARDS THE BOOKSHELF*): Where do I put it? (*He places the bookmarker back on the shelf.*)
> JUDY: I think that's fine. Thank you.
> MIKE (*IN LECTURE MODE*): As I was saying . . .

Likewise, when Jake slides over on the couch and inadvertently usurps Mike's seat, Mike pauses to reclaim it—"That's my spot"—and then continues to pace around, trying to remember where he left off.

> JUDY: How about the good guys and the bad guys. Who are they?
> MIKE (*SIGHING DEEPLY, THEN CONTINUING TO LECTURE*): The good guys, bad guys, good guys, Russians, bad guys . . .
> JAKE: Americans.
> MIKE: No. Good guys, Russians. And bad guys, um, German.
> JUDY: I see. And which side are you guys on?
> MIKE: We're on . . .

JAKE: Russian.

MIKE: Russian.

JUDY: Ah, so you're the good guys?

MIKE AND JAKE: Yeah.

JUDY (*TO MIKE AND JAKE*): Ah. And who's on your side?

ROB (*IN A BABY VOICE*): And me from Russian.

MIKE AND JAKE (*TO ROB*): What?

ROB (*IN A BABY VOICE*): Me from Russia.

JAKE (*REFERRING TO MIKE AND ROB*): Those two are from Russia.

JUDY (*TO JAKE*): And where are you from?

MIKE: America.

JAKE: Actually, my mom is from Washington, D.C.

JUDY: Oh.

MIKE: She's near the president of the United States?

JAKE: I think so.

JUDY: How about friends? Can you tell me what . . .

MIKE (*TO JUDY, IN HIS LECTURING TONE*): Excuse me. I'm not done.

JUDY (*YIELDING*): O.K.

When I ask about good guys and bad guys, Mike responds to my question (they're good guys) and allows the discussion to meander a bit as the boys discuss who's on which side. However, when I ask another question that changes the topic ("How about friends?"), Mike steps in and reclaims control ("Excuse me. I'm not done.").

Before continuing with his lecture, Mike tries to take his seat on the couch between Jake and Rob, but Jake sticks his leg out and Rob puts his hand down, playfully blocking Mike's efforts. Although Mike is momentarily taken aback, he recovers with a vengeance and ends up sitting on Jake's leg and Rob's arm.

JUDY: Oh my goodness, [be] careful before someone gets hurt. (*To Jake and Rob*) O.K., let Mikey sit on the couch.

ROB (*TO MIKE AND JAKE, WHO CONTINUE TO PLAY ROUGHLY*): Come on. You don't wanna, you don't wanna. (*Noticing a few bookmarkers that we neglected to pick up*) Oopsies. (*To Judy*) Look right there.

JUDY (*PICKING UP THE REMAINING BOOKMARKERS*): We'll put these up [on the shelf], too . . .

MIKE (*IN HIS LECTURING TONE*): So, as I was saying, military, when I grow up, I'm gonna get, when I'm ten, this is what I'm going to get: a can gun to shoot cans.

JAKE (*EXCITED*): And you can shoot cans . . . bang, bang, bang!

MIKE (*TO JAKE, STERNLY*): Not really . . . Well, I'll, so, as I was saying, the good guys . . . revolution, no, I already read that part . . .

In response to each interruption, Mike moderates authoritatively ("So, as I was saying . . . ") and then picks up where he left off.

It is worth noting that, although Mike takes it upon himself to speak on the boys' behalf and thereby saves Jake and Rob from having to respond to my questions, Mike doesn't exactly sacrifice himself. Rather, by putting on this act, Mike manages to appease me (or at least distract me) without actually revealing anything personal about himself or his own experiences. It's not that he represents himself dishonestly; in fact, he doesn't represent himself at all. Instead, Mike's posturing enables him to distance (and thereby protect) himself within this interaction where the option to disengage altogether is not apparent, and it allows him to transform his position from being uncomfortably subjected to my questions to being more or less in charge of the situation.

In many ways, the boys' posturing reflected how these boys were learning to be "boys" within a culture and society where boys and men are expected to be tough, confident, powerful, and in control. Through their exposure to media and in their everyday interactions with peers and adults, these boys were receiving messages about what it means to be a "real boy" and discovering how their masculine posturing, or adaptation to group and cultural norms of masculine behavior, could enhance their ability to influence other people (and shield their own vulnerabilities). To the extent that the boys found their alignment with conventions of masculinity to be useful and effective in their social interactions, they continued to incorporate gender-appropriate scripts into their speech and conduct. However, as the boys began to posture more (e.g., by using "pre-packaged" language and "imported" tones and gestures to express themselves and engage others), the qualities that had marked their full presence and genuine engagement in their interactions and relationships became more difficult to detect.

A Case Study: Jake

The boys did not tell me about their relational capabilities or the shift in their relational presence. Rather, these were things that I observed in the boys' interactions with each other and experienced in their interactions with me. To provide a better sense of what the boys' relational capabilities looked like and how the shift in their relational presence played out, I have therefore included case studies based on my observations and experiences of these boys. In this chapter, Jake's case study provides insight into the boys' ability and willingness to speak out and say exactly what they were thinking and feeling. Jake's example also highlights the boys' resistance against constraints on their self-expression and shows how their resistance began to wane as their group affiliation increasingly depended upon their adaptation to the interpersonal dynamics, rules of engagement, and norms of behavior within their peer group culture.

Tuning In and Speaking Out

Jake was the youngest boy in this class—along with Tony, who had the same birthday—and also the most sociable and outgoing. Although Jake mostly played with other boys while at school, he was friendly and supportive in his interactions with the girls as well as the boys, and seemed spontaneous and sincere in his interactions with adults as well as peers. During a meeting with Jake, Mike, and Rob on my fifteenth visit, when I bring out a bag of toys from my backpack, Jake recognizes the logo on the bag and exclaims excitedly, "Hey, that's from [the toy store] Henry Bear's Park! I've been there!" And when Jake learns that we both live in Cambridge, he responds with his usual warmth and enthusiasm: "Oh cool! So you live pretty close to me."

In addition to being amiable and easy-going, Jake was tuned in to others and could read his relationships with interest and accuracy. For instance, during my tenth visit, Jake notices Min-Haeng's sullen manner as they are playing together quietly in the block corner and expresses his concern. As Jake finishes his Duplo construction, he shows it to Min-Haeng and explains excitedly, "This part shoots out!" When Min-Haeng responds by nodding somberly, Jake remarks casually, "Min-Haeng, you don't seem to be very happy." As Min-Haeng replies softly, "I miss my mom," Jake gently reassures him, "That's O.K. You always have your friends." The two boys then return to working on their respective projects. They continue to play quietly at first. However, moments later when Jake exclaims gleefully, "Look at all these bombs!" Min-Haeng, who now seems in better spirits, responds readily, "This is a scare crow, a robot."

What impressed me about this exchange was not only that Jake was sensitive to subtle emotional cues in Min-Haeng's behavior but that he also was able and willing to respond in an appropriate and supportive manner. Similarly, I was impressed that Min-Haeng not only was aware of what he was feeling and why, but he also could communicate his feelings in a clear and straightforward manner. One could imagine that an older boy or man might not feel so free to comment, as Jake did, on a friend's apparent unhappiness (e.g., for fear of causing embarrassment or offense) or to admit, as Min-Haeng did, to feelings that could be viewed as vulnerable or shameful. Thus, beyond being attuned to emotions, Jake and Min-Haeng also exhibited a sense of entitlement and lack of self-censorship that enabled each boy to know what he knew, feel what he felt, and act on his knowledge and feelings. Moreover, while Min-Haeng seemed comforted by Jake's response, he did not seem compelled to cheer up instantly. Likewise, Jake's sympathy for Min-Haeng did not hamper his own good mood. Rather, they were able to stay with their own feelings and also be with each other.

While Jake's candor was admirable, his outspokenness could sometimes be misconstrued as being too assertive or even aggressive. For instance, during my fourteenth visit, Jake comes under suspicion when, after a dispute with Dan is unfairly settled, he persists in trying to confront Dan directly. The dispute arises as the boys are playing in the block corner. As Dan keeps telling Jake what to do, Jake becomes annoyed and protests by putting his foot on Dan's thigh. When Lucia approaches and asks what is going on, Dan immediately assumes the role of victim and begins to cry.

DAN (*IN TEARS*): He put his feet on my lap.
JAKE (*ANGRILY*): 'Cause he was bossing me around.
DAN: He ruined me and Robby's game.
JAKE (*SARCASTICALLY*): Yeah, right. I started the game.

Dan misrepresents the situation, and Jake points this out. However, without knowing all the facts, Lucia is influenced more by Dan's distress than by Jake's anger. As Lucia tries to mediate, she aligns herself with Dan's story and suggests that maybe Jake unknowingly intruded on Dan and Rob's "two-person game." Dan quickly agrees, even though Jake actually did start the game. Lucia then suggests that Jake and Dan shake hands to make up, but Jake refuses to cooperate. Not surprisingly, Jake is unhappy with Lucia's interpretation, which implies that he is essentially, if unintentionally, at fault.

Although Jake is not interested in reconciling with Dan on these terms, he also does not disengage or walk away from this interaction. Instead, Jake remains staunchly focused on confronting Dan, even when Lucia tries to distract Jake by changing the topic. Concerned about Jake's persistence and determination, Lucia remains nearby to keep an eye on the boys. When Lucia eventually turns her attention elsewhere, Jake finally manages to confront Dan: "Danny, you always boss me around." Dan neither confirms nor denies Jake's accusation. However, Dan does appear to be listening and that is all that seems to matter to Jake. Just minutes afterwards, the two boys join Min-Haeng to look at a comic book, and it is as though the dispute never happened.

> MIN-HAENG: Calvin and Hobbes.
> DAN (*CHEERFULLY*): I like this one.
> JAKE (*CHEERFULLY*): Yeah, I like this one, too.

It seemed that Jake's goal was simply to speak his mind and be heard. Once Jake had a chance to tell Dan how he felt, the dispute was soon forgiven and forgotten.

Advocating for Agency

Just as Jake was determined to speak out when he felt he was not being treated fairly, he resisted being told what to think or do, especially by his peers. During my eleventh visit, as Jake, Mike, and Min-Haeng are looking through a Calvin and Hobbes comic book together, they stop to discuss one scene in which a person resembling Calvin's dad is wearing an orange jumper.

MIKE: These are bad guys. I like the bad guys.

MIN-HAENG: It's his mom and dad.

JAKE: It's a helper.

MIN-HAENG (*TO JAKE*): It's his dad. He disguised himself.

JAKE (*TO MIN-HAENG, MATTER-OF-FACTLY*): You may think that, but I
don't.

Comfortable with individual differences, Jake could acknowledge other people's opinions without feeling compelled to conform (or insisting that others see things his way).

Jake's resistance against constraints on his self-expression was so strong that he sometimes chose to disengage from an interaction rather than surrender his right to say and do what he wanted. During my fourteenth visit, Jake joins Dan, Tony, and Miranda in the reading corner as they perform silly variations of the "Happy Birthday" song. Miranda makes a game of singing the words "Happy birthday" and then flinging herself onto the futon and saying, "Ouch." Miranda seems very pleased with herself and, encouraged by Dan's amused expression, repeats the sequence several times, referring to it as the "Happy Birthday Ouch." When Jake, who has been playing with Rob in the block corner, wanders over and cheerfully offers his own silly version—"Happy birthday to you. You live in a zoo. You act like a monkey and you look like one, too"—Dan rejects Jake's contribution, saying that he does not want Jake to sing that, "Not in this part of the room." In response, Jake says, "I can sing if I want . . . " and tries to rally Miranda's support: " . . . Hey Miranda, did you hear my song?" However, when the other kids remain silent and seem unreceptive, Jake decides to leave and runs back to play with Rob, who asks Jake what happened and, when Jake doesn't answer, assures him, "You don't have to talk about it."

Jake was so comfortable with and accustomed to defending his right to make his own decisions that his reactions to coercive language seemed almost automatic. For instance, during my fourteenth visit, when Rob tells Jake, "You have to be this [character]," Jake instantly replies, "I don't *have* to," even before he sees to which character Rob is referring. And during my eighteenth visit, when Jake accidentally rips one of my plastic bags (in which I keep my toys) and I casually remark, "I'll have to get new bags," Jake immediately corrects me: "You don't, like, *have* to get new bags, but you should, you could get new bags."

Showing and Telling

Given Jake's tendency to be very direct and upfront in expressing his feelings and opinions (and his assumption that other people would do the same), engaging him was usually a come-as-you-are affair. For instance, when Jake is feeling out of sorts during my sixteenth visit, everything about his appearance and conduct reflects his mood. As the other kids line up to attend a school assembly, Jake remains lying on the floor and does not budge, even after Lucia calls for him specifically. When I approach him and offer to let him sit in my lap during the performance, Jake accepts and, with some effort, hoists himself up to join the rest of the group. He seems drained and stands with his shoulders slumped. I comment that he has had a tough week, and he agrees. When I ask whether he is tired, he sighs and answers, "Yeah." Jake knows and shows how he feels and he tells it like it is.

As with the other boys, I appreciated that Jake could be frank with me. During a one-on-one meeting that he requested on my eighteenth visit, Jake is attentive and cooperative while responding to my questions, but he also feels free to assert his own agenda, which is to play with my toys. As I bring out my toys at the start of the meeting, Jake is ecstatic and giggles with glee: "Oooh! Hee-hee-hee!" When I immediately launch into my questions, he begins by responding thoughtfully and patiently. For example, when I ask him about differences between boys and girls, he pauses and asks me to clarify: "Like um, girls in our class or girls, like, all over the world?" However, when my questions persist, Jake begins to look out for his own interest. After each of my questions, he returns his attention to the toys, but I don't catch on. So, when I follow up on a series of questions about hurt feelings by asking Jake, "Can you tell me about that?" he replies firmly but politely, "Well, not right now while I'm setting up all the [toys]," and proceeds to play. A moment later, Jake takes the large plastic bag in which I keep my toys and playfully places it over his head. When I warn him, "Careful. You don't want to put that on your head," Jake seems to understand my concern and assures me, "I can still breathe." When I caution him anyway saying, "Sometimes it's dangerous," he qualifies the risk, "Yeah, sometimes, but not always." Rather than simply accepting (and complying with) what he is told, Jake likes to think things through and decide for himself what he believes and how to proceed. As our meeting comes to an end, Jake asks if he can listen to himself on my tape recorder. When I turn it on, Jake tells a joke: "Where do sheep go to cut their hair? At the bah-bah shop." After we listen to the recording together, I ask Jake, "Does the microphone [and tape recorder] bother you when I have it on?" and he tells me in a casual and unaffected manner: "Nah, it just, um, gets me a little shy sometimes."

Jake's ability to be attuned, outspoken, and comfortable with individual differences seemed to be largely enabled by his parents, who cherished his exuberance and individuality, gave him language to identify and understand emotions (his own and other people's), and encouraged him to be considerate, trusting, and generous in his relationships. Even as the other boys began to distort their voices (e.g., using a baby voice) in their efforts to influence others and get their way, Jake continued to use his regular speaking voice to communicate his thoughts, feelings, and desires. In fact, Jake was the only boy whom I did not observe to use a baby voice during the course of my study. So, when Jake began to express himself in ways that seemed less direct and less upfront, the changes in his manner and behavior were all the more conspicuous.

Modifying Presence across Relationships

Although Jake remained capable of speaking candidly and had the requisite vocabulary to express his views unequivocally, over time his ability to do so began to vary across his relationships. Whereas Jake had tended to be equally outspoken whether he was interacting with boys or girls and peers or adults, his ability to voice his opinions increasingly depended on the person or persons with whom he was interacting and on the circumstances (e.g., where they were, who else was there) of that interaction. In particular, Jake's self-expression when interacting with boys appeared to be influenced by the other boys' status, as compared to his own, within the boys' hierarchy.

With boys whose status was similar to his (e.g., Rob, Min-Haeng, and Dan), Jake seemed free to be open and forthright. With these peers, Jake also tried to be cooperative and inclusive, and he took offense when others did not reciprocate. For instance, during my nineteenth visit when Rob tries to prevent Jake from joining our discussion, Jake does not hesitate to express his displeasure. Upon arriving at class, Rob comes to show me his Playmobil catalog and points out which toys he thinks I should get for my meetings with the boys. As we look through the catalog, Rob uses his baby voice (whereas he generally speaks to me in his regular voice) to make a request: "Me want to play with them when you first buy 'em." When Jake arrives and joins us in looking at the catalog, Rob becomes territorial and tells Jake, "You've looked at this a long time." Rob seems worried that Jake will interfere with his plans to convince me to buy new toys and to let him be the first to play with them. When Jake replies indignantly, "You're not really guarding it," Rob decides, "You're bothering me, Jake." Angered by Rob's attempts to exclude him, Jake walks over to the classroom set of Playmobil toys, which Jake knows are important to Rob, picks up the plastic bin in which the toys are kept, and holds the bin high over his head to show Rob what he has. I am not sure whether Jake intends to make Rob jealous by playing with the toys or to upset Rob, who likes to store the toys in a particular way, by spilling them on the floor. I never find out because Jake's mom intervenes by calling Jake over to give her a hug and thereby distracting him from his course of action. Just as Jake sought to confront Dan when he violated the assumption of equality (by bossing Jake around) and the expectation of honesty (by misrepresenting their exchange to Lucia), Jake was inclined to retaliate when Rob betrayed his trust (by trying to exclude him).

Whereas Jake did not hesitate to take action when his same-status peers failed to act like friends, over the course of their pre-Kindergarten year Jake gradually became uncharacteristically tentative in his interactions with Mike, the self-proclaimed leader of the boys. In addition to Mike's high status, his domineering manner made it difficult for Jake to have much leverage in their interactions. Mike's dismissive attitude towards Jake was evident as early as my first visit to this class. While the kids line up to return to class after recess, Jake tries to engage Mike by pointing his hand like a gun and playfully "shooting" him. When Mike refuses to play along (probably because he doesn't want to play the role of victim) and says coldly, "Shoot me. I'm not dead," Jake responds by threatening to withdraw his friendship: "You're not my buddy." As it turns out, Mike is actually quite sensitive to and concerned about the possibility of being rejected and abandoned by his peers. Nevertheless, he undermines Jake's threat by responding coolly, "That's O.K. I have other buddies."

Resisting and Yielding to Dominance

Although Jake's experiences of being devalued in his relationship with Mike undoubtedly made an impression on Jake, Mike's influence did not appear (at first) to affect the way that Jake treated others. During my seventh visit, Jake joins Rob and Mike as they are using Duplo blocks to construct guns in the block corner. As Jake realizes that there are not enough Duplo blocks for him to construct a weapon, he asks Rob and Mike directly, "Guys, why aren't you sharing with me?" When Mike (who generally is unwilling to give up any advantage he might have) replies defensively, "I'm not going to give you any of mine," Jake seems disappointed but does not say anything. In the meantime, Rob breaks off some blocks from his gun and hands them to Jake.

Despite Mike's refusal to share (or because of Rob's willingness to share), Jake continued to be generous and fair when he was in a position to be helpful. For instance, during my tenth visit when Min-Haeng needs some wheels in order to complete his Duplo construction, Jake and Rob go out of their way to search for extras, and when they cannot find any, Jake removes the wheels from his own construction and gives them to Min-Haeng. Also, when Jake, Rob, and Min-Haeng are constructing guns during my twelfth visit and Rob complains, "Jakey, you're using too many of those (Duplo blocks). I just have a little gun," Jake immediately removes some blocks from his gun and gives them to Rob. The boys then continue with their play, with no trace of resentment or bad feelings. So, for a while, Jake's behaviors continued to reflect his beliefs (e.g., that friends should support each other), and he was able to follow Mike's lead without necessarily following Mike's example.

Although Jake's experiences of being dominated in his relationship with Mike may not have diminished his willingness and tendency to be supportive of others, he became less likely to speak out and to stand up for himself, particularly in interactions involving Mike. During circle time on my eleventh visit, Jen reads a detective story to the kids and then asks them questions about it afterwards. When Jake provides several correct responses in succession, Jen suggests that he would make a good detective. Encouraged by Jen's compliment, Jake happily agrees, "I'm a detective and Mike, too!" When Mike remarks harshly, "I'm better than you," Jake lowers his head and concedes in a soft voice, "Yeah, I know." Mike proceeds to explain why he is better than Jake but, perhaps because he notices (or anticipates) Jen's disapproval, he stops mid-sentence and says to Jake, "Actually, I'm not better than you." In response, Jen smiles approvingly at Mike and cheerfully suggests that Mike and Jake are both good detectives who may just do things differently. By correcting himself and refraining from making further claims of superiority at Jake's expense, Mike avoids Jen's criticism, earns her praise, and incidentally acquires for himself the positive attention that Jen had originally bestowed upon Jake.

Oftentimes, Jake seemed caught off guard and confused by Mike's domineering manner, probably because it was not what Jake expected from someone who was supposed to be a friend. At the end of recess during my twelfth visit, the kids are lined up and waiting to return to class. Once again, Jake tries to engage Mike through gun play. As they stand face to face, and with their hands positioned as guns, Jake aims at Mike and fires first:

JAKE (*PLAYFULLY*): Boom!

MIKE (*IN A STERN VOICE, WITHOUT FIRING*): Drop dead.

JAKE (*FIRING ANOTHER PLAYFUL SHOT*): Boom!

MIKE (*FIRMLY*): Drop dead. When I say, "Drop dead," you have to go like . . . (*He demonstrates how he wants Jake to fall over.*)

JAKE (*ENTHUSIASTICALLY*): How 'bout you . . .

MIKE (*CUTTING JAKE OFF, SPEAKING IN A HARSH TONE*): No. Now you drop dead when I say "Drop dead."

As Jake ponders his next move, Mike notices that I am watching and immediately changes his tone from threatening to playful as he says lightheartedly, "Oh, Jakey," sings innocently, "Dum da dum da dum," and tells Jake nonchalantly, "That was our chance." Although Jake seems perplexed by the sudden change in Mike's manner, he gamely follows along and mimics Mike's playful tone, "O.K., mister. You don't look very funny. You look like a bum-bum."

In this exchange (and others like it), Mike makes it clear that he is in charge, he gets to make the decisions, and he expects Jake to comply with his demands immediately and without question. In this example (and in the previous one), Mike backs off because an adult happens to be watching, which suggests that he knows that he is doing something wrong and has learned to retract sentiments and cover up behaviors (at least when adults are around) that could get him into trouble. Yet, even as Mike learned to regulate his self-expression and modify his behaviors to avoid negative consequences, his sense of entitlement (e.g., to express his preferences and impose them on others) appeared to persist.

For Jake, however, the dynamic of his relationship with Mike—within which he was compelled to confirm Mike's opinions while his own opinions were often ignored, dismissed, or denigrated—began to undermine his ability to be open and honest in expressing himself. In contrast to Jake's confidence and determination to speak his mind and make his own decisions in his other relationships, Jake seemed unsure about how to respond to Mike, who expected to be supported but did not necessarily offer his support in return. Whereas Jake usually resisted his peers' attempts to tell him what to do, he rarely if ever accused Mike of bossing him around, even when this was clearly what Mike was doing. Jake also began to display a negative attitude towards himself, even without being prompted by Mike to do so. For instance, later during my twelfth visit, I overhear Jake chanting to himself, "Two, four, six, eight, who do we appreciate? Mike! Two, four, six, eight, who do we eliminate? Jake!" Unable to avoid Mike's dominance, Jake makes it into a game, perhaps in an effort to make light of his situation.

Seeking Accountability

Although he was becoming accustomed to Mike's domineering manner, Jake still would try to undermine Mike's dominance by speaking out whenever he had the chance and in whatever ways he could. During a meeting with Mike, Jake, and Rob on my fifteenth visit, Jake uses every opportunity that arises to talk about Mike's misconduct. First, when I ask the boys, "Has anybody ever done something that you didn't like?" Jake points at Mike and says bluntly, "He threw a punch at me." When Mike starts to defend himself against Jake's accusation, "No, I didn't do an upper cut. That was an accident . . . " but ends up bragging, " . . . O.K., I know karate. And so . . . ," Jake challenges Mike's grandiose claims (albeit under his breath): "He took it, anyway." Seeming mildly irritated with each other, Mike and Jake then start to engage in rough play. When Mike pinches him, Jake feels free to retaliate, citing fairness to justify his response: "Now I get to do it to you, since you got to do it to me."

In an effort to get the boys settle down, I ask them another question, and Jake again reports on Mike's past offenses.

> JUDY: O.K. . . . Have you ever done something that other people didn't like?
>
> MIKE: Um, well, once.
>
> JAKE (*NODDING*): A lot of times . . . he does that a lot.
>
> ROB (*NODDING*): Yeah.
>
> JUDY (*TO JAKE AND ROB*): Like what?
>
> MIKE: Actually, I got this little dart gun. It shoots these little rubber things . . . You pull this thing back. It's a little gun. You can make it into a big gun, but I just use the little part. I put the darts in, I pull the thing back . . . and I sneaked to my mom's car and bang, bang, bang. I shot her.
>
> JUDY (*FEIGNING ALARM*): You shot your mom?!
>
> MIKE: No, I shot my mom's car. Actually, I shot my mom. And the sticky part, it was like this (*pretending to stick a dart on his forehead*). She was like this, stuck to the wall. She was stuck to the wall. (*Jake giggles*).

By accusing Mike of more offenses than he is willing to admit, Jake and Rob effectively back Mike into a corner, so to speak. However, before Jake and Rob can tell me about Mike's misdemeanors, Mike deflects their accusations by telling his own story, which centers on masculine posturing and transforms his admission of guilt into another chance to show off. Mike carefully crafts his response to serve his purposes. When I express surprise that he shot his mom, Mike begins to present a milder version of his story ("No, I shot my mom's car"), but then proceeds with his original version and even embellishes it to enhance its entertainment value ("She was stuck to the wall"), which, considering Jake's amused response, seems to bring about the desired effect.

Despite Mike's diversions, Jake continues to hold Mike accountable for his transgressions.

> JUDY (*TO THE BOYS*): How about hurting people's feelings? Have you ever hurt somebody's feelings?
>
> JAKE (*PLAINLY*): Um, yeah (*to Mike*) you have.
>
> JUDY (*INTERESTED, TO MIKE*): You have?
>
> MIKE (*DEFENSIVELY*): No.

JUDY (*INTERESTED*): Can you tell me about that?

MIKE (*ACCUSINGLY, TO JAKE*): You have.

JAKE (*UNFAZED*): Yeah. We both have, right?

Jake and Mike then launch into a back-and-forth exchange, with Mike protesting, "No," and Jake asserting, "Yes." Although Jake focuses on reporting Mike's offenses, he is willing to admit his own guilt as well ("We both have, right?"). However, Mike remains staunchly in denial and, as usual, refuses to give in. Within a minute's time, Jake and Mike's squabble turns into a "slap" fight, with each boy slapping the other's thigh. When I tell them, "Please keep your hands to yourself. I don't want anybody to get hurt," they begin to tap each other instead while chanting playfully, "Tap, tap, tap," and they soon seem to lose sight of the cause of their dispute.

As Jake and Mike's chant evolves from "tap" to "ch-yeah" and takes on a lively rhythm, Rob joins in and—responding to a question that I had asked earlier in this meeting about what it's like to be a boy—smiles and says in a sly voice, "This is what we [boys] like to do." When I seek clarification, "What do you like to do? Tap each other?" Rob smiles and continues, "Ch-yeah, ch-yeah." The three boys continue chanting merrily, "Ch-yeah, ch-yeah, ch-yeah," until Mike suddenly declares in a gruff voice, "This is what I like to do to my friends . . . " Mike then slaps his hands together and declares sternly, " . . . I kill 'em." When Mike proceeds to demonstrate by slapping Jake on the thigh (again), Jake retaliates and, sounding annoyed, retorts, "That's what it felt like." I tell the boys, "No more hitting, please," and Jake and Mike return to chanting "no" and "yes" until I change the subject and bring out my toys.

Backing Down

Despite Jake's efforts to undermine Mike's dominance and diffuse Mike's defensiveness, Jake's challenges only fueled Mike's determination to remain in control, and Mike usually found ways to regain his advantage. Thus, whereas Jake was very susceptible to Mike's influence, Jake's influence on Mike was rarely and barely detectable. Given this power imbalance (and Jake's insistence in his other relationships on fairness and mutuality), I expected Jake to withdraw from his relationship with Mike. However, Jake chose instead to remain in this relationship in which he was continually at a disadvantage, and, possibly as a result, his resistance (e.g., against being imposed upon) began to wane. For instance, during my sixteenth visit, Jake initially protests when Mike behaves disrespectfully towards him. However, when Mike is unapologetic, Jake goes out of his way to appease and please Mike. On this occasion, Mike, Jake, and Min-Haeng are reading quietly in the block corner. Mike is looking through a Lego catalog, Min-Haeng is looking through a Tin Tin book, and Jake is looking through a Star Wars book. When Mike suddenly grabs the Star Wars book from Jake, Jake complains, "Hey!" and Mike explains hastily, "I want to show Min-Haeng something." When Jake objects to having the book grabbed out of his hands, Mike simply repeats himself, "I want to show Min-Haeng something," as though his motive justifies his means, and does not apologize. Whereas Jake might have pursued the matter with his other peers, he succumbs to Mike by immediately dropping his accusatory tone and trying to engage Mike amiably, "Look, the light saver." When Mike responds by correcting him sternly, "Light saber, not saver," Jake remarks playfully, "Saber-tooth tiger?" and Mike replies flatly, "No." Despite Mike's dismissive attitude towards him, Jake continues to be supportive, as when Mike points out something in the book that interests him, "Look at, gun." and Jake replies brightly, "Cool." Moreover, when Tony approaches and tries to join in by saying, "Let me see," and pushing towards Mike, Jake mediates on Mike's behalf, "Stop crowding around Mike." In contrast to Jake's refusal in his other relationships to be bossed around, Jake not only puts up with Mike's domineering behavior, but also remains loyal to and is protective of Mike.

Although Jake seemed to suspect that his relationship with Mike was not the way friendships are supposed to be, he did not know what he could do about it. During a meeting with Jake on my eighteenth visit, Jake talks with me about the dilemma that he faces in being friends with Mike.

JUDY: Has anyone ever hurt your feelings before?

JAKE (*PLAINLY*): Yes, Mikey has.

JUDY: He has? What did he do?

JAKE: Well, like, once he did an upper cut on me. Goes like (*in slow motion, he punches his jaw from bottom-up*).

JUDY: Ouch.

JAKE: It really hurt. And I told on him.

JUDY: Yeah?

JAKE: It's a good thing to do.

JUDY: What's a good thing to do?

JAKE: Instead of hurting him back. Tell somebody.

JUDY: Who's your favorite play buddy?

JAKE: Mike.

JUDY: Yeah?

JAKE: But sometimes he hurts me, too. Kind of a problem.

JUDY: Why does he hurt you?

JAKE: Well, he's angry.

JUDY: Angry at you?

JAKE: Yeah.

JUDY (*INTERESTED*): Why would he be angry at you?

JAKE (*THOUGHTFULLY*): Well, I don't know. I have no idea. But any-
ways . . . (*He returns his attention to the toys.*)

As Mike's anger could be unpredictable and the reasons for Mike's
aggression unclear, Jake reached an impasse in this relationship and
seemed to focus his efforts on coping with and adapting to (rather than
trying to change) his situation.

Adopting a Cynical Attitude

While it was mainly in his relationship with Mike that Jake struggled to
understand what he could expect from friends and peers and how he
should act with them, Jake's submission to Mike eventually appeared to
impact Jake's attitude and behaviors in his other relationships as well.
Whereas Jake had been remarkably upbeat and optimistic about everything and everyone earlier in the school year, he began to adopt a more
cynical attitude towards others and towards himself as the school year
progressed. For instance, during my nineteenth visit, Jake mocks and discounts his peers' contributions, and in doing so deviates drastically from
his previous tendency to be accepting and encouraging. First, when Jen
reads a story during circle time about some people dancing in a tub and
Rob demonstrates by standing up and joyfully wiggling his body, Jake
says derisively, "Oh, shut up, Rob." Jake's derogatory remark and tone are
surprising, as Rob's actions seem like something Jake himself would be

inclined to do. Next, when Jen directs the children's attention to the calendar and mentions that "Gabriella updated the calendar today," Jake criticizes Gabriella's efforts: "And not very good either." Even if Jake is simply stating his honest opinion, it is not like him to be so judgmental. Usually, Jake is the one to remind his peers that they could make their own decisions about what to do and how to do it. Jake does, however, seem to be aware of and to hold himself accountable for his poor attitude. At the end of circle time when Jen tells the kids to give themselves a pat on the back for having behaved so well, Jake adds, "Except me," and does not pat himself on the back. All the same, Jake's disgruntled mood and manner persist as he and the other kids head to recess. Outside, Jake joins Mike and Rob, who have decided to look for arrowheads in the dirt. When Rob tells Jake excitedly, "Look at all the arrowheads I found," Jake replies sternly, "No, they're stones," and swiftly discounts Rob's discoveries. Jake's newly acquired cynicism was also evident during a meeting with Jake and Rob on my twenty-first visit. When I ask the boys if there is anything special about being a boy and Rob eagerly reports, "My mom buys me lots of toys in one day," Jake dryly informs Rob, "That's not special."

Jake had always felt free to disagree with his peers, but he had usually managed to remain respectful (and even appreciative) of differences in their opinions. While Jake still seemed to say what he was thinking in these examples, his dismissive manner and condescending tone were a departure from his trademark open-mindedness and delight in simple pleasures. Although Jake may not have necessarily replaced his positive outlook with a negative one, he seemed to take on a less fantastic (but possibly more rational and practical) view of himself and his world, such that he no longer considered it possible for unabashed enthusiasm to be celebrated, for stones to be construed as arrowheads, and for a mother's indulgence to be considered special. At the age of five, Jake had begun to espouse a more sober sense of reality and to adopt a voice of reason that dampened his exuberance and left him discontented.

Assuming a Dominant Stance

As Jake found (mainly in his interactions with Mike) that it did not serve him well to presume cooperation, at least not when others were focused on competition, he began to look out more for his own interests and to try to get his way when possible. For example, Jake was occasionally bossy and demanding in his interactions with Tony (who had the lowest status among the boys and was eager to please Jake), even as he continued to yield to Mike and to cooperate with Min-Haeng, Rob, and Dan.

In a meeting with Jake and Tony during my twentieth visit, the boys start out on equal footing, so to speak. As I bring out my toys, they decide which toy characters they want to be and gather their respective accessories. However, when Jake covets a toy that Tony happens to pick up first, Jake adopts a domineering manner (not unlike the one that Mike adopts with him) in his efforts to claim the toy for himself.

> JAKE (*CHEERFULLY*): I'm gonna, I'm gonna be [Dark Knight].
> TONY (*CHEERFULLY*): I'm gonna, I've been [Viking] before.
> JAKE (*MATTER-OF-FACTLY*): Oh. You're being a bad guy.
> TONY (*QUICKLY CHANGING HIS MIND*): No. I'm being [Blue Prince].
> JAKE (*CASUALLY*): Oh, you're a good guy. I'm a good guy, too.
> TONY: Because you're a knight . . . I get to have a sword and a shield and a . . .
> JAKE: I get to have a sword, an axe, a cape . . .
> TONY (*MUMBLING*): Where's the sword? Where's the sword? Where's the sword? Where's my sword?! . . . (*Singing triumphantly*) There it is. Here it is. Here it is my sword.
> JAKE (*PROUDLY*): Look at [my character].
> TONY (*SINGING*): I am the king.
> JAKE (*MATTER-OF-FACTLY*): No, you're a prince.
> TONY (*PLAYFULLY*): So I get to ride horses, horses. Actually, I'm a guard.
> JAKE (*EXPLAINING*): No, you're actually a prince [*the character's given title*].
> TONY (*SCANNING THE TOYS AND NOTICING*): There's only one horse.
> JAKE (*DEMANDING*): No. I get to have this [horse]. (*Suddenly frantic*) I get to have [the horse]!

Jake and Tony are silent. Jake's outburst seems to have surprised them both. Jake takes a moment to calm down, adopts a more casual tone, and tries to reason with Tony (even though Tony has not challenged him).

> JAKE (*CASUALLY*): Hey, I was gonna have [the horse]. Princes don't usually have horses. Princes don't have horses, you know. If I was a prince, I wouldn't have a horse. In real life, if I were a prince, I wouldn't have

a horse. (*Jake looks to me, as though wondering whether I am going to call him on his bluff.*)

JUDY (*MORE INTERESTED THAN DOUBTFUL*): Oh yeah?

JAKE: Yeah.

JUDY: What would you use instead?

JAKE: I would walk on feet.

JUDY: Yeah?

JAKE: Or I would ride in a carriage.

TONY: The carriage is right here. (*Picking up a toy cart*) Ooh, what's this? Is this for the . . .

Prompted by Jake's claim (that if he were the prince, he would ride in a carriage), Tony looks for a carriage. As there are no carriages among my toys, Tony settles for a toy cart ("The carriage is right here"), which he presumably intends for his prince (so that Jake's knight can ride the horse). However, Jake seems to think that Tony is offering the cart/carriage to him (and refusing to give up the horse). So, Jake intensifies his efforts by issuing a threat.

JAKE (*STERNLY*): Princes wouldn't really ride a horse that goes on a cart. (*decidedly*) O.K., . . . then next time I get to go, next time I come [meet with Judy], I get to go alone, without you.

TONY (*PLEADING*): Yeah, but when I come, you can use the horse.

Although Tony has now explicitly relinquished the toy in question, Jake doesn't realize this and continues to make threats: "You either, you don't come over to my house or let me have the horse. If you let me have the horse, then I . . . " At this point, Tony quickly hands the toy horse to Jake, who accepts it with an air of self-righteousness.

JAKE (*IN A HAUGHTY TONE*): . . . Well, then, thank you.

TONY (*HOPEFULLY*): So, can I come over to your house?

JAKE (*TRIUMPHANTLY*): Yes!

TONY (*SPEAKING FOR HIS CHARACTER, THE PRINCE*): Well, I'll walk with my feet.

JAKE: Yeah.

TONY (*SPEAKING FOR THE PRINCE*): I am the walk. I need my sword.

Given that Tony has surrendered the disputed item and Jake now has what he wanted, I expect Jake to resume a more cooperative attitude. To the contrary, Jake proceeds to flaunt his character's advantages and undermines Tony's efforts to claim equal or comparable provisions for his character.

> JAKE: Look at me! I have two weapons [*an axe and a sword*]. You only have one [*a sword*].
>
> TONY (*MEEKLY*): Yeah, but I use someone else's [axe].
>
> JAKE: Actually, well, there are only long axes. Princes don't usually have long axes.
>
> TONY: But I have a sword.
>
> JAKE (*IN A SNEAKY VOICE*): Well, you can use the [bad guy's] axe. (*Laughing wickedly*) Heh, heh, heh.
>
> TONY (*HESITANT*): So I can get the axe? I, pretend you're on my side.
>
> JAKE (*IN HIS NORMAL VOICE*): Yeah, I am.

It is only when Tony explicitly asks Jake to join him ("pretend you're on my side") that Jake finally abandons his domineering manner and returns to being supportive.

Accommodating to Circumstances

Whereas Jake maintained his confidence and sense of entitlement (to be treated with respect and at least as an equal) in his other relationships, he seemed to become increasingly submissive in his interactions with Mike. I wasn't the only one who noticed a change in Jake's manner and outlook. On my eighteenth visit, Jen tells me that since spring break, Jake has started saying that he is stupid. Jen then describes an interaction that she observed wherein Mike told Jake, "You're stupid," and Jake agreed, "Yeah, I know I am." Jake also became increasingly cautious in his relationship with Mike and seemed to go out of his way to avoid saying or doing anything that might offend Mike. For instance, during my twenty-third visit, when Jake accuses Min-Haeng of being a tattletale, Jake makes a point to assure Mike (who is sitting next to Min-Haeng) that the accusation is not directed at him: "You're not a tattle-tale, but Min-Haeng is."

Concerned that Jake's subordination in his relationship with Mike might be hurting his self-esteem, I ask Jake about it during a meeting with him, Rob, and Tony on my twenty-fourth visit.

JUDY (*TO JAKE*): You know what I heard the other day? I heard you say that you are stupid and I was wondering why you said that.

JAKE (*PLAINLY*): 'Cause I think I am.

JUDY: You think you're stupid?

JAKE (*PLAINLY*): Yeah, I do.

JUDY: Why do you think that?

JAKE (*PLAINLY*): Well, I dunno, I just do.

JUDY (*CONCERNED*): I think you're very smart.

ROB (*TO JUDY, REASSURINGLY*): No, it's a little game he plays.

JUDY (*TO JAKE*): Oh, it's a little game you play?

ROB: Mike and Jake.

JAKE (*PLAYFULLY*): Two, four, six, eight, who do we eliminate? Jake!

JUDY: Why?

JAKE: 'Cause, you know what eliminate means?

JUDY: Yeah, it means get rid of.

JAKE: Yeah.

JUDY: Why do you want to get rid of Jake? Jake is great.

JAKE (*PLAINLY*): No.

Although Rob reassures me that Jake's self-deprecation is just in jest, Jake's responses when I ask him why he says he's stupid ("'Cause I think I am") and whether he thinks he's stupid ("Yeah, I do") seem plainspoken rather than contrived. At some level, Jake may believe it. Or maybe Jake has come to expect criticism and preemptively puts himself down in order to undermine anyone else's attempt to do so. Either way, I find it unsettling that Jake has taken to making this claim, and I worry about its impact.

My uncertainty about what to make of Jake's self-deprecatory remarks raises another point regarding the shift in his relational presence, or changes I observed in his conduct and styles of engaging others. During the first half of his pre-Kindergarten year, there had been no need to second-guess Jake's meaning because he usually said what he meant and meant what he said. It was easy to know what he was thinking and how he was feeling because he could and would tell you, and in a clear and straightforward manner. However, as Jake found (especially in his relationship with Mike) that being open and forthright could have negative repercussions, he learned to tone down his enthusiasm and became more cautious about what he expressed and how he expressed it. Jake also adapted to his situation (and avoided undesirable consequences) by learning to anticipate and deliver what other people expected of him. As a result, it became difficult to know whether, or to what extent, his behaviors still reflected his beliefs, including what he really thought and how he really felt.

* * *

Jake's case study illuminates boys' relational capabilities—including their capacity to be fully present and genuinely engaged in their relationships—and how these may become less apparent as boys adapt to interpersonal dynamics and norms of masculinity within their peer group culture. We saw how Jake tried to preserve his connection to self (e.g., his sense of integrity, agency, and choice) as he negotiated his peer interactions, and how Jake's determination to voice to his opinions (e.g., sing his version of the birthday song) could sometimes result in disconnections from others (e.g., when Jake decided to disengage from the interaction after Dan and Miranda were unreceptive of his contributions). We also saw how Jake began to rein in his exuberance and outspokenness as he ascertained how it was possible for him to express himself and engage in his relationship with Mike. Moreover, we saw how the effects of his subordination to Mike could carry over to his other relationships. Although earlier in the school year, Jake had fervently resisted any and all constraints on his self-expression (e.g., through speaking out and refusing to be bossed around), he was becoming more savvy and strategic in his social interactions, for his own protection and for his own good.

3

Socialization and Its Discontents

The shift in these boys' relational presence—from presence to pretense via posturing—reflected in part how the boys were actively reading, taking in, and responding to their gender socialization at school. Although boys' gender socialization often begins at home, their exposure to cultural messages about masculinity and societal pressures to conform can intensify during early childhood when many children enter schools for the first time. Through observing and interacting with adults and peers in their school settings, boys acquire their sense of what is considered appropriate and desirable behavior for boys, and also how their conformity to and deviance from group and cultural norms can affect their social status (especially among their same-sex peers) and their relationships (with girls as well as boys). Moreover, through their experiences of gender socialization, boys come to understand that being a "real boy" is not simply a matter of who they are but also how they act. Namely, boys learn that they must prove their masculinity,[1] for instance through the ways in which they conduct themselves and engage with other people. Boys also learn that they must continually prove their masculinity, which can be called into question by anyone and at any time.[2]

One way that boys can prove their masculinity is by aligning with masculine ideals, as defined within their broader cultural and social contexts and as manifested within their specific family and peer group cultures. In their desire to identify with their peers (e.g., be one of the boys) and relate to their peers (e.g., be with the boys), boys learn both to emphasize qualities and display behaviors that liken them to other boys and to downplay or conceal those that set them apart. In cultures and societies where masculinity is defined in contrast to, or as the opposite of, femininity, boys also learn to show that they are boys (and not girls) by distancing and differentiating themselves from girls, women, and anything associated with femininity.[3]

Aligning with Masculinity

The most common way that the boys in my study proved their masculinity and established themselves as being one of the boys and with the boys was by expressing an interest in "boys' toys and activities." For these boys, at this age, this meant focusing on guns and gun play, as opposed to dolls and doll play. The boys' focus on guns was apparent as early as my first visit to this class, which took place during the second week of the school year. When Carol and I explained to the teachers, Lucia and Jen, our interest in studying boys' experiences and exploring central themes and issues in boys' lives, they immediately warned us that the boys in this class "are *very* interested in guns." The boys' parents were also aware of the boys' focus on guns and tried to discourage the boys' gun play by expressing their disapproval both implicitly and explicitly. During my first visit while Mike and Min-Haeng are playing in the block corner at the start of the school day, Mike notices Min-Haeng's construction and comments excitedly, "What a long gun!" Before Min-Haeng can respond, Min-Haeng's mom, who has come over to say goodbye to Min-Haeng, gently interjects, "It's not a gun." Both boys remain silent until Min-Haeng's mom leaves, at which point Min-Haeng reveals to Mike that his construction is indeed a gun.

By my fourth visit, the teachers had decided to ban guns and prohibit gun play in the classroom. Although this new rule presumably applied to the girls as well as the boys, it was primarily directed at the boys because the girls had not really shown any interest in guns or gun play. The teachers were concerned that the boys' gun play had become "all-consuming," as the boys were spending most if not all of their free time constructing toy guns and engaging each other through gun play. Lucia even put away the Duplo blocks that the boys were using to make their weapons, in hopes that the boys would explore other options for play. However, rather than discouraging the boys' gun play, the teachers' ban seemed only to enhance its allure. When the Duplo blocks were put away, the boys simply used whatever materials were available (e.g., their hands, pieces of fruit from their lunches) to construct their guns. Aware that they risked getting into trouble, the boys continued to play with guns but learned to hide or disguise them when adults were around. For example, when the teachers asked about the boys' constructions, which looked very much like guns, the boys claimed that their constructions were not guns but "dinosaurs," "rocket ships," "microscopes," and "old-fashioned cameras." As soon as the teachers left, the boys would then reveal that their constructions were actually guns and surreptitiously resume their gun play. If anything, the boys' gun play became more exciting after guns were expressly forbidden and even strengthened the boys' bond with each other as they engaged in this forbidden activity together as a group. More than anything, the boys seemed to enjoy the thrill of doing together what they were not supposed to do.

It is easy to understand why the boys' teachers and parents would be concerned about the boys' focus on guns and want to discourage their gun play. As adults, we tend to associate guns with violence and aggression, and we worry that a boy's enthusiasm for guns may reflect or lead to a proclivity towards these vices. However, based on what I observed in this class, the boys' focus on guns and gun play was not necessarily indicative of violent or aggressive tendencies. Although the boys' gun play could definitely appear aggressive (e.g., when they used their "guns" to "shoot" each other), the idea that guns are linked with actual violence, injury, and death did not seem fully formed in these boys' minds. Moreover, the purpose of the boys' gun play was rarely if ever to express anger, hostility, resentment, or other malevolent feelings. Rather, these boys seemed primarily interested in playing and being involved with each other, and one way they did this—at this age and in this setting—was by constructing guns and engaging in gun play together.

Please note that I am not suggesting that adults embrace or encourage gun play. Rather, given the possibility that young boys may not regard guns in the same ways or as having the same connotations as adults do, I wish to emphasize the importance of considering how boys themselves view guns and gun play and of trying to understand what it is about guns and gun play that appeals to boys in particular before we decide what it means and dread its implications. For example, in focusing on the boys' perspectives, I found that their interest in guns and gun play did not necessarily reflect (nor limit) their personal preferences. When playing on their own, individual boys were as likely to choose other toys and activities as they were to choose guns and gun play. Rather, the boys' interest in guns and gun play was primarily evident when two or more boys were playing together, and the main allure of guns and gun play seemed to be that they provided (and proved to be) a quick, effective, and distinctly "masculine" way for the boys to engage and bond with each other. For instance, during my eighteenth visit as Mike and Rob are standing at one of the tables, where dozens of colorful wooden cubes lay scattered on the table top, Mike notices a cluster of cubes that forms an "L" shape and remarks, "Oh, cool!" To show that he sees it too, Rob confirms, "Gun!" and the boys' shared interest in guns allows them instantly to reinforce their sense of connection to each other.

In addition to helping the boys relate to each other, the boys' interest in guns and gun play also became a way for the boys to identify as boys. For instance, during my twenty-second visit, Jake suggests that one of the main differences between boys and girls is their expressed interest (or lack of interest) in guns.

> JUDY: Are the boys different from the girls, or are they the same?
> JAKE: They're a lot different.
> JUDY: They're a lot different? Can you tell me how they're different?
> JAKE: 'Cause the boys in our class really like guns and stuff.
> JUDY: Oh.
> JAKE: And the girls, like, hate them.
> JUDY: The girls hate guns?
> JAKE: Yeah.

To the extent that these boys considered guns to be a "boys' toy" (and not a "girls' toy"), the boys' gun play was not only an interest that the boys shared but also something that defined them as boys. This may explain why the teachers' efforts to discourage the boys' gun play were unsuccessful. Despite the teachers' ban, the boys continued to construct and play with guns, not because they were especially interested in guns per se, but because gun play had become the primary means for them to affirm their group affiliation and confirm their masculine identities. Of course, the boys also engaged and bonded with each other through other interests and activities. They drew pictures together, ran around together, read together, and constructed narratives for their fantasy play together. However, compared with gun play, these things did not seem to instill as automatically or as strongly the same sense of group identity and camaraderie among the boys, maybe because they are not considered specific nor exclusive to boys.

As it turned out, the boys' interest in guns lasted only as long as it helped them to bond with each other and be a part of the group. Although the boys' desire to identify with and relate to each other persisted, their interests and group activities changed over time. For instance, after the boys found out about the school shootings in Jonesboro, Arkansas (which occurred during March of the boys' pre-Kindergarten year), the boys' interest in guns decreased significantly, and soon thereafter they abandoned their gun play in favor of other activities, like playing with Playmobil and collecting Pokémon cards. And during their Kindergarten year, the focus of the boys' play changed again as they became more interested in sports, especially soccer and basketball, which appeal to (and can facilitate the sense of connection among) men as well as boys and are still considered masculine despite increases in women's and girls' participation.

Distancing and Differentiating from Femininity

Whether driven by their own interests and inclinations, by their desire to identify and relate to each other, or by both, the boys' displays of stereotypically masculine behaviors were further encouraged by the boys-versus-girls dynamic that had emerged in this class. This dynamic manifested in two ways: as a division, wherein the boys acted against the girls, and as a distinction, wherein the boys acted differently than the girls.

In terms of a division, the boys-versus-girls dynamic not only separated these two groups but also pitted them against each other. Viewing themselves as being on opposite sides, the boys and girls engaged each other accordingly, for instance, by chasing and planning "attacks" against each other during recess. Although it was mainly the boys who instigated these oppositional encounters, the girls also played a role in perpetuating them. During recess on my nineteenth visit, for example, the girls run around screaming as though they are being chased, even though they are not. Sure enough, the boys soon notice the girls' behavior and begin to chase them. Moreover, it was not always the boys who played the role of aggressor and the girls who played the role of victim. The girls also chased the boys and could be intimidating in their own right. For instance, during a one-on-one meeting on my twenty-third visit, Rob tells me that sometimes the boys need protection from the girls because "the girls sometimes do make us [boys] a little bit afraid."

Not surprisingly, this division had implications for the boys' interactions with each other and with the girls. By positioning and defining themselves in opposition to the girls, the boys effectively strengthened their bonds with each other and hindered their relationships with the girls. Near the end of my first visit, I am sitting with Tatiana and Gabriella on the floor when I notice Rob (who had just come from playing with the boys) sneaking up on us. Whereas Rob had been shy upon arriving at class with his dad, his mood is now playful as he approaches us with a furtive smile on his face. Stopping a couple feet away from us, Rob (playing the role of bank robber) aims his toy weapon at us and declares, "This is a stick up." Rob is delighted when I exclaim, "Oh no!" and Tatiana screams, gets up, and leads me by the hand as we try to escape. Encouraged by our lively response, Rob proceeds to chase us around the room. As Rob closes in on us with his weapon in hand, I ask him why he wants to shoot Tatiana and Gabriella, since they are his friends, and he immediately corrects me by informing me in a casual tone, "I don't have friends who are girls." When I ask him why not, he replies matter-of-factly, "Because I play with the boys."

In addition to providing a reason and means for distancing themselves from the girls' femininity, these interactions wherein the boys engaged the girls as adversaries also provided the boys with opportunities to enact their masculinity. For instance, during playtime on my eleventh visit, Rob approaches Miranda, scrunches up his face in an effort to look scary, and growls, "We're tough. We're a tough guy." Although Rob is acting on his own, his use of the collective "we" suggests that he is representing the boys as a group, as he assumes the role of aggressor in this interaction.

Whereas there had been some intermingling at the start of the school year, the boys and girls gradually separated and began to play almost exclusively with their same-sex peers. As Rob demonstrated when he explained, "I don't have friends who are girls . . . Because I play with the boys," the boys were learning that they could be friends with either the boys or the girls but they could not really be friends with both. Likewise, although the boys and girls could play against each other, they were not supposed to play with each other. Therefore, as the division between the boys and the girls was increasingly emphasized, it literally became a matter of girls against boys and boys against girls.

In terms of a distinction, the boys-versus-girls dynamic fed into the view that boys and girls are not only on opposite sides but they are also each other's opposites. To the extent that the boys adopted this view, they learned to behave in ways that showed, on the one hand, that they are boys and, on the other, that they are not girls. They also showed that they are boys *by* showing that they are not girls. During my eighteenth visit, while explaining the differences between boys and girls, Jake suggests that the boys' and the girls' interests are not only specific to each sex but also exclusive by sex.

> JAKE: Well, there's like, 'cause boys really like weapons and stuff and the girls really like dolls and stuff like that.
> JUDY: Oh really? Do the girls ever play with the weapons, too?
> JAKE (*SUCCINCTLY*): No.
> JUDY: How about the boys? Do they play with the dolls, ever?
> JAKE (*DRAMATICALLY, ADDING A "W" SOUND AT THE END*): No.

Accordingly, the boys could demonstrate their masculinity and differentiate themselves from the girls not only by expressing an interest in weapons, which were considered "boys' toys," but also by rejecting dolls and doll play which, as Jake describes, are for girls.

The girls also understood this distinction and similarly had developed rigid notions about what boys and girls could and should want to play with. For instance, during a meeting with Gabriella on my nineteenth visit, I offer to let her play with my Playmobil toys but she is not interested.

> GABRIELLA: Do you have any dolls?
> JUDY: Well, there are little people in the Playmobil. What kind of dolls do you like to play with?
> GABRIELLA: Um. Good dolls.
> JUDY: Why do you like to play with dolls?
> GABRIELLA: Because girls play with dolls.

Like Jake, Gabriella has learned that there are "boys' toys" and "girls' toys" and that it is important to display a preference for toys that are considered appropriate to one's gender. Indeed, the reason that Gabriella gives to explain why she likes dolls is "because girls play with dolls." Thus, even though the Playmobil figures include girls as well as boys, these toys are unlikely to appeal to girls like Gabriella so long as they are regarded as a "boys' toy."

In addition to expressing gender-appropriate toy preferences, the boys further distinguished themselves from girls by disparaging and avoiding anything that they associated with girls. For instance, during my eleventh visit, while Min-Haeng, Mike, and Jake look through a book of Calvin and Hobbes comic strips together, Min-Haeng fervently declares his distaste when he sees depictions of girls and "feminine" displays of affection. While scanning each page of the comic book, the boys point out what they like, including "the alien part" and "the gun part." They also point out what they dislike, as when Min-Haeng sees a girl and remarks emphatically, "Ew! Girlfriend!" Just then, Jake's mom comes to give Jake a kiss goodbye, which prompts Min-Haeng to exclaim, "Ew! Kissing! I hate kissing! Jake kissed his mom!" When Jake's mom smiles and asks him, "Don't you like it when your mom kisses you?" Min-Haeng replies bluntly, "No, I hate it."

As with their shared interest in "masculine" objects and activities (e.g., guns, gun play), the boys' shared aversion to femininity became a way for them to bond with each other while confirming their masculinity. During a meeting with Tony, Jake, and Rob on my twenty-first visit when Tony mentions that, "Once I saw [the Disney movie] *Pocahontas*," Jake replies neutrally at first; "I saw *Pocahontas*." However, when Rob expresses a negative attitude towards the title character, "Ew, the girl. Ew," Jake instantly agrees, "I know!" Likewise, during my twenty-first visit, Mike and Min-Haeng support and encourage each other as they describe their contempt for girls. When Min-Haeng tells Mike, "Girls make me sick," Mike enthusiastically concurs, "Me, too!" Min-Haeng then jolts back suddenly, as though overwhelmed by an unpleasant memory, and exclaims, "Yuck! Girls give me kisses!" In response, Mike sympathizes, "Yeah, Tatiana said she loved me." While the boys' declarations of disgust are exaggerated to the point of being comical, they allow the boys to maximize the perceived chasm that separates them from the girls and to demonstrate to each other that they are on the same side.

Although the boys were especially careful to avoid engaging in affectionate displays with girls and women, it appeared that even symbols of "feminine" affection could incite the boys' objections. For instance, during my fourteenth visit as Min-Haeng and Dan look through the Calvin and Hobbes comic book together, Min-Haeng recoils dramatically whenever he comes across anything he associates with femininity.

MIN-HAENG (*JOLTING BACK*): Ew! Love.

DAN (*PLAINLY*): It's a Valentine.

MIN-HAENG (*JOLTING BACK*): Ew! A girl!

Some of the boys also tended to avoid engaging in affectionate displays with boys and men, at least in public settings. For instance, during my twentieth visit, when Mike's dad prepares to leave by asking Mike for a hug and kiss, Mike walks slowly and self-consciously towards his dad, stands with his arms at his sides, and allows his dad to hug him. While in his dad's embrace, Mike makes a face like he is slightly annoyed or feels inconvenienced by this exchange and lets his body go limp like a rag doll. However, there is a brief moment when Mike smiles slightly and returns his dad's hug (by placing his hands on his dad's back) before letting his arms fall loosely at his sides again and resuming his air of indifference. As Mike and his dad finish their hug and begin to pull away from each other, Mike's dad gives Mike a kiss on the cheek, which Mike subtly wipes away by gently brushing his cheek with his fingertips. When Mike's dad catches him in the act and asks playfully, "What are you doing?" Mike responds with a guilty smile, and they separate affably.

Amidst his displays of indifference, Mike's minute gesture of returning his dad's hug suggests that Mike is not actually averse to being close and affectionate but is instead putting on a show for anyone who might be watching. Although Mike may desire and seek his dad's attention at home, at school where he is the leader of the boys, Mike carefully crafts and painstakingly projects his tough guy image. Whereas Mike's dad may feel free to be tender and affectionate with Mike in this context, Mike cannot—or he may feel as though he cannot—reciprocate without jeopardizing his status and reputation among the boys.

For the other boys as well, masculine posturing appeared to be mainly a performance for their peers, and the boys were clearly making an impression on each other and influencing each other's conduct. During my sixteenth visit when Mike's dad prepares to leave and asks Mike for a hug and kiss before he goes, Mike replies firmly, "Not a kiss," but allows his dad to hug him. Aware that Min-Haeng, Tony, and Gabriella are watching, Mike tries to appear disinterested by rolling his eyes upwards and wearing an exasperated expression on his face while his dad hugs him. When Mike's dad gives him a kiss anyway, Mike squints his eyes as though pained by the gesture. With an amused look on his face, Mike's dad gently pats and rubs the top of Mike's head until Mike says defiantly, "Don't mess up my hair." Soon after, Min-Haeng's mom approaches to say goodbye as Min-Haeng is playing with Mike, Jake, and Tony. Just as Mike did with his dad, Min-Haeng resists his mom's displays of affection. When Min-Haeng's mom squats down and leans towards him, Min-Haeng protests, "No! No! Please don't give me a kiss!" Seeming amused by Min-Haeng's dramatic reaction, Min-Haeng's mom laughs and agrees not to kiss him and instead touches the top of his head, to which Min-Haeng responds by telling his mom, "Now you messed up my hair."

Maintaining Appearances

As the boys began to understand that femininity could undermine their masculinity, they learned to exhibit an appropriately negative attitude towards girls and to avoid displaying qualities and behaviors that are considered feminine. On occasions when the boys had no choice but to engage in "feminine" acts, they were quick to compensate for their digressions. For instance, during my seventh visit, after Jen solicits a public display of affection from Mike, Mike seems eager to re-establish his masculinity and re-position himself among the boys. On this day, Rob, Jake, and Mike are engaged in gun play in the block corner when Jen arrives, remarks that she hasn't yet had a chance to greet Mike today, and asks him to come and give her a hug. Although Mike complies with Jen's request, he does so reluctantly and literally drags his feet as he walks self-consciously towards Jen, who is kneeling on the floor with outstretched arms. While in Jen's embrace, Mike rolls his eyes and then looks around to see if anyone is watching. Although Mike tries to convey his cool detachment, Jen foils his efforts by cheerfully assuring him that he gives great hugs before letting him go. As Mike returns to join Rob and Jake, he immediately recounts a scene that he saw on television in which a robber stabbed a policeman in the back, "And there was blood." Emasculated first by Jen's request and then by Jen's compliment, Mike tries to recover by describing a hyper-masculine incident.

Given their efforts to avoid "feminine" displays of affection, the boys could even construe unwelcome expressions of affection as antagonistic. For instance, during my sixteenth visit, Tony unintentionally provokes Mike when he playfully kisses Mike on the cheek. Caught off guard, Mike becomes angry and tells Tony firmly, "Don't." To my surprise, Mike then retaliates by planting several kisses on Tony's face. Although Mike clearly intends this as a hostile act, Tony does not understand and responds by giving Mike another friendly kiss on the cheek. This time, Mike gets even angrier and pushes Tony. As Tony stands looking confused, Lucia calls for all of the kids' attention, and this interaction promptly comes to an end.

To the extent that the boys associated the need or desire for closeness and comfort with femininity and/or immaturity, they could feel conflicted when their need or desire to be close to and comforted by others would surface. During my twelfth visit, Min-Haeng approaches me as I am sitting on the floor in the meeting area and sits in my lap without saying a word. All of the kids are rather hyper today, and he just seems to need some downtime, or a moment to be calm. While sitting in my lap, Min-Haeng alternates between making himself cozy and seeming like he might get up at any moment. Although Min-Haeng wants to be held, he does not want to be coddled. I suspect that he would protest and leave immediately if I were to say explicitly, "Oh, do you need a hug?" So, instead, I place my arms loosely around him and sit with him quietly while we wait for circle time to begin.

As the boys learned to demonstrate their masculinity and maturity by acting tough, stoic, and self-sufficient, they also could become defensive when they were offered help or care, or when they were by other means made to feel feminized or infantilized. During a meeting with Min-Haeng and Mike on my twenty-third visit, Min-Haeng inadvertently calls attention to himself by complaining, "Ow! I hit my head," while crawling out from under the table (where he had gone to fetch a toy that fell on the ground). When I respond my expressing (too much) concern, "Are you O.K.? You hit your head? Uh-oh. Are you O.K.?" Min-Haeng becomes annoyed and responds angrily, "Don't say that! I'm all right. I don't care if I hit my head." Again, Min-Haeng makes it clear that he does not want to be coddled, which he may experience as condescending and/or as suggesting that he is vulnerable or weak. In retrospect, I imagine he might have preferred for me just to say, "You're all right. Walk it off," which would have implied that I thought he was tough enough to handle it and thereby would have left his masculinity and pride intact.

Separating from Mothers

In addition to (or possibly as a part of) their efforts to distance themselves from the girls and distinguish themselves from the girls' femininity, the boys also made a point to separate themselves physically and emotionally from their moms (e.g., by turning away from or acting indifferently towards their moms), at least in the public setting of school. This need for boys to separate from their mothers in particular was different from the need for children to separate from their parents (mothers and fathers), for instance at the start of the school day. In Western cultures, a child's ability to be independent is often regarded as a marker of social growth and emotional maturity. To the extent that a progression towards individuation and separation is considered normative in children's development, boys and girls may be encouraged and rewarded when they begin to assert their individuality and separate from their parents. The goal of easy separations becomes especially important when a child enters school, where parents cannot stay for the duration of the school day, and teachers cannot attend endlessly to children who continue to be distressed after their parents' departure.

The boys' parents and teachers mentioned that the boys (and girls) had experienced difficult separations (e.g., feeling sad or distressed when it was time for their parents to leave) during the previous year when they were in day care and at the beginning of pre-Kindergarten when this school and this class were new to them. However, after the first few months of school, many of the boys were able (and had learned to take pride in their ability) to say goodbye to their parents with confidence and ease at the start of the day. For instance, in the moments after his dad leaves on my ninth visit, Jake proudly informs Jen, "I see my dad's gone and I'm not sad." Jake's comment surprised me, as I had never seen him struggle when it was time for his dad or mom to leave. Whether or not separating from his parents was a challenge for him, Jake knew that the ability not to feel sad about these separations was something of which he could be proud.

The girls also were learning to separate easily from their parents upon arriving at school and to take pride in this accomplishment. For instance, during my fifteenth visit, Nicole notices that Tatiana is having a hard time saying goodbye to her mom for the day, and boasts about the ease with which she separated from her mom earlier on. As Tatiana sits on her mom's lap, cuddling close and giving her mom frequent hugs, Nicole approaches them and announces triumphantly, "You know what? I pushed my mom out the door." To underscore the significance of her accomplishment (and to offer further proof of her maturity), Nicole adds, "I don't need a car seat."

Beyond demonstrating maturity, however, a boy's ability (or inability) to separate easily from his mother in particular—and to deny his need for the kind of nurturance and care that the mother-child relationship represents[4]—is believed to have further implications for his ability to establish and develop a "healthy" masculine identity. For instance, psychoanalytic theory[5] emphasizes early childhood as a critical period in boys' identity development when a boy must learn to separate from his mother (and from her feminine influence) and identify with his father in order to acquire masculine qualities, learn masculine behaviors, and become a "real boy," as opposed to a "mama's boy."

Whether or not the boys in this class were familiar with the term "mama's boy" and its negative connotations, most of them learned to distance themselves from their moms, just as they learned to distance themselves from girls, at least while they were at school. During my fourth visit, Jake arrives at class with his mom and sits down at one of the tables to paint with watercolors. Although his mom stands behind him and watches him work, Jake doesn't pay much attention to her and focuses instead on his task. When his mom leaves the room momentarily, Jake doesn't seem to notice. And when it's time for Jake's mom to leave, Jake acknowledges her departure but doesn't go out of his way to see her off, as he usually does with his dad. Although Jake engaged his mom comfortably and was happy to comply with her requests for hugs and kisses, he did not actively seek her company nor initiate affectionate displays in this setting. However, I knew from visiting Jake's family at home that, in contrast to the restraint he showed at school, he could be very loving and overtly affectionate with his mom in the privacy of their home. Thus, while cultural norms and societal expectations may discourage public displays of affection between boys and their mothers, boys' closeness and intimacy with their mothers are not necessarily disrupted but may be allocated to times and places that are more private.

Implications for Status

The boys' ability to display gender-appropriate qualities, attitudes, and behaviors—including an aversion to femininity and a cool indifference towards their mothers—appeared to be linked to their status within the boys' hierarchy. For example, Mike and Min-Haeng, who were the most determined to show that they are boys (not girls) and big kids (not babies), also happened to have the highest status among the boys. These two boys were the quickest to leave their moms upon arriving at class in the mornings and they rarely made any effort to engage their moms while at school. They were also the most emphatic in avoiding "feminine" displays of affection, especially with their mothers but also with their fathers, as when Min-Haeng instructed his mom not to kiss him and when Mike wiped away his dad's kiss.

Jake and Rob, who seemed less focused on proving their masculinity and maturity, were in the middle of the boys' hierarchy. Although they tended to be less affectionate with their moms than they were with their dads, they occasionally remained with their moms after arriving at school, and they were receptive to "feminine" displays of affection. Jake and Rob also were less likely (as compared to Mike and Min-Haeng) to disparage "feminine" objects and interests, even though they clearly associated these things with girls and made a point to separate and differentiate themselves from the girls, as when Rob explained that he doesn't have friends who are girls (because he plays with boys) and when Jake explained that boys and girls are "a lot different."

Dan and Tony, who sought to remain close to their moms and occasionally played with girls and "girls' toys," had the lowest status among the boys. It is difficult to know whether Dan and Tony had lower status because of their attachment to their moms, which could make them appear infantile and therefore less desirable as playmates, or if they were especially attached to their moms because of their low status, which could make their peer relationships less accessible or less satisfying. Either way, these boys' tendency to be uninhibited and unabashed in expressing how much they still wanted, needed, and depended on their moms set them apart from their peers, who were learning to take pride in their emerging autonomy and increasing competence. Even in the public setting of school, Dan and Tony insisted on being close to their moms and struggled (sometimes dramatically) when it came time for their mothers to leave. For instance, on my twentieth visit, as Mike, Rob, and I head back to class after a meeting, we see Dan fussing and clinging to his mom, who is carrying him and trying to say goodbye to him in the hallway. Although Dan sees us approaching, he neither changes nor curbs his behavior. When Jen comes to help and gently pries Dan from his mother's arms (to carry him into the classroom), Dan screeches and reaches for his mom, who slowly backs away. Comparably, Tony would also beg his mom to stay with him when it came time for her to leave, and he would openly request his mom's hugs and kisses, whereas the other boys had learned to downplay their attachment and avoid affectionate displays with their mothers.

A Case Study: Tony

While Jake's case study (in chapter 2) illustrates how boys' ability and willingness to speak out in their relationships (and their resistance against constraints on their self-expression) may be undermined as they adapt to interpersonal dynamics, rules of engagement, and norms of behavior within their peer group culture, Tony's case study highlights boys' capacity and desire for close relationships (and their resistance against losing their relationships). Tony's case study also shows how, despite their relational capabilities, boys may neglect to present themselves and engage others in ways that foster meaningful connections.

Craving Closeness

Unlike the other boys in this class, Tony didn't really go through the routine of arriving at class with his mom (or dad) each morning and then separating for the day. As his mom was a teacher at his school and her classroom was directly across the hall from his, Tony usually wandered into the classroom on his own or with his stepsister Gabriella, and his mom would come by later on (sometimes without his noticing) and pop her head in to check that he was all right.

On the few occasions that I observed Tony's mom accompany him to class, Tony made every effort to keep her with him for as long as possible. For instance, on my eleventh visit, when Tony and Gabriella arrive at class with his mom, Tony wraps his arms tightly around her leg and clings to her for the entire time that she is in the room. When it comes time for her to leave, Tony's mom gives Tony a kiss, extracts her leg from his grasp, and heads towards the door. As she reaches the door, Tony whines and calls for her, "Mommy! Come here!" With a sigh, she turns around, walks slowly towards Tony, and patiently asks him what he wants. When Tony replies playfully, "I want a kiss," she reminds him, "I just gave you a kiss." Nevertheless, she complies with his request and kneels down to give him another kiss. As she pulls away from him and begins to get up, Tony quickly adds, "and hug." With another small sigh, Tony's mom kneels once more and, when Tony is slow about delivering his hug, urges him to "make it quick." As soon as Tony finishes giving his mom a hug, she rises to her feet and heads out the door, at which point Tony calls for her again, but this time does not get a response.

Although Tony's frequent requests for his mom's attention sometimes seemed to wear her down, she usually responded to him with warmth and affection. During my nineteenth visit, when Tony's mom quickly checks on him (after he arrives at class in the morning) and starts to head back to her own classroom, Tony follows her into the hallway, asks her not to leave, and tells her that he needs to show her something. Her pace suggests that she is in a hurry, but she indulges him and comes back into the classroom with him. As Tony shows her a couple of water bottles that create miniature tornadoes when turned upside-down, his mom watches attentively and remarks enthusiastically, "Oh, I love this. Oh, cool."

At home, Tony was struggling with having to share his mom with his new stepdad, three stepsisters, and a baby on the way. Despite his mom's efforts to reassure him of her availability to him, Tony seemed to feel insecure and constantly sought to be near her. In short, Tony simply could not get enough of his mom. It didn't help that Tony had access to his mom throughout the school day. Since neither his mom nor his teachers seemed to discourage him, Tony was virtually free to visit his mom in her classroom whenever he wanted, and he would leave his class to do so not only during "free play" but also at times when the children were gathered for structured lessons and activities. Of course, Tony's mom had other obligations and responsibilities in this context (e.g., tending to her students), which made it difficult for her to give Tony her undivided attention. As a result, Tony became caught in a vicious cycle wherein he would seek his mom's undivided attention at times when she could not give it to him, feel disappointed and frustrated by his unsuccessful attempts, and subsequently become even more determined to have her all to himself. At the time, I had wondered why Tony didn't try making fewer and more strategic attempts as he sought his mom's attention (e.g., when she could actually be available to him), but I can now see how his approach was in some ways adaptive to his situation. Given that Tony perceived his mom as becoming less available to him, that he wasn't sure when she would be available (e.g., sometimes she was, sometimes she wasn't), and that he felt increasingly desperate for her attention, it made sense that he would choose to make more frequent, albeit haphazard, attempts to capture her attention and thereby increase his chances of getting what he wanted.

Requiring Assistance

As Tony tended to be unselective about his reasons for visiting his mom, he seemed to visit her whenever the urge struck him or at the slightest provocation. For example, during my fifth visit, when he and Gabriella get in a small dispute over a toy that they both want to play with, Tony slaps Gabriella's hand as she reaches for the toy and goes to seek his mom's intervention. Similarly, during my twentieth visit, when Gabriella accidentally splashes Tony as they are playing together at a tub filled with water, Tony gets angry and runs to his mom's classroom to tell on Gabriella, who follows along to defend herself.

Tony also sought his mom's help to resolve conflicts that didn't involve his stepsister, as when he accidentally causes a scab on Mike's knee to come off during free play on my twenty-fourth visit. When Mike's knee begins to bleed, Mike bursts into frantic tears, and Tony immediately leaves to find his mom (not for Mike but for himself). Lucia brings Mike to see the school nurse but cannot stay with him, so I go to check on him as the other kids settle down for naptime. On my way, I see Tony sitting in the gym with his mom, who has left her own class in order to comfort him. When I arrive at the nurse's office, Mike is no longer crying, and the nurse is attaching a new bandage to his knee. I sit down next to Mike and talk with him about a game that he is playing (a wooden labyrinth where the object is to roll a small metal ball from the start point to the end point while avoiding the many holes along the way). After a minute or two, Tony's mom enters with Tony, who looks sullen and remains silent as his mom tells us that he wants to apologize by doing something he thinks will help to make things better. With his mom's encouragement, Tony then proceeds to give Mike a "high-five." However, because Tony's intentions are unclear, Mike does not know what to expect, and Tony ends up slapping Mike's hand. When Mike looks upset, Tony's mom steps in again to explain what Tony was trying to do. Having failed at his attempt to apologize, Tony begins to fuss and whine, so his mom picks him up and carries him out of the room. A few moments later, they return to try again. After Tony apologizes and all seems forgiven, his mom tries to bring him back to class, explaining that she needs to return to work, but Tony refuses to go. I tell Tony's mom that he can stay with us until Mike is ready to return. After his mom leaves, Tony suddenly grabs the game that Mike was holding and, when the ball gets stuck, becomes frustrated. Tony may be trying to engage Mike but, without his mom's help, he does not quite manage.

Although Tony's attachment to his mom may be appropriate for this age, his reliance on her to help regulate his emotions and facilitate his social interactions was hindering his ability to cultivate and feel confident about his own interpersonal skills. As Tony was quick to disengage from his interactions and seek his mom's help, especially when conflicts arose, he had fewer opportunities (as compared to the other kids) to learn how to communicate effectively with others and to develop strategies for working through and resolving problems on his own. And the more that Tony depended on his mom's intervention and guidance, the more he seemed to feel that he was incapable of engaging and getting along with others on his own.

Resisting Exclusion

Tony's regular departures from class (to visit his mom or to seek her help) also were hindering his peer relationships because either he was not around when the other boys formed their playgroups and began their activities or he could not be relied upon to remain engaged for the duration of an interaction. It therefore became easy for his peers to overlook him and discount his presence. Oftentimes, Tony would return to class and find that he had been left out of, or (when he ran off in the middle of an interaction) subsequently excluded from, the boys' plans, and that he could participate, at best, from the margins of the boys' interactions. Although Tony sometimes ended up doing what the girls were doing (e.g., helping the teachers), unlike Dan, Tony didn't get along with the girls and was an outsider among them as well.

Occasionally, the other boys would block Tony's attempts to join (or re-join) them. When this happened, Tony became even more determined to be included in (and avoid being excluded from) that particular interaction. For instance, during my fourth visit, as Mike, Jake, and Rob are playing with Playmobil toys on the floor and Mike refuses to let Tony join them, Tony immediately reports to Lucia, "Mike said, 'You can't play.'" When Lucia comes to investigate, Mike explains to her that they just don't need any more help. In response, Lucia reminds Mike that "You can't say, 'You can't play,'"[6] and sees to it that the boys make room for Tony. More often, however, it seemed that the other boys simply neglected to include Tony. So, Tony would seek out possible points of entry by watching what the other boys were doing, following them around, and trying to join in their activities in whatever ways he could, as when Rob, Jake, and Dan are playing together during my fourteenth visit and Tony tries to participate by asking hopefully, "Can I be [this character]? [Which character] can I be?" until the boys assign him a role.

Even though the boys usually made room for Tony to join them, Tony often ended up with less desirable characters and roles because he tended to arrive after the boys' play was already underway and thus could choose only from whatever was left over. During recess on my nineteenth visit, Mike, Jake, Rob, and Min-Haeng gather at the tire swing and climb on. By the time Tony arrives, there is no more room on the tire swing, so the boys instruct Tony to push them. Tony could decide not to comply with the boys' instructions, but then he would forfeit his participation in the boys' activities, which he generally was unwilling to do. In this case, Tony relents and begins to push. After a few minutes, Mike turns to Min-Haeng and cautions him to "Hold on really tight." Mike then pretends to fall off. Rob also decides to get off the tire swing. Mike and Rob then join Tony in pushing Jake and Min-Haeng on the tire swing. Thus, by accepting whatever roles the boys offered him, Tony could sometimes end up engaging the boys on more equal terms.

Engaging Sporadically

Despite Tony's determination to be included by the other boys, he often seemed uncertain about how best to approach and engage them. In addition to wandering in and out of class to visit his mom, Tony tended to wander in and out of his social interactions. Although most of the kids changed activities and play partners several times each day, their interactions generally occurred in episodes that had (more or less) beginnings, middles, and endings. Tony's approach, however, was more like "channel surfing," or flipping through television programs in rapid succession. While milling around the room, Tony would occasionally try to join an interaction that was already in progress but he rarely committed his full attention or stayed long enough to see an interaction through to the end. Rather, Tony seemed to spend most of his time drifting from one interaction to the next, as though continually in search of something that might interest him more. During my second visit, Gabriella joins me as I am sitting at one of the tables in the work area. She asks what I am doing, and when I tell her that I am taking notes, she goes to get some chalk and a chalkboard so she can join me. Gabriella then draws on her chalkboard while I continue to write in my notebook. When Tony wanders over and sees what Gabriella is doing, he also grabs some chalk and a chalkboard and begins to draw. However, Tony is not really interested in drawing or in engaging me and soon wanders off. Tony also engages half-heartedly while playing with Min-Haeng on my seventh visit. As the two boys use Duplo blocks to build a castle, Min-Haeng thoughtfully places each of his blocks while Tony seems to add his blocks randomly. Consequently, the castle looks rather unbalanced. When Min-Haeng suggests that the castle needs reinforcements and asks Tony to help him carry out this plan, Tony loses interest and wanders off.

As a result of Tony's tentative and unpredictable presence, nobody pays much attention to him when he is around, and nobody really notices when he is gone. During my seventh visit, Tony leaves the classroom as everyone else gathers in the meeting area. Standing just outside the door, Tony peeks in and watches his teachers and classmates as they proceed with circle time. Tony looks very pleased with himself, as though he has managed to play a great trick on everyone by sneaking away and hiding. However, when his teachers and classmates begin a fun jumping exercise without him, Tony realizes that no one is looking for him and he returns to class looking sad and disappointed. Accustomed to his frequent comings and goings, Lucia assumes that Tony is upset about missing out on the fun jumping exercise and, in an effort to cheer him up, promises to repeat the activity later. However, as this is not the reason he is upset, Tony is not consoled by Lucia's promise and continues to mope at the edge of the meeting area. Tony seems to be waiting for someone to welcome him back (and maybe apologize for having overlooked his absence). When no one pays him the special attention he seeks, Tony sulks for a bit and, seeing that everyone else has moved on, reluctantly rejoins the group.

In addition to drifting physically from one interaction to the next, Tony also tended to drift mentally once he gained access to an activity or interaction. Sometimes he would tune out, so to speak, at the very moments when his peers were trying to engage him. Consequently, Tony often missed subtle (or even obvious) cues within his social interactions, and his behaviors frequently were mismatched or out of sync with those of his peers. For instance, during a meeting with Tony, Min-Haeng, and Dan which occurred on my seventeenth visit, Min-Haeng expresses his support for Tony, but Tony doesn't notice because his mind has wandered elsewhere.

JUDY: Can you guys tell me what's going to happen when you grow up? Tony, what are you going to be when you grow up?

TONY: A policeman.

JUDY (*INTERESTED*): You are? Why do you want to be a policeman?

TONY (*IN HIS BABY VOICE*): 'Cause they have a gun and I love gunnies.

JUDY: You love guns?

TONY: Yeah.

JUDY (*TO DAN AND MIN-HAENG*): Dan and Min-Haeng, did you know that Tony wants to be a policeman when he grows up?

MIN-HAENG (*IN HIS BABY VOICE*): Well, I want, when I grow up, I want to be one of [Tony's] partners . . . (*Tony suddenly gets up and tries to leave the room.*) . . . When I grow up, I want to be Tony's partner policeman, 'cause policemen need partners.

It's not clear why Tony suddenly tries to leave the room but his urge to leave seems to subside as abruptly as it came on, so the only outcome of his distraction is that he fails to recognize (and benefit from) Min-Haeng's supportive comment ("I want to be one of [Tony's] partners"). By neglecting to stay focused and becoming easily distracted, Tony could find it difficult to connect with the other boys, even when they included him.

Asserting Himself

As Tony could not be certain of his acceptance by and place among the boys, he seemed to be continually negotiating his participation in the boys' activities and interactions. To his credit, Tony was not easily discouraged, and he persisted in his efforts to be included and valued by others, despite any obstacles that he perceived and setbacks that he experienced. With some of his peers, Tony was also confident enough to assert himself when others did not respond to his efforts to engage them. For instance, during the same meeting with Tony, Min-Haeng, and Dan (after Tony tries to leave the room), Tony calls for Dan's attention when Dan becomes distracted during their play. As Dan focuses on assembling one of the toys, Tony first tries to recapture Dan's attention by instructing him, "Danny, you need to watch this." Tony then tries to elicit Dan's interest by getting into character (Dan loves to role-play) and using a deep, dramatic voice to entice him, "Come on, this way." When Dan still does not cooperate, Tony tries another tactic and says warningly, "Danny, I'm not playing." To this, Dan responds instantly by begging Tony to stay and play: "Please." Although Dan's plea seems more automatic than authentic, Tony seems satisfied and continues to suggest ideas for their play while Dan returns his attention to assembling the toy. Given that Tony spent much of his time trying to get the other boys to notice and include him in their play, he was not often in a position to influence his peers, much less by threatening to disengage from an interaction. However, Tony evidently believed (and Dan's response confirmed) that Dan valued his companionship; otherwise, Tony could not hope for his threat to work.

During a meeting with Tony and Min-Haeng on my twenty-second visit, Tony similarly asserts himself, first by boldly claiming the most popular toy figure for himself and then by standing his ground when Min-Haeng tries to convince him to trade.

TONY: I wanna be Black Knight.[7]

MIN-HAENG (*CALMLY*): I wanna be (*starting to whine*), uh, no, I wanna be the black (*whining*), I wanna be the black knight! Please!

TONY: I had the black knight . . .

MIN-HAENG (*PLEADING FRANTICALLY*): No, please!

TONY: Yeah, but Min-Haeng, I had . . .

MIN-HAENG (*FRANTIC*): Please!

TONY: . . . the black knight first.

MIN-HAENG (*FRANTIC*): Please, Tony, please!

TONY: Min-Haeng, I had the black knight first.

MIN-HAENG (*CALMING DOWN*): How about [Blue Prince]?

TONY: No.

MIN-HAENG (*FRANTIC*): But [Blue Prince is] better.

TONY (*TRYING TO PERSUADE*): Come on, Min-Haeng.

MIN-HAENG: No.

TONY: I had the black knight first. (*No response*) I had it first, Min-Haeng.

MIN-HAENG (*CALMING DOWN*): I just wanted to build it for you.

TONY (*SOOTHING*): I know. I know how to make it.

MIN-HAENG: But I want to build it for you. I first want to build it for you.

TONY (*ENTICINGLY*): Min-Haeng, if you be the guard, you'll get to ride the horse.

MIN-HAENG (*ADAMANTLY*): No. No way.

TONY (*TO JUDY, CHANGING THE SUBJECT, AND REFERRING TO DARK KNIGHT'S HAIR PIECE, WHICH HAD BEEN LOST DURING A PREVIOUS MEETING*): Did you find the hair? Judy? Did you find the hair?

JUDY: Yeah, I found it behind the couch. It took me forever to find it, so we've got to be careful with the pieces.

MIN-HAENG (*TO TONY*): O.K., you can play [with the black knight].

TONY (*SINCERELY*): Thank you, Min-Haeng.

MIN-HAENG (*BITTERLY*): I don't want it.

Whereas Tony readily surrendered a disputed toy in a previous interaction with Jake, Tony remains firm and debates with Min-Haeng until the dispute is settled in his favor.

One thing that may have enabled Tony to assert himself with Dan and Min-Haeng was that he viewed these boys as being similar to him, in terms of their status among the boys. Like Tony, Dan also was frequently left out of the other boys' plans and activities. Although Min-Haeng was more likely to be included by the boys (especially Mike, who respected and was particularly fond of Min-Haeng), his decisions to disengage from the boys' activities (e.g., to work on his drawings) had the same effect of displacing him from the center of the boys' social circle. Tony's sense of entitlement (e.g., to have, pursue, and defend his own interests) within these relationships may also have been bolstered by the fact that Dan and Min-Haeng actually considered Tony's suggestions, incorporated his contributions, and responded to his requests. In turn, Dan and Min-Haeng would negotiate and plead with Tony (rather than assume his compliance) when proposing their suggestions, offering their contributions, and making their requests. As a result, Tony could feel that he had equal sway in these relationships and expect these boys to acknowledge (rather than ignore or dismiss) his opinions.

Following Jake's Lead

In contrast to Tony's interactions with Dan and Min-Haeng, which were balanced in the sense that each of the boys could express his own opinions and expect to be heard, Tony's interactions with Jake were often skewed in Jake's favor. Of all the boys (and girls), Jake was the one whose friendship mattered the most to Tony. Whereas the other boys were sometimes annoyed by and dismissive of Tony (e.g., when he would become unavailable, literally or figuratively, during their interactions), Jake didn't seem to mind Tony's idiosyncrasies and tried to help Tony when he could. For instance, during my tenth visit, Jake encourages Tony to participate when Tony becomes reluctant to engage in a fun activity. On this day, the learning specialist, Bonnie, has come to teach the kids about syllables. The kids are familiar with Bonnie and seem to like her very much. She draws their interest by speaking to them in a soft voice, but she is also firm and expects the kids to pay attention and follow directions. After explaining the instructions, Bonnie leads the kids in an activity where she pairs them up, says their names, and asks each pair to tell her how many syllables are in each name. At the end of their turn, each pair of kids gets to chase and pop some bubbles that Bonnie blows for them. Most of the kids enjoy this activity, and some even try to get a second turn. However, when Bonnie calls Gabriella and Tony to task, Tony replies shyly, "I don't want to."

Although Bonnie tries to persuade him, Tony takes his turn only when Jake helpfully reminds him, "[Bonnie] won't be around later."

Grateful for Jake's acceptance and support, Tony willingly aligned his views with Jake's, even when it was clear that disagreements would not jeopardize their friendship. For instance, during a meeting with Tony and Jake on my twentieth visit (after Tony surrendered the disputed toy horse to Jake), Tony eventually changes his response to match Jake's when they give different responses to my question.

> JUDY: Do you ever need to protect your moms?
> TONY (*IMMEDIATELY*): Nn-yes. Don'tcha know?
> JUDY: What do you protect your moms from?
> JAKE (*PLAINLY*): No, we don't.
> TONY (*DECIDEDLY*): Monsters.
> JUDY (*TO JAKE*): You don't protect your mom?
> TONY (*FIRMLY*): Yes, we do.
> JUDY: Tony says "Yes," and Jakey says "No"?
> JAKE (*CONFIDENTLY*): Right.
> TONY: No. Usually, we don't protect our moms.
> JUDY: What do you protect her from, Tony?
> TONY (*FIRMLY*): I don't protect my mom.
> JUDY: You don't?
> TONY: No.
> JUDY: Does she ever need some protection?
> TONY: No.

Tony initially expresses his own opinion ("Nn-yes. Don'tcha know?") and defends his view ("Yes, we do"), even when Jake disagrees with him ("No, we don't"). However, Tony becomes uncomfortable when I point out that he and Jake have different opinions ("Tony says 'Yes' and Jakey says 'No'?"). While Jake seems fine with this difference ("Right."), Tony reverses his position ("Usually we don't protect our moms."). When I try to follow up on his original response ("What do you protect her from, Tony?"), Tony sticks with his new position ("I don't protect my mom"). Whereas earlier in this meeting Jake had threatened to cancel their play date unless Tony yielded to his demands ("You either, you don't come over to my house or let me have the horse"), Jake's tone here suggests that he doesn't really care whether Tony agrees with him or not on this matter. Nevertheless, Tony insists on siding with Jake.

Later during this meeting, while they are playing with Playmobil characters, Tony again chooses to follow Jake's lead.

> TONY (*PICKING UP THE TOY PIRATE*): I'm a pirate. I have one eye. Look at me. Arg!
> JAKE: Wait. Wait.
> TONY: Jake, look at [the pirate]. He has one eye.
> JAKE (*FIRMLY*): No, not that guy. [The pirate] isn't in the game.
> TONY: Yes, he is.
> JAKE: Well, not in this part of the game.
> TONY (*PICKING UP A TOY BIKER*): Is this guy in this part of the game?
> JAKE: Hey, . . . he can't be in the game. (*Glancing at Judy*) It's up to us . . . We can decide.
> TONY: . . . Biker, biker, I need a biker guy. Jake, do you want a biker guy? You want a biker man?
> JAKE: No, [the bikers are] stupid.
> TONY: No, they're not . . . Pretend the biker man came.
> JAKE: No, bikes weren't invented.
> TONY (*CONFUSED*): Huh?
> JAKE: Bikers weren't invented.
> TONY: They weren't? Pretend . . . just, he said, "Hi." (*Tony directs the toy biker towards Jake.*) "Hello." (*Tony's biker guy then rides away.*)

When Jake rejects Tony's toy figures ("[The pirate] isn't in the game," "[the bikers are] stupid"), Tony at first defends his choices ("Yes, he is," "No, they're not"), but then gives in and the pirate and bikers are cast aside for the rest of this meeting. Even though Jake says, "We can decide," and Tony continues to propose ideas, Tony—in his eagerness to remain on good terms with Jake—allows Jake to decide whether to incorporate his proposals and readily complies with Jake's rules.

Fighting for Relationships

In addition to trying to be like Jake, Tony also was willing to go to great lengths to be with Jake. For instance, on my twenty-first visit, Tony barges in on my meeting with Rob and Jake, endures Rob and Jake's efforts to exclude him, and tries repeatedly to distract Jake and disrupt Rob and Jake's play until he is able to entice Jake to join him instead. When I arrive at class on this day, Rob and Jake are waiting for me and immediately ask to meet with me. After I check with Jen to make sure it's all right if I take them, we head out the door, with the boys leading the way. When Tony follows us into the hallway and says that he wants to come, too, I explain that I can take only two boys at a time (because my meetings with three boys have been chaotic and overwhelming) and promise to meet with him next. Rob, Jake, and I then continue towards a staff member's office that we have been given permission to use.

As we enter the office, Rob and Jake comment excitedly because they realize that it belongs to Bonnie, the learning specialist.

ROB: We're in Bonnie's office where (*to Judy*) Bonnie comes into our classroom.
JAKE (*TO ROB, EXCITEDLY*): I know! And she has goldfish. And look! There's her bubbles! There's her goldfish!

The boys and I sit down on the floor and I bring out my Playmobil toys.

ROB: I want to be Dark Knight.
JAKE: I'm gonna be Blue Prince.
ROB (*VERY EXCITED*): Oh! That's the wrong sword! [Dark Knight is] supposed to have a black sword! . . . Look at, black. I need that.
JAKE (*LAUGHING*): Wrong swords!

Suddenly, the door (which I had closed and luckily was not heavy) comes flying open and hits Jake on the back. Tony is standing in the doorway, and Jen arrives soon after. Jen apologizes for interrupting and asks if Tony was supposed to come with me. Apparently, this is what Tony told her. When Jen asks whether this is correct, I tell her that Tony was not supposed to come to this meeting and that I will meet with him next. Jen then explains to Tony that I will meet with him in a few minutes and tries to convince him to return to class with her, but Tony refuses to leave. As Jen seems unsure what to do, I try to help her out by allowing Tony to stay.

Although Rob and Jake say nothing during my exchange with Jen, they have been listening and probably detect my displeasure at Tony's disruption and deception. After Jen leaves, Rob and Jake return to their play, and they make a point to ostracize him. They begin by degrading the toy figure that Tony picks out for himself.

> ROB (*TO JUDY*): Jakey's being the, Tony's gonna be the Viking.
> JUDY: Oh.
> JAKE (*TO JUDY*): Yeah and he's the bad guy.
> ROB: Because Vikings are bad guys.
> JAKE (*TO TONY*): Yeah. Vikings are bad guys, Tony. If you're gonna be a
>   bad guy, then be a Viking. We're good guys.
> ROB: Yeah.
> JAKE (*TO TONY*): We're good guys, you're a bad guy.
> TONY (*SUBDUED*): No, I can still be a good guy.
> JAKE (*TO TONY*): No, Vikings are early pirates.
> ROB (*TO JAKE*): Yeah, and pirates are bad, right?
> JAKE (*TO ROB*): Oh yeah. (*To Tony*) So, you're a pirate.
> TONY (*SADLY, QUIETLY*): I'm bein' [a different] guy.
> ROB (*TO JAKE*): I have this guy, Jake. Do you have this guy?
> TONY: Now do you have a lot of biker men?
> JAKE (*TO ROB*): Oh yeah, I have, no I don't have. You mean at my house?
> ROB (*TO JAKE*): Yeah.
> JAKE (*TO ROB*): No.

When Tony claims a different toy figure and tries again to join in, Rob and Jake continue to block Tony's attempts to participate in their play.

> TONY: I'm being a biker man.
> JAKE: Oh. There are no bikers invented.
> ROB: Yeah, all the bikers like that [*the one Tony is holding*].

Tony angrily throws the biker figure across the floor.

> ROB: Oh, you can still be [a biker].
> JAKE: Yeah, but you just won't be able to play in our game.

ROB: Yeah, you can play your own game. You can be more, lots of more [biker] guys than us. You could be lots of [bikers], one [biker] girl also. [*The bikers include a man, a boy, and a girl.*]

Tony throws another the biker figure across the floor.

ROB: Or you can use the [pirate] that goes in prison.
TONY (*HOPEFULLY*): Here?
JAKE: Yeah, [the pirate and the Viking] go in prison.

As though to punish Tony for his intrusion, Rob and Jake basically offer Tony the undesirable options of being a bad guy in their game or playing his own game.

At first, Tony resists Rob and Jake's efforts to devalue and exclude him, but he becomes frustrated and is gradually defeated as Rob and Jake alternate between ignoring him and rejecting his contributions. It is only when Tony surrenders that Rob and Jake finally allow him to join their play on amiable terms.

TONY (*RESIGNED*): I don't have to play.
JAKE (*TO TONY*): You can be . . .
ROB (*TO TONY*): I'm making a Viking for you.
TONY (*MEEKLY*): Yeah, but I want to be on the nice team [*with the good guys*].
JAKE (*TO TONY*): Oh, you can be [the guard].
TONY (*TENTATIVELY*): Is he on the nice team?
ROB AND JAKE: Yeah.
ROB: Get him his axe. He needs a axe. Do you want to be a guard, Tony? You're being a guard.
TONY: I'm being the guard of the castle.
ROB: Yeah. And you killed the Viking, right?
TONY (*CHEERING UP*): Yeah.

Even though Rob and Jake have now allowed Tony to join them, they still neglect to incorporate Tony's suggestions.

TONY: Pretend this is the doorway. Right here . . .

Jake and Rob remain focused on gathering and assembling accessories for their characters and do not respond.

> TONY: You guys, pretend this is . . .
> JAKE (*TO ROB*): Oh, wait.
> ROB (*TO JAKE*): No, this is extra pieces. These are extra pieces.
> TONY (*IN A SINGSONG TONE*): You guys. Pretend this is the doorway right here.
> JAKE (*TO ROB*): And that's the castle . . .
> ROB (*TO JAKE*): And pretend I'm gonna make some . . .
> TONY: Pretend, um, this is where the, this is inside here . . . (*In a deep voice, picking up a toy figure*) "Hey, what's here? Someone's here. Someone's here." (*To Jake, in his regular voice*) You need him. You need him.
> JAKE (*TO TONY*): No, that's the prince.
> TONY: I know. The prince is supposed to come.
> ROB (*TO JAKE*): Yeah, but then the guards were banging with their axes on the drawbridge and then the drawbridge comes down.

While Rob and Jake continue to construct their play narrative, Tony—unable to be of influence—begins to lose interest in their play.

Given that the main reason why Tony insisted on coming to this meeting was that he wanted to be with Jake, and that his attempts to join in Rob and Jake's Playmobil play do not enable him to do this, it makes sense that Tony would search for other ways to engage with Jake. For example, Tony tries to distract Jake and disrupt Rob and Jake's play by whispering in Jake's ear, interjecting silly comments, and calling for Jake to look at him. Tony occasionally succeeds in capturing Jake's attention, as when his exclamation "O.K.! O.K.! My bud . . . the king" leads Jake to laugh and reply in amusement, "I'm not king!" For a while, however, Jake continues to focus on constructing the Playmobil narrative with Rob.

> ROB (*TO JAKE*): I wanna be king.
> JAKE (*TO ROB*): Sorry, but . . .
> TONY: Where's my axe? Where's my axe?
> JAKE (*TO ROB*): . . . [Blue Prince] is the only royal guy.
> TONY: Jake, watch this.

JAKE (*SMILING AT ROB, HIS EYES WIDENING WITH EXCITEMENT*): There *is*
no king.
ROB (*SMILING AT JAKE*): Oh yeah, there is no king. The king died, right?
TONY: Jake! Watch this! (*Balancing precariously on one foot*) Whoa!

At one point, Tony picks up a toy lance, takes a stab at Rob's eye, and just
misses. When I tell Tony firmly not to do that, he replies flippantly, "I really
liked it." When I explain to Tony that he almost poked Rob in the eye, Tony
seems strangely aloof as he smiles and says dreamily, "Yeah." Whereas
Tony had seemed grounded and sincere while he tried to join in Rob and
Jake's play just moments before, he now seems alarmingly distant.

As Tony persists in his efforts to amuse Jake (and Rob becomes more
controlling), Jake's interests and loyalties within this interaction begin
to change.

ROB (*TO JAKE*): Hey, we need to put this . . .
TONY (*REFERRING TO SOME TOY FIGURES THAT LAY SEPARATE FROM THE
REST*): They escaped.
JAKE (*TO TONY, PLAYING ALONG*): Oh nuts, I could've known.
ROB (*TO JAKE, IN A SINGSONG TONE*): Put the sword in his case, you know.
I have my sword in my case.
JAKE (*TO ROB*): I know, but we just . . . (*Jake and Tony engage in toy sword
play.*) . . . ching-ching-ching . . .
ROB (*TO JAKE*): Oh wait, we need the reins . . . The reins, we need the reins.
JAKE (*TO ROB*): No, we don't.
ROB: Yeah.
JAKE: No.
ROB: We do!
JAKE: No.
ROB: He holds onto them, so he won't fall off.
JAKE (*PRETENDING TO FALL*): Whoa!
ROB: We *do* need the reins.
TONY (*PRETENDING TO FALL*): Whoa!
ROB (*TO TONY*): Stop it. This isn't like in the royal day.
TONY: Don'tcha know that?
JAKE (*TO ROB*): Stop bossing us around.

Jake and Tony proceed to goof off and end up rolling around on the floor. When Tony gets up and flies his toy figure around the room, Rob tries to restore order, but it is too late.

> ROB: No. No! Stop it, Tony.
> TONY (*PLAYFULLY*): I'm flying in the air.
> ROB: No, Tone, stop it.
> JAKE (*TO ROB*): You said, "Job it." (*Tony giggles*).
> ROB (*ANGRILY*): I meant I was gonna chop you.
> JAKE: Me?
> ROB (*TO JAKE*): No, him.
> TONY (*SURPRISED*): No, me? For real?
> ROB: Yeah.

Undeterred by Rob's annoyance, Tony continues to make mischief, and now Jake joins him. As Tony wiggles and squirms, Jake positions his hand like a gun and "shoots" Tony. Happy to have Jake's attention (and determined to keep it), Tony responds to Jake's gesture by exclaiming dramatically, "I'm the king, I'm the king," and then pretending to die by lying motionless on the floor. Amused by Tony's performance, Jake playfully pinches Tony's bottom and tells him to get up.

Rob giggles as he watches Tony and Jake's horseplay, but when Tony pokes Jake's leg with a toy sword, Rob becomes serious and asks, "Can you please, guys, play nice and stuff?" When Tony and Jake pick up their toy swords and start to "duel," I join Rob in trying to get them to settle down.

> ROB (*TRYING TO BE FIRM*): Stop it.
> JUDY: No, no, no. No sword fights.
> ROB: Can everyone please quiet down?
> JUDY (*TO TONY AND JAKE*): Careful.
> JAKE (*TO JUDY*): They're not sharp. Those aren't very, very sharp,
> JUDY: But they're still sharp and you could still hurt yourself.
> TONY (*SASSY*): No, I can't.
> JAKE (*AGREEING WITH TONY*): Yeah.
> JUDY (*FIRMLY*): Yeah. You can.

With Jake on his side, Tony feels free to ignore Rob and to challenge my "authority." As Tony and Jake become increasingly rowdy and start poking each other with the toys, I finally announce, "I think it's time to clean up now and go back to class." Rob and I then put the toys away while Tony and Jake lie on the ground, tickling and hugging each other. On our way back to class, Rob walks quietly by my side while Tony and Jake run and shout as they lead the way.

Adopting a Misguided Approach

Although Tony's antics could enable him to capture Jake's attention and win Jake over for the moment (as shown in the example above), Tony's approach to engaging Jake, which centered on trying to amuse and impress Jake, was not necessarily conducive to establishing enduring bonds. Rather, Tony's alliance with Jake often lasted only as long as their fun did, as Tony became so focused on aligning his opinions with Jake's and keeping Jake entertained that he undermined his own presence in their relationship and thereby impeded his chances of developing a close relationship with Jake in which both boys could feel truly known, accepted, and supported.

In his other relationships as well, Tony appeared to resort increasingly to displaying silly and hyperactive behaviors in his efforts to connect with others, even though he was still capable of engaging in ways that felt focused and grounded. For instance, during my twenty-second visit, Tony is attentive and responsive at first but then changes gears, so to speak, for reasons that are not clear. After meeting together that morning, Tony, Min-Haeng, and I return to class to find the classroom empty (because everyone else is in the auditorium attending a school assembly). When the boys say that they don't want to go to the assembly, I tell them they can stay in the classroom with me, if they promise to be quiet. The boys then head over to the reading corner and sit down on the futon. I follow and sit down next to them. In the peacefulness of this setting, Tony is calm and thoughtful (just as he was during my first visit) as he engages me in conversation.

> TONY (*TO JUDY*): Are you a sister?
> JUDY: Yeah, I have a brother . . .
> TONY: Are you a sister?
> JUDY: . . . and I have a sister, too. And I'm their sister.

At this point, Tatiana arrives at class with her grandfather. She is wearing a black felt cape with red lining and holding a Batman mask in her hand. When I explain where the rest of the class is, Tatiana decides that she also does not want to attend the assembly and joins us in the reading corner.

Noticing Tatiana's mask, Min-Haeng says to her softly, "Tatiana, I can draw a Batman for you." When I ask Tatiana, "Would you like him to?" she replies, "Yeah," and Min-Haeng says, "O.K. I'll try." The four of us then walk over to the drawing table, where colored construction paper and colored chalk have been laid out for the kids to use. As Min-Haeng begins to work on his drawing, Tony picks up Tatiana's Batman mask and wants to try it on but struggles to adjust the strap.

> TONY (*TO TATIANA*): How can you fit it?
> TATIANA (*CHEERFULLY*): Do you want me to help?
> TONY (*HANDING THE MASK TO TATIANA*): I'm five years old.
> TATIANA (*REASONING*): You're a little bit bigger than me.
> TONY: Can you fix it?
> TATIANA: Yeah. Maybe it would go one more [notch]. You could try that.
> TONY (*TRYING ON THE MASK*): No.
> TATIANA: It still doesn't fit you. But it has to be tight so it fits on you real good. I tried it on tight and it fit me real good, so it doesn't fall down when I'm, you're wearing it at home and you're running around in the house with it. (*She laughs.*)
> TONY (*PUTTING ON THE MASK*): There. (*Tatiana laughs.*)

Tony is patient and pleasant as he engages Tatiana and asks for her help.

In a moment of silence, we hear music from the assembly. When I point out one song that will play at my wedding in two weeks, Tony seems especially interested (perhaps because of the recent changes in his family's composition).

> TONY: Your sister and you are going to get married?
> JUDY: No, I'm getting married. But my sister's gonna be there. And my brother's gonna be there. You wanna see their pictures?
> TONY: Yeah. (*I take out my wallet and show Tony the photos inside.*)
> TONY: Are you gonna get married with him?

JUDY: No, that's my brother. I'm getting married with . . . (*I flip through the photos.*)

TONY: Who?

JUDY: I'll show you.

TONY (*LOOKING AT THE PHOTO THAT I'M SHOWING HIM*): That's you?

JUDY: That's me. And that's him.

TONY (*FLIPPING TO ANOTHER PHOTO*): Hey, are they getting married?

JUDY: That's my mom and dad.

TONY (*LOOKING AT THE NEXT PHOTO*): Is that your mom and dad?

JUDY: No, that's my brother and that's a girl that he went to a dance with.

TONY (*CONCERNED*): Did your mom, is that O.K.?

JUDY: Yeah, she said it's O.K.

When Tony finishes looking through my photos, he closes my wallet carefully and hands it back to me saying, "I closed it." I tell him, "Thank you," and mean it, as I really appreciate his interest and consideration.

Tony then turns his attention to some punch-out stamps, which are used to create holes of various shapes. Tony picks out a sheet of construction paper and punches out five sun-shaped holes.

TONY: I have one, two, three, four, five suns. I'm five.

TATIANA: I'm five.

JUDY (*TO TATIANA*): You're five, too?

MIN-HAENG: I'm five.

JUDY (*TO MIN-HAENG*): Wow.

TATIANA (*TO JUDY*): Are you five?

JUDY: I'm twenty-five.

MIN-HAENG: Oh my gosh! Yikes! I thought you were 142!

TONY: I thought you were twenty-four.

JUDY (*TO TONY*): Oh, well that's close.

When Tatiana finishes her drawing and gives it to me, Tony also offers me the paper from which he punched out five suns. As I thank them both, Tony suddenly becomes antsy and begins to kick the table.

JUDY (*TO TONY*): Oh, don't kick the table, please. Min-Haeng's drawing and you're gonna mess him up.

MIN-HAENG (*TO JUDY*): No, it's O.K. I could erase.

JUDY (*TO MIN-HAENG*): Oh, O.K. (*Tony continues to kick and eventually disturbs Min-Haeng.*)

MIN-HAENG (*TO TONY*): Stop, Tony! Tony, stop.

JUDY: Tony, don't kick it, O.K.?

Tony stops kicking the table and sings a silly song instead, "I love to eat butt, butt, butt." When Tatiana laughs, Tony continues to sing, "I really don't love to eat butt. I love to eat wieners." When Min-Haeng also laughs, Tony is further encouraged and continues to make up silly song lyrics.

TONY (*SINGING*): I love to eat the sun so high. I love to eat this whole school.

MIN-HAENG: Ew! That would taste so yucky!

TONY (*SINGING*): I would love to eat this whole wide . . .

MIN-HAENG: You can't. It's too, too big.

TONY (*SINGING*): I can eat this whole world, if I had a big humungous mouth.

TATIANA: Then you'd be a dinosaur. (*She giggles.*)

TONY (*SINGING*): I will eat this whole world. And then you guys will be crushed up. In my mouth. (*Tatiana laughs.*)

MIN-HAENG (*TO TONY*): You would be crushed up!

TONY: I would love to eat . . . I love to be Godzilla.

MIN-HAENG (*SPASTICALLY*): Yeah, Godzilla, he's a monster, he's like (*shouting*) yah, yah, yah!

I remind the kids that they need to be quiet because the assembly is still going on, which prompts Tony to run out to check.

When Tony returns, I ask the kids if they would like to go to the assembly now, and they all say that they would not. Min-Haeng then begins to work on another drawing while Tony runs around the classroom giggling and yelling.

TONY (*TO JUDY, FROM ACROSS THE ROOM*): I said, I hurt my butt!

JUDY: O.K., but you have to be quiet or else they'll come and get us and take us to the concert. So you have to be quiet, 'cause we're hiding.

TATIANA (*CHEERFULLY*): I'm a good hider. I could hide almost anywhere. I can hide anywhere.

JUDY (*TO TONY, WHO IS STILL RUNNING BACK AND FORTH*): Tony, they're gonna hear you running around and they're gonna take you to the concert.

TONY (*SURPRISED*): Me?

JUDY: Yeah, so you gotta be quiet and stop running like that, O.K.?

With this warning, Tony stops running, heads to the reading corner, and sits down on the futon. Noticing a reflection of light on the ceiling, Tony calls for Min-Haeng to come take a look. Min-Haeng walks over to where Tony is, takes a look, and explains to Tony, "It's just sunlight." Tony agrees and then proposes, "Min-Haeng, let's have a race." Before Min-Haeng can respond, Tatiana and I join the boys and I offer to read a book to them. As Tony and Min-Haeng scramble to pick out a book, they end up spilling a pile of books all over the floor. Min-Haeng grabs one of the books, gets up, and runs off, and Tony chases after him.

As the two boys run around the room giggling, I ask them to quiet down but they ignore my requests. I turn to Tatiana, who is sitting quietly by my side, and ask her jokingly, "What am I going to do with these boys?" To my surprise, Tatiana tells me exactly what to do, step-by-step. First, she tells me to give them three chances. When I ask her how to do that, she tells me to say, "You have three chances." I repeat her words and magically Tony and Min-Haeng stop dead in their tracks and turn to face me. I ask Tatiana what to do next and she tells me to say, "This is your first chance." With each chance, the boys calm down a little and drift slightly in our direction but then regain momentum and continue to chase each other. After I have given the boys three chances, I turn to Tatiana and ask, "What do I do now?" and she tells me to give them a time out. Again, I ask her what to say, and she tells me the exact words to use. As she did during my first visit, Tatiana is able to consider my novice perspective and tells me what I need to know in order to navigate the rules and culture of this class. When I repeat her words, both Tony and Min-Haeng immediately stop what they are doing and join us on the futon. Amazing.

Just as he did during the meeting with Jake and Rob, Tony shifted his presence in this interaction with Min-Haeng and Tatiana. Once again, Tony demonstrated the ability to engage earnestly with others and to interact in ways that are appropriate and appealing, as when he asked Tatiana to help him adjust the Batman mask and when he took an interest in my photos. However, as Tony began to focus on trying to amuse and impress his peers, in this case by darting in and out of the classroom and shouting absurdities ("I said, I hurt my butt!"), his conduct felt flighty and his contributions seemed haphazard.

Although Tony's impulsive behaviors may have annoyed his peers at first (e.g., when his table-kicking disrupted Min-Haeng's drawing), Tony persisted with this approach because it sometimes got him what he wanted (e.g., when Tatiana and Min-Haeng seemed entertained by Tony's silly songs and when Min-Haeng eventually joined Tony in running around the room). Thus, Tony was learning to seek connections through disconnected and disconnecting behaviors, or behaviors that seem absent-minded and disengaged from the interaction at hand and that foster neither self-awareness nor close relationships with others. And so long as this approach occasionally yielded desired results, Tony was unlikely to change his ways.

Getting away with It

While I was not surprised that Tony's flighty and haphazard behaviors could be effective in getting his peers' attention, I was surprised that these behaviors seemed to go unnoticed or uncorrected by the adults at school. Jake had been tested for Attention Deficit Hyperactivity Disorder (ADHD) because at times he seemed unable or unwilling to contain his exuberance. Mike had been enrolled in a behavior management program to learn to control his aggressive impulses. And during my twelfth visit, when Mike cannot sit still during circle time, his teachers punish him by denying him his duties as line leader and making him stay back while the other kids head out to recess. At times, Tony also seemed restless and displayed aggressive behaviors when he didn't get his way. However, whereas Jake and Mike were carefully policed and promptly criticized, Tony's disruptive conduct was rarely acknowledged, much less addressed.

Occasionally, Tony was even rewarded, albeit unintentionally, for his outbursts and bad behavior. During my seventeenth visit, a conflict arises when Tony insists on playing with Tatiana's toy wolf after she tells him that she does not want to share. When Tatiana continues to refuse, Tony throws a tantrum. He whines, pouts, and knocks over chairs. He punches and kicks angrily at the air. He walks towards the sink, picks up a wooden stepping stool (that the kids stand on to reach the faucet), and hurls it to the ground. Just as Tony picks up two stuffed animals and prepares to throw them on the floor as well, Jen intervenes and talks to him and also to Tatiana. Jen resolves the situation by explaining to Tatiana that she should not bring to school toys that she does not want to share with others. Jen says nothing to Tony about his tantrum. Rather, Jen takes the disputed toy from Tatiana and offers it to Tony, who grabs it, heads to the reading corner, and handles it roughly while Tatiana watches anxiously. Later, when I ask Tony how he felt when Tatiana would not allow him to play with her toy wolf, Tony's response ("Yes, happy") seems oddly detached and suggests that, despite having gotten his way, he is still distracted and unsettled.

Although the other children could expect the teachers to praise their good behaviors and admonish their bad behaviors, Tony seemed to escape being monitored in this way. Just as no one seemed to notice or remark on Tony's comings and goings (e.g., when he left class to visit his mom), no one seemed to hold Tony accountable for his misconduct. As a result, Tony was often allowed to "get away" with behaviors that were discouraged in the other kids. In the end, this did not help Tony, as he consequently did not receive the feedback he needed in order to learn how to behave appropriately and engage others effectively.

Conforming to Group Norms

Another thing that set Tony apart from the other boys was his interest in dolls. Just as the boys in this class learned to take (or fake) an interest in guns in order to identify with and relate to each other, they learned to express an aversion to dolls in order to distinguish themselves from the girls. This was not a problem for boys who were not interested in playing with dolls. However, boys who were interested in dolls had to find a way to reconcile this "feminine" interest with gendered expectations regarding appropriate toys for boys. As it turned out, Tony liked dolls and enjoyed playing with dolls, and this got him into trouble at home. During a meeting with Gabriella (Tony's stepsister) on my nineteenth visit, Gabriella tells me that Tony is not allowed to play with dolls because Tony's stepdad (Gabriella's dad) does not approve.

JUDY: Can boys play with dolls, too?

GABRIELLA: No!

JUDY: How come?

GABRIELLA: Because always, when Tony plays with dolls, and my dad sees him, he yells at [Tony].

JUDY: And what does your dad say to Tony, like when he's yelling at him?

GABRIELLA: "Don't play with the dolls!"

JUDY: And how does Tony feel about that?

GABRIELLA (*WHISPERING*): Sad.

JUDY: He's sad? What does your mommy say?

GABRIELLA: She says, "Let Tony play with the dolls." And Daddy says, "No. He's a boy. He can't play with dolls."

JUDY: And then what happens?

GABRIELLA: Um, [Tony] plays with his own stuff.

JUDY: Like what?

GABRIELLA: Playmobil. So, I like to play with girls' stuff and [Tony] likes to play with boys' stuff.

Although Gabriella concludes that Tony "likes to play with boys' stuff," it seems that Tony doesn't really have a choice. However, Tony was not so easily deterred. Despite his stepdad's disapproval, Tony continued to play with dolls at home. He just learned to be careful not to do it when his stepdad was around. Rather, it was mainly within his interactions with peers at school that Tony began to feel conflicted about (and to consider seriously the implications and potential consequences of) his interest in dolls.

Like Tony's stepdad, the other boys made it clear through their expressed attitudes and beliefs that playing with dolls—like most activities associated with girls—was not something in which they, as boys, were (or should be) interested. Whereas his stepdad's restrictions had not stopped Tony from playing with dolls, Tony quickly learned to accommodate his attitude and behaviors to masculine norms when he realized that his interest in dolls could undermine his ability to be accepted and included by his peers. For instance, during a meeting with Jake and Tony on my twentieth visit, Tony immediately mimics Jake's negative response (and even takes it a step further) when I ask the boys about doll play.

JUDY: Do you guys ever play with dolls?

JAKE (*SOON JOINED BY TONY*): No! No way!

TONY (*EMPHATICALLY*): We'd kill 'em and we don't like dolls.

JUDY: Oh, so boys aren't supposed to play with dolls, then?

JAKE: No, actually, we *could* play with dolls, but we don't *want* to.

JUDY (*TO JAKE*): What would happen if a boy did play with a doll? 'Cause you said he could, right?

JAKE: Yeah.

JUDY: What would happen? Would people say things?

TONY: "We don't like him."

JAKE: Yeah.

JUDY: But what if you saw a boy who was playing with a doll? What would you think of him?

JAKE AND TONY: Um,

JAKE (*IN A SEMI-PLAYFUL TONE*): A mutt.

JUDY: A mutt?

TONY: Yeah, a mutt.

JUDY: He's a mutt.

JAKE: We would think he's a mutt.

At this school, no one explicitly forbids the boys (or girls) from playing with dolls. Even so, Jake and Tony both know that a boy who plays with dolls would not be well received ("We don't like him," "We would think he's a mutt"). Jake, who does not seem interested in playing with dolls anyway, suggests it is a matter of choice ("we *could* play with dolls, but we don't *want* to"). For Tony, however, the situation is more complicated. Although Tony is interested in playing with dolls, he also has learned that this could jeopardize his relationships with the other boys. Unwilling to risk his relationships, especially with Jake, Tony denies that he plays with dolls ("No! No way!") and makes sure to display an appropriately (and extremely) negative attitude towards dolls ("We'd kill 'em").

While in Jake's company, Tony similarly denies that he plays with Gabriella, which contradicts Gabriella's complaint that Tony always asks her to play with him.

JUDY: Do you play with Gabriella at home?

TONY: No! . . . way, José.

JUDY: How come?

TONY: I don't like girls.

JUDY: Really?

JAKE: Yeah, neither do I.

JUDY: You don't like girls?

JAKE: We go against them. It's sorta like a war against girls.

JUDY: Oh really? A war against girls?

JAKE: Yeah, girls against boys, boys against girls.

Again, the boys are attuned to the boys-versus-girls dynamic in this class and, in order to confirm their identities as boys and demonstrate their masculinity, they have learned to conceal any associations they may have with girls or femininity.

Despite learning to display gender-appropriate attitudes and behaviors, Tony's own interests and preferences still emerged occasionally. On my twenty-first visit, Tony, Gabriella, and three Kindergarteners (two girls and one boy) are playing with Barbie dolls in the block corner at the start of the school day (before the other kids arrive). Barbie dolls are an unusual sight because, like guns, they are not allowed in this class. Other kinds of dolls, however, are allowed and can be found in the house area. Jen explains to me that the Kindergarteners have different rules about toys, and they are allowed to bring Barbie dolls to school. At first, the children simply play together quietly and contentedly. No one seems to notice or care that boys as well as girls are playing with dolls. However, when Gabriella sees me watching from the front of the room, she greets me from where she is sitting, holds up one of the Barbie dolls, and—referring to a previous conversation when she told me that she likes to play with "good dolls"—yells to me, "I like to play with these." Probably recalling that conversation (when she also told me that her dad does not allow Tony to play with dolls), Gabriella suddenly turns to Tony and informs him, "Tony, you can't play with girls' stuff." When Tony asks why, Gabriella replies firmly, "Daddy said." Although one of the Kindergarten girls interjects, "It's not really girls' stuff," Gabriella remains firm: "Last time, Tony wanted to play and Daddy said it's girls' stuff." In her father's absence, Gabriella takes it upon herself to monitor Tony's behavior and enforce her father's rule. Now that the issue of gender-appropriate play has been raised, the other boy gets up and heads back to his class, which leaves Tony sitting with the three girls amongst a pile of Barbie dolls. Reluctant to be the only boy playing with girls and with "girls' toys," Tony also gets up and leaves soon after.

I suspect that Tony might have been more willing to reveal his interest in dolls if he could know that his deviance would not result in his being outcast and alone. For example, if another boy played with dolls, then Tony wouldn't be the only one who was different from the rest of the boys, and that might be enough to support and sustain his resistance against pressures to conform to gendered norms. During a meeting with Jake, Tony, and Rob on my twenty-first visit, Tony seems hopeful when Jake picks up the Blue Prince and remarks in a neutral tone, "Look at his [long] hair. He's a girl." Focusing on the possibility that Jake is playing with a girl doll (or a "girls' doll"), Tony asks tentatively, "You're playing with a girl, Jake?" Given that Tony looks up to Jake, a positive response from Jake could enable Tony to feel validated and perhaps reveal his own interest in dolls. However, before Jake can respond, Rob interjects, "No. Boys can have long hair," and inadvertently dashes Tony's hopes of finding an ally.

Without someone to join him, Tony seemed less able or less willing to take the risk of deviating from group norms, so he continued to deny his interest in dolls when he was among his peers. During a meeting with Tony and Min-Haeng on my twenty-second visit, Tony resumes a firm stance against dolls and doll play.

> JUDY (*GENTLY*): You know what? I know a little boy who likes to play with Barbie dolls . . .
>
> MIN-HAENG (*SOON JOINED BY TONY*): Ew!
>
> JUDY: . . . but his dad won't let him. I thought it was O.K. for boys to play with dolls.
>
> MIN-HAENG: No, they only, only girls play with them.
>
> JUDY: If you were this little boy's dad, what would you tell the little boy?
>
> TONY: "No."
>
> JUDY: You'd tell him he can't play? But what if that makes him very sad, 'cause he really wants to play with them?
>
> TONY (*SIGHING, IN A SOFT VOICE*): Yeah, but we can't. Boys can't play with dolls.
>
> MIN-HAENG: And they don't want to.

JUDY: Who says that? Who says that boys can't play with dolls?
TONY: Daddies. Mommies.

Like Jake, Min-Haeng emphasizes that boys do not (and should not) want to play with dolls, whereas Tony explains that boys are not allowed to play with dolls. Although Tony says that it's parents ("Daddies. Mommies") who prohibit boys' doll play, Tony's behaviors indicate that it is mainly his peer group culture and his desire to fit in with and be like the other boys (and not merely a need to comply with adults' rules or prove his masculinity in a general sense) that motivates him to give up, or at least hide, his interest in dolls.

* * *

By the end of the year, Tony's strategy for relating to others resembles what Janie Ward calls "resistance for survival."[8] This short-term strategy aims to protect a fragile sense of self rather than affirm a sturdy sense of self, and is described as an attempt to put (or keep) together what others have tried to take apart. In contrast, "resistance for liberation" is designed to affirm rather than protect the self, and is considered to be a more healthy form of resistance. In Tony, resistance for survival is reflected in his flighty manner and haphazard behaviors and in his accommodation to group norms that do not reflect his personal preferences. Tony's mode of resistance is partly a consequence of being in an environment wherein he feels that no one is listening to him, attending to his needs, and paying enough attention to him. Although Tony's strategy occasionally enables him to achieve the ephemeral result of getting the attention and acceptance he seeks (and may protect him from the pain of being overlooked or ostracized by his peers), it will eventually cost him as he fails to engage with people in meaningful ways, becomes disconnected from others (even as he tries to be close), and is given negative labels (e.g., disengaged, disruptive) that will not serve him well as he moves through the school system.

Tony's case study sheds some light on why and how boys who seek and are capable of close relationships might nevertheless struggle to connect with others. It was not necessarily the things that made Tony different from the other boys—including his intense desire for closeness and his interest in dolls—that led to problems in his relationships. Rather, it was that Tony came to express his desire for connection through disconnected behaviors and disconnecting relational styles. Whereas Tony demonstrated the ability to be attentive and responsive and had the capacity and desire to establish close relationships, he began to approach his relationships in ways that involved and/or resulted in his becoming detached from his sensibilities and alienated from others. For example, Tony's focus on capturing people's attention and interest often prevented him from paying attention to and taking a real interest in what people were saying and doing. Even if Tony sometimes managed to entertain his peers, his tentative and unpredictable presence ultimately undermined his efforts to develop and maintain the kinds of relationships in which he could feel confident and secure and which he seemed to seek so desperately. In turn, without the support of close relationships in which he could feel accepted, understood, and joined, it became difficult for Tony to remain grounded in his own thoughts, feelings, and desires while interacting with others. Thus, Tony's presence was impacting his relationships and his relationships were impacting his presence.

4

Boys versus the Mean Team

In this pre-Kindergarten class, the process wherein boys became "boys" was probably best illustrated by the boys' participation on the Mean Team—a club created by the boys, for the boys, and for the stated purpose of acting against the girls. For these boys, the Mean Team appeared to play a central role in establishing a notion of masculinity that is defined both in opposition to and as the opposite of femininity. The Mean Team also emphasized and reinforced the hierarchy that had emerged among these boys. The requirements and implications of the boys' membership on the Mean Team—as dictated and enforced by the boys themselves—exemplified the challenges that boys may face and the costs for boys as they negotiate their identities, behaviors, and styles of relating to others within contexts that emphasize hierarchy, competition, and conformity to group and cultural norms.

I first learned about the Mean Team during a meeting with Rob on my sixteenth visit when I asked him about expectations for boys.

JUDY: Are there things that, like, boys have to do?
ROB: Yeah, because I'm in a club at school.
JUDY: Oh really? What kind of club?
ROB (*SOFTLY*): The Mean Team.
JUDY (*MISHEARING*): The man team?
ROB: No, the Mean Team, which is a very silly game that we, all we do is we bother people. We go over and we disturb someone else's game and we bother them.

Until this moment, I had not been aware that these boys had formed an official club. As it turned out, the boys' parents and teachers also did not know about the Mean Team at this time. Given that its name and purpose (to "bother people") imply aggression, I was not surprised that the boys would try to keep the Mean Team a secret from adults, who would likely disapprove. I was impressed, however, that the boys had succeeded in keeping their club a secret—because, at this age, they still tended to foil their own attempts to be secretive—and I was glad that Rob was willing to let me in on it.

JUDY: Who else is on this team?

ROB: Like, Mike is the boss, and Tony and Min-Haeng, Jake [and Dan].

JUDY: What's this team for?

ROB: It's for boys . . . but Mikey's the whole point, 'cause he wanted to do it.

JUDY: Hmm, why do you think he wanted to do it?

ROB: I don't know.

JUDY: Why do you do it?

ROB: Because [Mike] told me to do it.

JUDY: Oh . . . So, what does this team do? You go around and bother people, how?

ROB: We just disturb their game.

JUDY: You mess things up?

ROB: Yeah, like, if they were playing something? They were playing house and this grass was soup once. We did this. (*He uses his hands to pretend to scoop something up off the floor.*) We messed it all up and threw it at them.

JUDY: And that's why it's called the Mean Team? Because you do mean things in this group?

ROB: Yeah.

JUDY: Do you like being in this group?

ROB: Yeah, 'cause I like being mean.

JUDY: Yeah? Do you feel like [there are] a lot of times when you're not allowed to be mean?

ROB: Yeah, so, I like to [be on the Mean Team].

According to Rob's description, being mean involves engaging in annoying but harmless mischief. Although Rob says the Mean Team was mainly Mike's idea ("Mikey's the whole point, 'cause he wanted to do it") and that he participates "Because [Mike] told me to do it," Rob also likes being on the Mean Team ("'cause I like being mean").

However, as Rob explains further, there are some drawbacks to being on the Mean Team, as when the boys do things that he doesn't really like or want to do.

JUDY: So, there's this Mean Team and Mikey's the leader.

ROB: Yeah.

JUDY: And you go around doing mean things. Do you ever hurt people?

ROB (*IN A DISTRESSED VOICE*): Yes. I'm not very interested, because I don't usually do stuff then, with hurting. (*In his regular voice*) But I do like to throw stuff at people.

JUDY: You throw stuff at people?

ROB: And bother them. But I don't really, like, hurt 'em. But the other team, people on the team [who] are mean, sometimes hurt people.

JUDY (*MISUNDERSTANDING*): Who's the other team?

ROB: No, people on our side sometimes hurt people.

JUDY: Oh yeah? Like who?

ROB: Like Mikey, got a shark tooth.

JUDY: What do you think about that shark tooth?

ROB: It's sharp and stuff. You can poke people with it.

JUDY: Does he poke anybody with it?

ROB: He poked my brother.

JUDY: He did? Your baby brother or your older brother?

ROB: My older brother.

JUDY: And how did [your brother] respond to that?

ROB: It didn't really hurt, but he did get a little scratch.

JUDY: And how did that make you feel?

ROB: Um, sort of sad.

JUDY: Yeah? How come?

ROB: Because, he was sort of, I don't really wanna do it.

JUDY: You don't really want to hurt people?

ROB: Yeah.

JUDY: Is there somebody you can talk to when you're feeling like you want to be mean or when you don't feel like being nice?

ROB: Yeah.

JUDY: Who's that?

ROB: My boss. 'Cause he's really, he decides if I can be, my boss decides if I can be mean, if I can be nice or mean.

JUDY: Who's your boss?

ROB: Mikey. He leads the whole gang. He decides *every*thing. We don't get
to say *any*thing.

JUDY: Is that, what do you think about that?

ROB: It's O.K. with me.

JUDY: Really?

ROB: Yeah.

JUDY: Is it ever not O.K. with you?

ROB: No. It's O.K. with me.

JUDY: What happens if [Mike] tells you to do something that you don't want—

ROB (*CUTTING ME OFF, REPLYING FIRMLY*): I do it.

JUDY: You do it anyway, even if you don't want to?

ROB: Yeah, I'm 'posed to do it.

According to Rob, Mike is in charge ("He leads the whole gang. He
decides *every*thing."). Despite not being allowed to have any say ("We
don't get to say *any*thing"), Rob says that he's "O.K." with this arrangement and implies that he feels obligated to comply with Mike's orders
("I'm 'posed to do it").

Reinforcing the Boys versus Girls Dynamic

Although Rob didn't specify who were the targets of the Mean Team's
mischief ("we bother *people*," "we disturb *someone else's* game," "we
bother *them*"), and although the example he gave (of Mike poking his
brother with a shark tooth) indicated that the targets could be boys as
well as girls, it soon became clear that the Mean Team's intended targets
were primarily the girls. During a subsequent meeting with Rob on my
eighteenth visit, Rob mentions the Mean Team again and confirms that
all of the boys are members and the girls are not.

JUDY: Are there things you have to do? Like people tell you, "You have to
do it"?

ROB: Not always, but sometimes.

JUDY: Oh yeah? Who tells you those things?

ROB: Sometimes the teacher, sometimes Mikey, 'cause Mikey's the boss of
the Mean Team.

JUDY (*REMEMBERING*): That's right. And who's on the Mean Team again?

ROB: Jake, Tony, Min-Haeng . . . (*He becomes distracted by my Playmobil toys.*)

JUDY: Mikey and you?

ROB: Yeah, Mikey and me and that's all.

JUDY: Not Dan?

ROB: Oh yeah, Dan.

JUDY: So all six boys?

ROB: All six boys and there's four girls.

JUDY: [The girls are] on the Mean Team, too?

ROB: No, they're not on the Mean Team.

JUDY: Oh.

ROB: 'Cause we don't have room for them. We need some enemy.

JUDY: Oh, so the girls are your enemy?

ROB: Yeah and they, sometimes we're their enemy.

JUDY: Oh.

ROB: Sometimes we are, but not always.

Rob's description suggests that the boys have (or view themselves as having) the upper hand in this relationship (between the boys and the girls) because—assuming that the girls want to be in their club—the boys get to decide whether to include the girls.

In addition to viewing girls as their enemy, the boys also viewed the girls as their opposites and made a point to define and position themselves accordingly. For instance, during a meeting with Rob and Mike on my twentieth visit, the boys explain how they renamed the Mean Team to contrast with its counterpart, the girls' Good/Nice Team.

JUDY: Mikey, was it your idea to form the Mean Team?

MIKE: Yeah, it was.

ROB: Yes.

MIKE: Me and Jake.

JUDY: Yeah? How did the idea come up? How did you get that idea?

MIKE: I don't know. We just made it up.

ROB: The Mean Team. At first we thought it could be the Good Team.

MIKE: No. Well, the girls are the Good Team. We're the Mean Team.

ROB: I know.

JUDY: The girls are the Good Team and you're the Mean Team? So, is the Mean Team the same thing as the bad team?

MIKE: We're actually pretty not nice.

JUDY: The Mean Team?

MIKE: We're posh.

JUDY: You're posh?

ROB: Yeah.

JUDY: What does that mean?

MIKE: It means you never smile. And I'm posh.

JUDY: I see.

ROB: Yeah, we never smile.

Both boys are silent for a moment as they pucker and pout their lips and try not to smile.

MIKE (*A LITTLE EMBARRASSED*): I just smiled. It's hard not to smile. (*Judy laughs.*)

ROB (*STILL PUCKERING HIS LIPS*): We're supposed to be posh.

MIKE (*RESUMING HIS POSH STANCE*): Posh.

ROB: Yeah.

Ironically, the boys demonstrate what it means to be a member of the boys' Mean Team by imitating Posh Spice, a member of the all-women band Spice Girls and a character in *Spice World* (the Spice Girls movie), which Mike had watched recently. Nonetheless, the trait is an appropriate choice for the boys' masculine posturing because, as personified by Posh Spice, it involves being confident and cool.

When Mike, Rob, and I return to class after our meeting, Mike and Rob try to explain and demonstrate to Jen how—because they are boys—they are opposed to and also the opposite of girls. As Jen joins the boys at one of the tables, Mike looks around the classroom and notices that Nicole is absent today.

MIKE (*DREAMILY*): A day without Nicole.

JEN: I miss Nicole. I really like Nicole and Nicole likes you.

MIKE: You have it mixed up because Nicole likes us, but we don't like Nicole.

ROB: The boys all play together.

JEN: Do you ever play with girls?

MIKE AND ROB: No.

ROB: We have a team. Mikey, tell her the name of our team.

MIKE: The Mean Team. And they are the Nice Team.[1]

JEN: So, the girls are the Nice Team?

MIKE: Yes.

JEN: Why is that?

MIKE: Because they always do nice things.

ROB: Yeah. And we do bad things.

JEN: Do you ever do nice things?

ROB: No.

JEN (TO MIKE): Can you tell me what's a bad thing to do?

MIKE: Kicking and punching at school.

ROB: One time I ripped a cover from a book.

JEN: Were you angry about something?

ROB: No, I ripped it and threw it at someone.

JEN: What's something nice you've done?

ROB: Nothing.

Mike also doesn't respond. Neither of the boys wants to admit to doing nice things, especially since they have just asserted that girls do nice things and boys do bad things. When Jen insists, "I know you've both done nice things," Rob tries to demonstrate how he is bad (and therefore a boy) by taking Min-Haeng's nametag off the wall and hiding it so that Min-Haeng won't be able to find it later. However, Jen thwarts Rob's attempt by suggesting calmly and cheerfully that when Min-Haeng comes and cannot find his nametag, Rob will be able to tell him where it is. As Jen points out that this is a nice thing, Rob immediately replaces the nametag. He is determined not to do a nice thing, not when his masculinity is at stake.

Was the Mean Team Mean?

Considering the name of the boys' club and its practice of bothering and disturbing people, the question inevitably arises: Was the Mean Team mean? According to Rob, the boys' participation on the Mean Team did sometimes involve doing mean things. However, the Mean Team appeared to serve as more than just an outlet for boys' stereotypical aggression. For the boys, being a member of the Mean Team also became an important indicator of their status as boys, and seemed (at least to them) important to their ability to identify with and relate to their same-sex peers. Just as the boys learned to show that they are boys (and not girls) by embracing gun play and rejecting doll play, so their membership on the Mean Team became another way for them to affirm their group affiliation and confirm their masculine identities. For instance, during a meeting with Rob, Jake, and Tony on my twenty-first visit, the boys indicate that being a member of the Mean Team has become a proxy for being a boy.

> JUDY: If I wanted to learn how to be a boy (*the boys giggle*), what would I
>   have to learn to do?
> TONY: Be on the Mean Team.
> JUDY: Yeah? And how could I do that?
> JAKE: Be mean.
> TONY: Be mean.
> JAKE: That's all.
> JUDY: That's it?
> TONY: No, and then you need to capture the girls.
> JAKE: At least try.
> TONY: And then you need to capture yourself.
> JAKE: No, first you at least have to *try* to capture them.
> TONY: Yup, we captured them.

Like Mike and Rob, Jake and Tony suggest that, in this class, being a boy involves being on the Mean Team and acting mean. Conversely, they also have learned that being on the Mean Team and acting mean are ways to show that they are boys.

In addition to enabling the boys to be *one of the boys*, membership on the Mean Team could also instill a sense of inclusion, belonging, and being *with the boys*. For instance, during a meeting with Jake and Tony on my twentieth visit, the boys refer to themselves as being Mike's "men" and "in his army" when they tell me about people they have to protect (a topic that I ask about because other boys had brought it up previously).

> JUDY: Do you ever protect anybody?
> JAKE AND TONY: Yes. Yeah.

JUDY: Who do you protect?

JAKE: Mikey.

JUDY (*SURPRISED*): Mikey? You protect him?

JAKE: Yeah, we're his men!

JUDY: Oh.

TONY: Don'tcha know?

JAKE: We're in his army, don'tcha know?

Given that Mike was by far the toughest and most domineering of the boys, I had not expected that he would need protection nor that the boys would feel inclined or obligated to protect him. Regardless, the boys seemed happy to go along with this scheme, as it enabled them to have a place among the boys and to be a part of the group. During a meeting with Mike and Rob on my twentieth visit, Rob similarly mentions the sense of camaraderie that comes from being on the Mean Team and following Mike's lead.

JUDY: Are you the boss of something, Mikey?

MIKE: I'm the boss of the Mean Team.

JUDY: What does that mean that you're the boss?

ROB: It means that he tells us to do stuff and then we do it. And then, if we can't do it, we all group together and do it.

JUDY: Oh.

ROB: Right, Mikey?

MIKE: Yeah.

Like Jake and Tony, Rob is willing to accept a subordinate position ("It means that he tells us to do stuff and then we do it") in exchange for the assurance that he has the support of the group, that he and the other boys are in it together, so to speak, and that therefore he does not have to act on his own or be alone.

Formalizing the Boys' Hierarchy

In addition to reinforcing the boys-versus-girls dynamic that was emerging in this class, the Mean Team also formalized the hierarchy that had been established among the boys. Thus, in appointing himself the boss of the Mean Team, Mike basically extended his role as the undisputed leader of the boys to a more "official" capacity and became further empowered (and may have felt even more entitled) to take charge, impose his preferences, and expect his peers to comply with his demands. Whereas the boys in this class generally resisted being bossed around, they hesitated to question or challenge Mike's authority (partly because Mike promptly punished them when they tried). Nevertheless, Mike seemed preoccupied with proving his worth and also his superiority, as when he declared (unprompted) on my twenty-first visit, "I'm stronger than Robby." As though trying to justify and defend his right to rule, Mike worked continually to project an image of strength and importance, especially in his interactions with other boys.

The boys' willingness to follow Mike's lead and to do what he asked, even at the cost of subordinating themselves, was not surprising given Mike's domineering and headstrong manner. In combination, Mike's dominant personality and high status made it hard for the other boys to refuse him. Although all of the boys resisted being bossed around, Mike adamantly refused to be told what to do, especially by his peers. And because the boys often ended up complying with his demands, Mike became accustomed to and would insist on getting his way. For instance, during a meeting with Mike, Rob, and Jake on my fifteenth visit, Mike is the first to claim Dark Knight (the most popular toy figure among the boys), and when Rob tries repeatedly to convince him to trade, Mike is clear and firm in expressing his preference "No. I don't want to trade him."[2] However, during a meeting with Mike and Min-Haeng on my twenty-third visit, when Min-Haeng is the first to claim Dark Knight and does not want to trade, Mike persists in his efforts to acquire Dark Knight until Min-Haeng finally surrenders the toy. Mike and Min-Haeng begin to argue about who gets to be Dark/Black Knight as soon as I bring out my toys at the start of our meeting.

MIKE: Where are the toys?
MIN-HAENG: The toys are in the bag. Here we go! I'm being Black Knight.
MIKE (*IN A BABY VOICE*): I am being Black Knight.
MIN-HAENG (*CAUTIOUSLY*): I wanna be . . .
MIKE (*IN A BABY VOICE*): No, but I never . . .
MIN-HAENG: You can be Blue Knight.
MIKE (*IN A BABY VOICE, POUTING*): I don't like Blue Knight. I only like Black
     Knight. Black Knight cooler than Blue Knight. Blue Knight a girl.
MIN-HAENG: No, he's not a girl.

> MIKE (*IN A BABY VOICE*): No, Blue Knight's a girl. Me don't want girl. Me want (*he points to the Black Knight*).
>
> MIN-HAENG (*SOFTLY*): Sorry, Mike.
>
> MIKE (*IN A BABY VOICE*): Me not play with you ever again if you not give me that.
>
> MIN-HAENG (*ANGRILY, HANDING THE TOY TO MIKE*): Oh fine. Here you go. Play with it.
>
> MIKE (*SURPRISED*): Oh?
>
> MIN-HAENG (*MUMBLING*): I'm not playing with you.
>
> MIKE (*INNOCENTLY*): What?
>
> MIN-HAENG (*MORE CLEARLY*): I'm not gonna play with you.
>
> MIKE: What?
>
> MIN-HAENG (*CLEARLY*): I don't wanna play with you.

Defeated and angry, Min-Haeng climbs out of his chair and sits on the floor under the table with his arms folded and crossed over his chest. Meanwhile, Mike begins to chant quietly, more to soothe himself than to communicate with Min-Haeng.

> MIKE (*IN HIS REGULAR SPEAKING VOICE*): It's no big deal. No big deal. It's no big deal.
>
> MIN-HAENG (*ANGRILY*): It's not fair.
>
> MIKE: I'm not gonna, it's no big deal, it's no big deal, it's no big deal, it's no big deal, it's no big deal, it's no big deal.
>
> MIN-HAENG (*ANGRILY*): It's not funny to me. When I get home, I'm gonna play detective without you, Mikey.
>
> MIKE: Well, I'm gonna ask your mom if I can come over to your house today.
>
> MIN-HAENG (*SUSPICIOUS*): Why? What do you want to see?
>
> MIKE (*PLAYFUL, IN A BABY VOICE*): *Winnie the Pooh's Grand Adventures*!
>
> MIN-HAENG (*LESS ANGRY*): Actually, that was a library tape.

Mike is actually quite fond of Min-Haeng and seems to respect that Min-Haeng is not easily intimidated. So, once Mike has what he wants (i.e., Dark Knight), he turns his attention to reconciling with Min-Haeng and manages to do so by changing the topic and assuming a playful stance to lighten the mood.

A Case Study: Mike

Even before Mike established the Mean Team and appointed himself its boss, his aggressive behavior and tendency to bully his peers made him a force to be reckoned with. For instance, during snack time on my second visit, Mike seems agitated in general and begins to harass Gabriella when she tries to sit at the table where Mike is sitting with Jake, Tony, Tatiana, and Miranda. As Gabriella takes her seat, Mike does his best to make her feel unwelcome. He begins by telling Gabriella that girls are not allowed at the table, although he says nothing to Tatiana or Miranda. Mike then suggests that Gabriella is a baby and declares that he and Jake are not babies. Seeming grateful to be included by Mike, Jake goes along with Mike's tirade, adding, "Gabriella's a weirdo." When Jen intervenes and tells the boys that these are not nice words, Jake responds by asking defiantly, "Why?" Jen explains, "Because they hurt people's feelings." As though trying to impress Mike, Jake replies in a sassy tone, "What's wrong with that?" Despite Jen's intervention, Mike continues to point out ways in which he is better than Gabriella, starting with his ability (and Gabriella's inability) to do karate. Jen suggests that there are things other people can do that he cannot, but Mike ignores her and mentions that he is also older than Gabriella. Mike then proceeds to list more things that he can do but Gabriella cannot. When Gabriella claims that she knows how to do some of those things, Tony interjects, "No, you don't, Gabriella," and undermines her efforts to defend herself. Mike, Jake, and Tony then continue to tease and taunt Gabriella, for example by saying that they would not invite her to their birthday parties because she's a girl. Although Gabriella retaliates by saying that she wouldn't allow boys at her birthday party, the boys are unfazed. Instead, they get up from the table and start demonstrating their karate skills, with Mike showing Jake and Tony certain moves that he has learned and Jake and Tony copying Mike's moves. Although Tatiana and Miranda witness this entire exchange, they don't say or do anything, maybe to avoid becoming the boys' next targets.

The girls were not the only ones who were subjected to Mike's domineering manner. Boys also could be targeted, particularly when they appeared to side against Mike. For instance, during free play on my ninth visit, Mike punishes Jake for choosing to play knights and castles with Rob, instead of joining Mike's city game. As Mike tended to regard every interaction as a zero-sum game, wherein one person's gain comes at the expense of another person's loss, he approached his interactions with a dominate-or-be-dominated attitude. So, when Jake chooses Rob's game over Mike's game, Jake unintentionally betrays Mike and incurs Mike's wrath. Unaware that he has offended Mike, Jake finishes constructing his weapon and announces cheerfully, "Hey guys, this is my throwing gun." In response, Mike says to Jake scathingly, "Guns are not allowed at school! You're not allowed at school!" Later on, when the game of knights and castles appears to be gaining more support than the city game that he had proposed, Mike seems to take it as a personal affront and says in an exasperated tone, "I can't believe I'm seeing knights." Although Mike teams up with Dan, who agrees to play Mike's city game after Mike threatens him ("If you don't play the city game, you're a dope") and then pleads with him ("Pretty please"), Mike gets annoyed when Dan unknowingly provokes him. As Mike and Dan gather props for their game, Mike shoves a dictionary into an old purse and decides that he will carry "the pack." When Dan suggests that they use wooden blocks instead of the dictionary and proceeds to make the replacement, Mike responds by shouting at him angrily, "You are not the boss of us!" Stunned by Mike's outburst, Dan remains silent as Mike reclaims the pack and restores its original contents. By trying to tell Mike what to do, Dan inadvertently missteps his bounds and is immediately put back in his place.

Making an Impression

While Mike certainly could be intimidating, he did not become the leader of the boys solely through intimidation; Mike also knew how to impress his peers. For instance during my twelfth visit, when Mike tells Rob about his recent diving excursion, Mike stretches the truth to present his story (and himself) in a more exciting light.

> MIKE: I even saw a big, big shark.
> ROB (*IN AWE*): Did you kill it?
> MIKE (*WITH AN AIR OF BRAVADO*): Yeah. That's how I got my shark tooth.

In addition to regaling the other boys with embellished accounts of his adventures and accomplishments, Mike also impressed them with his apparent knowledge of taboo topics. For example, Mike's exposure to media intended for adult audiences meant that he had information to which the other boys (who were not permitted to watch R-rated movies) might not have access. This put Mike in a position to "educate" his peers, as when Mike introduces Jake and Rob to the "F-word" during my fifteenth visit.

MIKE (*DESCRIBING A MOVIE THAT HE SAW RECENTLY*): So, this military movie, it was, like, really disgusting. There was blood everywhere, people getting ran over by tanks, people getting pushed into mud, these bald people . . . it was rated R. They said lots of swears . . .

JAKE: Like heck and God?

MIKE (*SIGHING*): Well, they said the F-word.

JAKE: What is that? What is the F-word?

MIKE (*MUMBLING TO HIMSELF*): My parents said I shouldn't say it.

JAKE: No, say it please.

MIKE (*TO JUDY*): Do you dare me to?

JUDY (*CONCERNED*): I don't know . . .

MIKE (*INSTANTLY*): O.K., it's f*ck, it's f*ck, it's f*ck.

Although Mike is tempted to tell Jake the forbidden word, he hesitates because he knows that saying a swear word could get him in trouble. So, he asks me if I dare him to say it, as though he would otherwise be unwilling to do so. This is a clever move on Mike's part, as he effectively protects himself from negative consequences by making me an accomplice to his misdemeanor. It is partly this ability—to read and anticipate other people's responses and to adjust his behaviors accordingly—that enables Mike to be such an influential leader among his peers.

Taking Care of His Men

Beyond showing off for the boys, Mike's role as leader also included being accountable to and responsible for his "men." For example, Mike could be protective of his "men," as when Min-Haeng unknowingly makes himself vulnerable to ridicule during my eighth visit and Mike immediately comes to his defense. While we are sitting together at one of the tables, I ask Mike and Min-Haeng what kinds of stories they like.

Mike says that he likes ones about robberies, and Min-Haeng says he likes ones with action heroes. As Min-Haeng begins to list his favorite action heroes, he decides to go to his locker to get his Power Rangers t-shirt. Upon returning with his t-shirt in hand, Min-Haeng starts to unbutton the flannel shirt that he is wearing (so that he can put on his Power Rangers t-shirt instead) and reveals what he has on underneath, "I'm wearing my pajamas." Min-Haeng does not appear to be embarrassed or to see anything wrong with this admission. However, when Dan sings mockingly, "He's wearing his pajamas," Mike interjects firmly, "It's not his pajamas. It's just a long-sleeved shirt."

Mike also tried to comfort his "men" when they appeared to be distressed. For instance, during my twelfth visit as Mike, Rob, Jake, and Min-Haeng are looking through a comic book together and co-constructing a narrative for a particularly violent scene, Rob asks sadly, "Did [my character] get blasted?" and Mike gently reassures him, "No." And during my sixteenth visit as Mike, Jake, and Min-Haeng are looking through a Lego catalog together, and Min-Haeng softly inquires about the characters' suffering—"It didn't hurt when it crashes?"—Mike says kindly, "It didn't hurt." Likewise, Mike could be attentive to and express concern about the other boys' feelings. On my twelfth visit, as Mike and Dan are playing together, Mike detects a change in Dan's tone of voice, asks, "Are you sad?" and seems relieved when Dan replies, "No, I'm just talking weird." And on my twentieth visit, when Mike notices Rob's attention wandering as they are playing together, he asks Rob, "Are you getting bored?" and when Rob replies, "No," seems glad to hear it: "Good."

Another way that Mike took care of his "men" was by helping them to avoid undesirable consequences. For instance, during a meeting with Mike, Jake, and Rob on my fifteenth visit, Mike tries to warn Jake that the character he has chosen is considered to be a bad guy.

> ROB (*TO JAKE*): Look at this [Viking] guy. Want to be this [Viking] guy instead?
> JAKE (*ACCEPTING*): Yeah, sure.
> MIKE (*TO JAKE*): If you have that [Viking] guy, you're a bad guy. Actually, those [Viking] guys are good guys.
> JAKE: No, Vikings. They're Vikings . . . Vikings are bad.
> ROB: No, this is Eastern Warrior. [*The character is listed as Northern Warrior in the Playmobil catalog.*]

JAKE: No, he's a Viking.

MIKE: No, Eastern Warrior. Eastern Warriors are, like, really nice. Actually, Vikings are really nice. They're not bad guys.

JUDY: So, are all three of you good guys, then?

JAKE: No, I'm actually, I don't want to be that [Viking] guy. I want to be this [good] guy.

Although Mike tries to change the rules so that Jake's character can be a good guy, Jake sticks to the "facts" ("They're Vikings . . . Vikings are bad," "he's a Viking") and eventually chooses to play with a different character so that he can be a good guy instead of a bad guy.

At times, Mike even took it upon himself to protect his "men's" possessions. During my twentieth visit, Mike notices Tony mishandling one of Dan's constructions—a circular object made out of Tinker Toys that resembles a wheel or web—and immediately intervenes.

TONY (*IN A BABY VOICE*): Whose is this? (*Picking it up and waving it in the air*) This is a Frisbee. Frisbee, Frisbee, Frisbee, Frisbee.

MIKE: That's Dan's. Put it down.

TONY: Is it a hat?

MIKE (*FIRMLY*): No, it's Dan's and he made it. It's a Frisbee. No. I don't know what it is. And don't touch it.

Later on when I ask Mike about this incident, Mike explains, "Dan wasn't there so I had to protect it. I thought [Tony] was going to break it, so I had to protect it." Thus, Mike's role as boss of the Mean Team and leader of the boys involved not only promoting himself (e.g., by projecting an image of toughness and dominance) but also helping his "men." While Mike's efforts to protect and look out for his "men" could seem condescending (because he viewed his peers as needing his protection), they also reflected feelings of genuine concern and attachment. During a meeting with Mike and Rob on my twentieth visit, when I ask the boys how they feel about Min-Haeng's leaving next year to attend another school, Mike replies in his baby voice, "Sad. He's one of my men,"[3] and for a moment reveals the importance he places on his friendships and his vulnerability in facing this loss.

Feeling Vulnerable

Whether Mike was taking advantage of others or taking care of them, he seemed especially sensitive to their vulnerability, perhaps because he was especially aware of his own vulnerability. In particular, Mike seemed to worry about the possibility that people could leave him or not want him around. Mike's concern resulted in part from his situation at home, where he was adjusting to his parents' separation (his dad had moved out but maintained frequent and regular contact) and where his older sister (whom he revered) sometimes discouraged his attempts to be with her and to be like her. During my eighteenth visit, when I ask Mike what makes him feel sad, Mike tells me about a time when his sister asked him to get out of her room.

> JUDY: Can you tell me about something that makes you feel sad?
> MIKE: Um, my sister, sometimes I like to jump on her bed and she's like, "Get out of my room, please!"
> JUDY: Oh, so you don't like [it] when she won't let you play with her?
> MIKE: Yeah. I don't want to play with her often.
> JUDY: You don't want to play with her often?
> MIKE: Uh-huh.
> JUDY: Do you like to play with her?
> MIKE: Um, no, not really,
> JUDY: But that makes you sad, when she kicks you out of her room?
> MIKE: (*pause*) Yeah.

Although Mike says that he does not often want to play with his sister and that he does not really like to play with her, it is her rejection (or her ability to deny him something he wants) that first comes to his mind when I ask him about what makes him feel sad.

As the younger sibling, Mike tended to have less power and influence in his relationship with his sister. Despite his strong personality, Mike viewed his sister as being not only older but wiser, and he was willing to acquiesce to her authority, even when she belittled him. During a meeting with Mike and Min-Haeng on my twenty-third visit, Mike animatedly recounts a time when he didn't recognize an old photo of his sister because her hairstyle had since changed.

MIKE: My sister, guess what, my sister has, um, what are those things when you travel? You bring this little book so you can get home?

JUDY: A map?

MIKE: No, a little book that you put stamps in? . . . I have one because I went to Mexico once. And I looked at my sister's one. And I could hardly recognize her.

JUDY: Oh, a passport!

MIKE: A passport, yeah. . . . Her hair's this short now (*he gestures with his hand*), and it used to be down to here on her shoulders. And I was like (*in a small, hesitant voice*), "C.C.? Who is that?" And she's like, "You stupid! That's me!"

Given how Mike swiftly punished peers who questioned or challenged him, I would have expected Mike to become angry or defensive at being called "stupid." However, the lightness of his tone (and the smile on his face) as he tells this story suggests that he sees the humor in this situation (and agrees with his sister that he should have known better).

Protecting Vulnerability

Whereas (or because) Mike was susceptible to being bossed around and criticized by his sister, he seemed determined to establish and maintain his advantage in most of his peer interactions. During my twenty-first visit, Mike heads over to the block corner where Rob is using blocks to construct a castle. Rather than asking Rob if he can join in (which would give Rob the power to accept or refuse him), Mike proposes his own participation by criticizing Rob's construction, "It doesn't look much like a castle. It looks more like a bridge," and then offering his assistance, "Let me build it to a castle." Having implied that Rob needs help, Mike then sits down next to Rob and does him a favor by working on the construction with him. Also, during my twentieth visit, Mike cleverly reverses the power dynamic in his interaction with Jake and Tony when he feels left out of their plans. At the start of the school day, Mike is playing in the block corner when Jake comes to join him. Following Jake's lead, Tony arrives soon after and starts talking with Jake about their upcoming play date. Although Mike generally takes Jake's companionship for granted and often acts as though he does not value

Jake's friendship, Mike seems to resent Tony who—in his eagerness to please Jake—unwittingly competes with Mike for Jake's attention. Excluded from Jake and Tony's discussion about their play date, Mike suddenly turns to me and asks if he can meet with me. As the boys now know that meeting with me involves playing with toys, they have come to view the meetings as desirable (rather than something to avoid). Upon hearing Mike's request, which Mike made sure was loud and clear, Jake and Tony chime in, "Me, too." When I explain that I can only take two boys because three is too many, Mike and Jake immediately pair up. Despite Tony's loyalty to Jake and Mike's apparent indifference towards him, Jake is quick to side with Mike. Tony tries to join in but Mike and Jake block his efforts, reiterating that I said two. I tell Mike that I need to get permission from Lucia and that we will go later. Mike seems fine with this, probably because his request to meet with me has already served its purpose: to change the boys' interaction from being one in which he felt excluded (from Tony and Jake's plans for their play date) to one in which he was in a position to exclude Tony (from his and Jake's plans to meet with me).

Even though Mike typically projected an image of confidence and self-sufficiency, he could still feel uncertain of his peers' acceptance and vulnerable to being excluded. As he sought to engage and influence his peers, Mike did whatever was necessary to shield himself from possible rejection. Most commonly, Mike adopted a domineering manner in order to urge his peers' compliance. However, there were also times when Mike—in what appeared to be a counterintuitive move—exaggerated his vulnerability in his efforts to influence his peers. For instance, on my nineteenth visit, after Min-Haeng and Tony side with Dan against him during recess, Mike cautiously approaches Min-Haeng and Tony (when Dan leaves to play elsewhere) and uses his baby voice to propose his participation, "Me play." As with his masculine posturing, Mike used his baby voice strategically to increase his chances of getting what he wanted. Whereas being bossy and demanding could lead other people to become defensive or resentful, Mike's use of a baby voice could make him appear meek, even as he asserted himself. Although subtler and less direct, this approach could be compelling and even coercive in soliciting other people's cooperation and support (e.g., when Mike pressured Min-Haeng into giving up Dark Knight). All the same, Mike seemed uncomfortable assuming this vulnerable stance and typically avoided situations where he had to rely on others not to take advantage of him. Sure enough, once Min-Haeng and Tony make space to include him, Mike returns to speaking in his regular voice and resumes his domineering manner.

Mike usually found ways to ensure his inclusion among the other boys, but there were still times when Mike was inadvertently excluded. When this happened, Mike was quick to seek revenge, usually through masculine posturing (e.g., acting tough and aggressive). Although posturing enabled Mike to express his hurt feelings without revealing his vulnerability, this strategy tended to obfuscate his point. During my twenty-first visit, Mike arrives at school late to find that Jake, Rob, and Tony are meeting with me, without him. Feeling left out and angry, Mike takes it out on Jake when we return from our meeting. As we walk into the classroom, Jake rushes to Mike's side and Tony follows, only to have Mike ignore both of them and walk away to search for Dan, who also was not included in the meeting (but didn't seem to mind). Moments later when Jake tries again to engage Mike, Mike pushes Jake. When Jake (who does not know why Mike is angry) protests, "Don't push!" Mike retaliates, "Well, I have to, if you do that," but doesn't explain what "that" is. Mike then continues to harass Jake. When Mike pulls on Jake's shirt, Jake goes and reports to Jen, "Mikey pulled me by the shirt."

With Jen following behind him, Jake returns to confront Mike, who lunges at him threateningly. As Jake retreats and hides behind Jen, he says to Mike warily, "I know what you're gonna do." Jen then squats down between Jake and Mike and tries to mediate.

JEN: So, Mike and Jake, I want you guys to look each other in the eye and talk to each other about how you're feeling. Jake, what was upsetting you?

JAKE (*MUMBLING*): [*Incoherent.*]

JEN: O.K. Were you able to hear that, Mike?

MIKE (*FLIPPANTLY*): Nope.

JEN: Jake is upset because you grabbed him on the shirt and could've ripped it. Mike, what upset you?

MIKE (*AGITATED*): I don't know, so can I play now?

JEN: Well, what I'm worried about is, if you start playing now, you'll still be upset with Jake about whatever it is.

MIKE (*SOFTLY*): I am. I'm still feeling left out.

JEN: So Mike, was it something Jake said or something he did that got you
   upset and led you to pull on his shirt?

MIKE: That is exactly.

JEN: That is exactly? Which one? Something he did?

MIKE (*STRANGELY PLAYFUL*): Yah.

JEN: And what was that?

MIKE (*IN A BABY VOICE*): I pulled him on his shirt.

JEN: You told him that you're? Sorry, Mike. I couldn't hear your words. You
   told Jake that you're upset?

MIKE: Yeah.

Mike initially puts up a front by claiming ignorance and trying to disengage ("I don't know, so can I play now?"). However, he then abandons his defensive stance for a moment and tells Jen exactly why he is
upset ("I'm still feeling left out"). Unfortunately, Jen doesn't hear him
and Mike—being unwilling to remain exposed by the admission of vulnerable feelings—distances himself once again from the interaction by
adopting a strangely playful manner, using his baby voice to respond to
Jen's questions, and retreating to the refuge of his pretense.

As the conversation continues to go nowhere, Jake also distances himself from the interaction by wandering over to the window. Although Jen
calls to him, "Jake, sweetie, we need to finish this conversation. Jake?"
Jake doesn't respond and Jen turns her attention back to Mike.

JEN: Mike, I know you pretty well by now, all this wonderful time in [our]
   class and I know that when you get upset, there's a good reason.

MIKE (*IN A COMMANDING TONE*): I'm ready for first grade.

JEN: You mean no Kindergarten even for you? You're going right to first grade?

MIKE: No, I want to go to first grade.

JEN: You want to. But I know that when you get upset, it's usually about
   something. Maybe something that someone did or someone said. So,
   do you remember what it was?

MIKE (*IN AN OBNOXIOUS VOICE*): I want to play.

JEN: I know you do, but what I'm thinking that might happen if we don't
   talk about this is that you'll still be upset with Jake.

MIKE (*HESITATING, THEN WITH CERTAINTY*): I won't.

JEN: O.K.

No longer interested in talking about his feelings, Mike offers distractions ("I'm ready for first grade") and then focuses on appeasing Jen (by showing that he has calmed down and is no longer angry) so that he can go play. Interestingly, it is when Mike and Jake are left on their own that they are finally able to resolve the matter. After Jen leaves, Mike walks over to Jake, taps him on the shoulder, and apologizes, "Sorry, Jakey." When Mike explains why he was upset, Jake responds amicably, "Is that all? That's what you're upset about?" and all seems forgiven.

Enforcing Rules for Engagement

Mike did not create the Mean Team just so he could boss people around; he did that anyway. Rather, the Mean Team—with its rules, which Mike determined, and its hierarchy, within which Mike was at the top—became a way for Mike to ensure his peers' loyalty and support and to protect himself against being abandoned or betrayed. For example, one of the rules of the Mean Team prohibited the boys from excluding each other and, ironically, was punishable by exclusion. Thus, a boy who tried to exclude a peer risked being banished himself.

Even though it was assumed and expected that all of the boys would be on the Mean Team, membership on the Mean Team was not guaranteed. As it turned out, it was possible for a boy to be fired from this boys' club. During my twenty-first visit, Mike is playing with Rob in the block corner when Dan approaches and whispers in Mike's ear (loudly enough to be overheard) that Rob wouldn't let him help to build a castle. Upon overhearing Dan's complaint, Rob immediately tries to explain.

> ROB: No, I said, "You're not involved with this." That's all I said.
> DAN (*IN HIS REGULAR SPEAKING VOICE*): But that is still excluding.
> ROB: No, it's not. Right, Mike?
> MIKE: Actually, yes it is.
> DAN (*WHISPERING TO MIKE*): So he has to go all by himself.
> MIKE: Yeah, fired.
> DAN (*TO ROB, IN HIS REGULAR SPEAKING VOICE*): You're fired from the Mean Team. You're on the Nice Team. You're a girl.

According to Dan's decree, a boy who is not on the Mean Team is by default on the Nice Team and therefore a girl. Thus, being fired from the Mean Team could jeopardize not only a boy's group affiliation (e.g., his ability to be with the boys) but also his masculine identity (e.g., his ability to be one of the boys). As Rob protests and tries to defend himself, the boys consider the likelihood that Rob can actually become a girl.

> ROB (*URGENTLY*): I can't be a girl!
>
> MIKE: I know, but you have the hair for it. You have the long hair for it. You have the curly hair.
>
> ROB (*TO MIKE, DEFENSIVELY*): You have long hair. Dan has long hair all the way down to his neck.
>
> DAN (*CHEERFULLY*): And we're still boys! Mike, you have hair down to your neck.
>
> ROB: Yeah.
>
> JAKE: Do I have hair down to my neck?
>
> ROB: Everyone gots that.
>
> MIKE: Well, you're not fired, but you have to . . .
>
> DAN: Rob, you have to challenge the girls . . .
>
> ROB (*SOUNDING INTRIGUED*): Yeah?
>
> DAN: . . . yourself. Robby, you have to challenge the girls yourself.
>
> ROB (*SMILING, IN A SCHEMING VOICE*): I know. I'm gonna challenge them.

Whereas Rob might otherwise have been intimidated by the task of challenging the girls on his own, he happily (and with an air of bravado) accepts this condition for remaining on the Mean Team.

Although the boys seemed to agree that being a boy involved being on the Mean Team, the extent to which these boys were interested and invested in its goals (e.g., being mean, acting against the girls) varied across individuals. Of the boys, Mike stood to gain the most from his (and the other boys') participation in this club. While Mike was influential in his own right, his position as the boss of the Mean Team gave him the authority to fire boys from the boys' club and thus empowered him to offer or withhold not only his support but also the support of the boys as a group. For the other boys, however, being on the Mean Team could have both advantages and disadvantages. On one hand, membership on the Mean Team could enable a boy to identify with and relate to the boys as a group, and to feel joined and supported instead of isolated and alone. On the other hand, because a boy's membership on the Mean Team could be revoked, the boys became even more susceptible to Mike's dominance and could find it even more difficult to challenge or disobey Mike's commands (as compared to when they were dealing with Mike alone, before he established the Mean Team). Drawn by promises of inclusion and daunted by threats of exclusion, the boys learned to comply with Mike's rules and conform to group norms, which helped them to retain their group membership but could also constrain their self-expression and hinder their relationships.

Constraining Possibilities (for Others)

While the boys were sometimes willing and happy to follow Mike's lead, there were also times when their cooperation seemed primarily motivated by their wish to avoid the negative consequences that their noncompliance and non-conformity might incur. For instance, during a one-on-one meeting with Jake on my twenty-second visit, Jake explains how he has learned to hide his friendships with the girls in order to avoid being fired from the boys' Mean Team.

> JUDY: Do you have any good friends who are girls?
> JAKE: Well, Nicole and Tatiana and Miranda are my friends.
> JUDY: Yeah? How about Gabriella?
> JAKE: All of the girls in the class are my friends, but I act as though they aren't.
> JUDY: Oh yeah? How come?
> JAKE: Well, because if Mike finds out, if Mikey finds out that I like the girls, he'll fire me from his club.
> JUDY: From the Mean Team?
> JAKE: Yeah. That would be a real bummer 'cause then I won't be on a team.

Concerned about being cast out by his peers, losing his group membership ("if Mikey finds out that I like the girls, he'll fire me from his club"), and ending up alone ("then I won't be on a team"), Jake opts to conceal the truth about his relationships.

Even when their membership on the Mean Team was not necessarily at risk, the boys made an extra effort to avoid offending or upsetting

Mike. For instance, during my twentieth visit, Jake ends up siding against his mom when he notices Mike's annoyance and sets out to appease Mike. At the start of the school day, Jake and his mom arrive at class. They appear to be in a good mood, as usual. As they greet me, Jake's mom encourages Jake to show me his new toy: a snake-in-a-can. Jake opens it near my face and the snake-spring pops out. When I react with surprise, Jake smiles and his mom laughs. Jake then walks over to the block corner to join Mike. Following Jake, Tony also heads to the block corner.

When Jake's mom arrives at the block corner, Tony takes the snake-in-the-can from her hand and pops the snake in Mike's face. Mike does not appreciate the gesture and asks in an irritated tone, "What is it?" Jake's mom explains cheerfully, "It's a snake-in-a-can! It's a spring. Mikey, you can feel it. It's a spring covered with plastic. And then you basically stuff it in the can. And when you take off the top, it comes popping out." As Jake's mom tries to put the snake back in the can, the snake pops out again, and she says happily, "It jumped out even before I got the top on!" Noticing that Mike does not look at all amused, Jake interjects playfully, "Mom, you big fart!" and in effect discounts her enthusiasm.

Jake's comment is mainly a response to Mike's displeasure and seems intended to alleviate the tension that he perceives (but his mom may not). It was not like Jake to insult either of his parents, whom he obviously adored. However, it makes sense that Jake would choose to side with Mike, instead of his mom, in this instance. Given Mike's tendency to punish those who displease him (and to be particularly hard on Jake), Jake is especially sensitive to Mike's moods and vulnerable to Mike's disapproval. Whereas Jake's relationship with Mike can feel tenuous and uncertain, Jake trusts his relationship with his mom to be resilient and secure. And it is precisely because of Jake's confidence in his relationship with his mom that he is able to side against her without fear of losing her love and support.

Nevertheless, Jake seems aware of his betrayal and immediately tries to make amends by gently taking the toy from his mom's hand and working to finish what she started (by stuffing the "snake" back in its can). In turn, Jake's mom also makes an effort to reconnect with him. As she prepares to leave, she says gently, "Jakey, before you do it again, can you give me a hug, Jakey?" Jake happily complies and the momentary rift in their relationship is instantly repaired. As it turns out, Jake was right to be concerned about Mike's annoyance. After Jake's mom leaves, I approach Mike to follow up on our plans to meet, and he tells me that he has changed his mind about which of his friends he wants to bring. Although he had originally asked to go with Jake, he now wants to go with Rob instead.

Just as Jake worried about losing his group affiliation if he deviated from norms of masculine behavior (e.g., by befriending the girls), Rob was concerned that the other boys would harass him if he tried to leave the Mean Team to do his own thing. When I ask Rob about the Mean Team on my twenty-sixth visit, which takes place in November of the boys' Kindergarten year, he indicates that his feelings about it have changed.

> JUDY: How about the Mean Team? How is that going?
> ROB: I don't really want to be in it anymore.
> JUDY: Why not?
> ROB: We had this election and the boys got to choose a new leader for next year. I wanted to be [the new leader], but the boys chose Ryan [*one of the new kids in class*].
> JUDY: Who's the leader this year?
> ROB: Mike.
> JUDY: Is that why you don't want to be on the Mean Team anymore? Because the boys chose Ryan instead of you?
> ROB: No, it's O.K. if Ryan be the leader.
> JUDY: Then why don't you want to be on [the Mean Team] anymore?
> ROB: I don't feel like it anymore.
> JUDY: Is it that you don't like being mean anymore?
> ROB: Yes. They make me go places, but I want to go where I want to, not where they tell me.
> JUDY: Does the Mean Team make you do things you don't want to do?
> ROB: Yes.

Rob is disappointed about losing the election, not because he won't get to tell the other boys what to do but because he won't get to make decisions for himself. However, despite having changed his mind about wanting to be in this boys' club, Rob doesn't see a way out.

> ROB: There's no way to get off the Mean Team.
> JUDY: What would happen if you tried to quit?

ROB: [The boys] would *just* be mean to me.

JUDY: Do you want to be off the Mean Team?

ROB: I sort of do, but sort of don't.

Rob then reiterates that he wants to quit so that he can do what he wants (instead of what others tell him to do) but he is afraid that, if he tries to leave, he will consequently become a target of the boys' attacks.

While Jake and Rob may have wanted to make their own decisions about whom they befriended and in what activities they engaged, they learned to go along with what the other boys were doing, in order to avoid being excluded and/or targeted by the boys as a group. For the time being, they resigned themselves to comply with the rules of engagement within their peer group culture, but they seemed dissatisfied with their situation and wondered about their options. Later in his Kindergarten year, Rob did manage to break away from the Mean Team and do his own thing, which included playing basketball during recess. As expected, Rob's decision to leave the boys' club—and his exit strategy of simply walking away from whatever activity the boys were engaged in as a group—did result in his being alone. However, Rob said this didn't bother him. Mainly, Rob was relieved that the other boys did not band together and come after him, as he had feared they would. Rob was willing to accept the consequence of being alone in exchange for getting to make his own decisions.

By the end of their Kindergarten year, the other boys also had become more interested in playing sports. Although they no longer operated as the Mean Team, the other boys still tended to follow Mike's lead, for example by choosing to play soccer (Mike's preferred sport). Thus, despite changes in the boys' group activities, the structure and dynamics of the Mean Team endured.

Creating Options (for Himself)

Whereas boys like Jake and Rob had to be careful to align (or at least appear to align) with group norms, Mike's position as boss of the Mean Team afforded him the freedom to express a wider range of interests and opinions and to engage in a broader array of activities. As it was usually Mike who made and enforced the rules (e.g., telling the boys what they could and could not do), he could also make exceptions to or change the rules as he saw fit. Therefore, Mike did not have to worry as much as the other boys did about how his choices might impact his masculine identity, social status, and relationships. During my sixteenth visit, as Mike, Jake, Min-Haeng, Tony, and Gabriella look through a Star Wars picture book together, Jake declares that he hates Princess Leia and looks expectantly at Mike (as though expecting him to concur), but Mike remarks casually, "I actually like her." While any other boy would risk being ridiculed for admitting that he liked a female character, Mike could deviate from the very norms of masculinity that he typically endorsed and imposed on his peers.

Also, whereas the other boys seemed inclined or compelled to demonstrate their allegiance to the boys by shunning and avoiding the girls, Mike could be warm and receptive when engaging the girls, if he wanted. During my fifteenth visit, Gabriella pays Mike a compliment, "Nice hair cut," as he walks past her. In contrast to his usual tendency to play it cool, so to speak, and feign disinterest, Mike turns around, smiles, and says cordially, "Thanks," before proceeding to the reading corner. Encouraged by Mike's sociable manner, Gabriella runs after him and pushes him playfully, to which Mike responds by falling dramatically on the futon, still smiling. When Gabriella pulls on his arm to help him get up, Mike adopts a formal but affable pretense, "Excuse me, ma'am. Could you get out of my way? Could you let go of me, please?" As Mike's dad watches the scene with interest, someone suggests to him that Gabriella and Mike are flirting. Mike's dad smiles as though amused by the suggestion, and then turns to leave.

Mike could even play with girls without jeopardizing his affiliation with and position among the boys. During my seventeenth visit, Tatiana and Miranda approach Mike while he is playing alone in the block corner. Each of the girls is carrying a toy animal that she brought from home. Miranda has a plastic bat and Tatiana has a wolf. Miranda shows her plastic bat to Mike, who responds by talking to it sweetly and telling Miranda, "He said, 'Come to my house.'" Encouraged by Mike's friendly response, Miranda asks Mike, "Wanna see the bat dance a funny way?" Miranda and Tatiana then sit down to join Mike. When Mike returns to narrating his own play, Miranda tries to recapture his attention by asking explicitly for permission to join him.

MIRANDA: Mike, can I play with you?

MIKE: Yeah, I'm playing baby catcher.[4] Miranda, look . . .

Given that Mike and the boys' Mean Team that he created were instrumental in perpetuating the boys-versus-girls dynamic in this class and enforcing the taboo against playing with girls, I would have expected Mike to try to disengage from this interaction as soon as possible. Instead, Mike graciously allows the girls to join him and even seems to enjoy their company. As Mike shows Miranda a contraption for catching babies that he constructed using Duplo blocks, Tatiana eagerly joins in.

TATIANA (TO MIKE, ENTHUSIASTICALLY): My wolf is for killing babies.

MIKE: I'm making lots and lots of—

MIRANDA (TO MIKE, EAGERLY): Can we make things to drop the baby?

TATIANA (WAVING HER TOY WOLF IN THE AIR): Look at me, Mike! Guess
    what my wolf's name is!

MIKE: What?

TATIANA: Balto.

MIKE: I have the movie Balto.

TATIANA: I have that movie, too!

Whereas Jake felt the need to hide his friendships with girls for fear of being fired from Mike's Mean Team, Mike apparently could play with whomever he wanted.

One reason why Mike could play with girls without undermining his masculinity and status was that, like the boys, the girls engaged him on his terms. For the most part, it was the girls who made an effort to initiate and maintain this interaction. Mike had the advantage in the sense that he had (or was given) the power to decide whether to let the girls join him and how much value to place on the girls' contributions. Although Tatiana and Miranda outnumbered Mike in this interaction, they willingly catered to Mike's interests (e.g., contributing to his "masculine" game of baby catcher). At times, Tatiana and Miranda even competed with each other for Mike's attention. For example, when Mike talks with Miranda about baby catchers and doesn't respond to Tatiana's suggestion (that her wolf is for killing babies), Tatiana tries to capture Mike's attention ("Look at me, Mike!") and, once she has it, changes the topic. In turn, when Mike and Tatiana proceed to recount scenes they liked from the movie, *Balto*, Miranda reclaims Mike's attention by interjecting, "I want to tell you something," and excludes Tatiana by whispering to Mike.

> MIRANDA (*WHISPERING TO MIKE*): This thing . . .
> MIKE: Shoots the babies.
> MIRANDA: Yeah.
> MIKE: And this thing is a double-decker baby catcher.
> MIRANDA (*EAGERLY*): This . . . is a vampire bat, and he can eat sixteen babies.
> MIKE: That's, that's a lot.
> TATIANA (*EAGERLY*): Guess what? My wolf, um, can eat a million babies in one day.
> MIRANDA: That's a lot.
> MIKE: Did you know wolfs, after they eat, they digest. If they eat one hundred babies, they blow up.
> TATIANA: Well, my wolf never blows up. It never ever because it . . . (*She whispers into Miranda's ear.*)

As the girls whisper and giggle together, they not only stop engaging Mike on his terms (e.g., by focusing on his "masculine" game of baby catcher) but they also exclude Mike, albeit inadvertently, by teaming up (i.e., girls versus boy). No longer in control, Mike suddenly seems self-conscious and immediately tries to disengage from this interaction. Springing to his feet, Mike hastily explains to the girls, "I'm, um, excuse me, I'm getting Jake. He loves baby . . . ," and calls out in Jake's general direction, "Jakey, want to play baby catcher?" as he heads to where Jake is playing on the opposite side of the room. Mike doesn't seem to mind when Jake (who may not have heard Mike's question) fails to respond, as Mike's primary objective was to remove himself from what had become an uncomfortable situation.

Having made his escape, Mike continues walking towards Jake but does not end up joining Jake, who is otherwise engaged. Instead, Mike meanders around the room briefly and eventually returns to the block corner (without Jake) to join Tatiana and Miranda, who welcome him back by once again making him the focus of their attention and efforts.

> MIRANDA (*EAGERLY*): Look, Mike! It caught a baby!
> MIKE: Cool.

TATIANA (*EAGERLY*): My wolf caught a baby! Mike! My wolf caught a baby!
MIRANDA: This is what I spy.
TATIANA: That's the baby crying.
MIKE: Look at, look at my double-decker baby catcher.
MIRANDA: Now I should put another double, of this.
MIKE: I got one, I got one. (*Talking to a toy figure*) And you go in the biggy—
MIRANDA: Bring that sucker.
MIKE: Suck their brains so they don't remember.

As this example suggests, it was not merely the act of playing with girls that could be emasculating for boys; the way in which a boy engaged with girls (e.g., as equals or otherwise, through "masculine" or "feminine" modes of interacting) could also have implications for a boy's public image. So, once the girls return to engaging Mike on his terms, he is again able to enjoy their company as much as anyone else's.

Maintaining His Advantage

Although the girls were not members of the Mean Team, they also had learned to play by Mike's rules and tended to align with Mike, when given the choice. During recess on my nineteenth visit, Dan, Tony, Min-Haeng, and Gabriella are playing together in the sand box when Mike, Jake, and Rob walk past. Noticing that he has a larger group and therefore an advantage over Mike, Dan boldly challenges Mike by saying in a taunting manner, "Sorry guys, it's four against three. We have more than you." When Mike responds with an angry grunt, Min-Haeng quickly assures Mike of his loyalty.

MIN-HAENG: Mike, I'm still on your side.
DAN (*LOOKING TO NICOLE AND TATIANA, WHO JUST ARRIVED ON THE SCENE*): But then I'll have Tony and the girls.
NICOLE: No, we're on Mike's side.
DAN: How 'bout you, Tatiana? (*Tatiana looks to Nicole.*)
NICOLE (*TO TATIANA*): I'm on Mikey's.
TATIANA (*TO DAN*): I'm on Mikey's.

It doesn't matter that it is Dan who thinks to include the girls and thereby introduces the possibility that alliances need not be based on sex. The girls still choose to side with Mike.

Incidentally, Dan appeared to be the least constrained by his participation on the Mean Team, in the sense that he did not seem as focused on or conflicted by the expectation to follow Mike's lead. As illustrated in this example, Dan's attitude and behavior suggested that if he were fired from the Mean Team, he would simply start his own group and appoint himself the leader. And because Dan was less invested in remaining on the Mean Team, he was not bound to comply with Mike's rules and therefore freer to say what he thought and to do what he wanted.

Whereas Mike's domineering manner, by itself, might have made him an outcast among his peers, his ability to be charming and charismatic as well as commanding made him not only influential among but also appealing to both boys and girls. Just as most of the boys would rather be with Mike than against him, the girls appeared to be drawn to rather than put off by Mike's tough guy persona. For instance, during my fourteenth visit, when Mike demonstrates his pirate impersonation by snarling at Tatiana, "Arg," she responds by smiling and gazing back at him lovingly. And on my twenty-second visit, Tatiana happily informs me, "Guess who I'm marrying . . . Mike."

Given that the girls as well as the boys tended to yield to his dominance and follow his lead, Mike had a certain amount of power and privilege within his peer relationships at school. Even so, Mike could (of course) feel hurt by other people's criticism and rejection. For instance, during my sixth visit, Mike seems dejected and embarrassed when Gabriella does not appreciate his earnest efforts to help her. On this occasion, Mike, Gabriella, and Tatiana join Rob and me in the work area to do some drawing. Rob wants to cut out his drawings but is having a hard time with the scissors, so I offer to help him. Mike draws what he says (in a self-deprecatory manner) is a "stupid spaceship," and then begins to work on a detailed depiction of his world—including his house, the local supermarket, and his self. Gabriella asks me to draw a princess for her. When I tell her that I can't right now because I'm helping Rob with his project, Mike immediately offers to draw a princess for her and puts aside his own drawing in order to do so. Gabriella accepts

Mike's offer but seems irritated (because I won't help her), sighs deeply, and slumps in her chair. While Mike works diligently to draw a princess for her, Gabriella complains, "You're doing it wrong." Although Mike explains what he is trying to do and points out the princess's accessories in his drawing, Gabriella remains dissatisfied, and Mike eventually gives up. Instead of becoming defensive or getting angry with Gabriella for dismissing his efforts, Mike seems to be mainly frustrated with what he perceives to be his own artistic shortcomings. Dispirited, Mike pushes the drawing aside and declares in an exasperated tone that he does not know how to draw princesses. Mike then returns to drawing his world while Gabriella pouts and glances frequently in my direction to let me know how upset she is with me for refusing to grant her request.

As the year progressed, it became apparent that Mike's artistic ability was a sensitive issue for him. For instance, as he and Min-Haeng are drawing together during my fourteenth visit, Mike lets down his guard, so to speak, as he openly admires and humbly concedes to Min-Haeng's superior artistic skills. When I ask the boys what they are drawing, Mike says, "I'm gonna draw a motorboat," and Min-Haeng says, "I'm drawing a police boat." Impressed by Min-Haeng's response, Mike asks Min-Haeng meekly, "Can you teach me how to draw a police boat?" and then disparages his own efforts: "I'm drawing a stupid Navy boat that this guy [*a figure in his drawing*] doesn't know how to drive." Unfortunately, Min-Haeng doesn't seem to hear Mike's request and, instead of responding to Mike, asks himself pensively, "What am I going to draw?" In turn, Mike, who rarely reveals his weaknesses and generally refuses to subordinate himself in his peer interactions, immediately resumes his guarded visage and disengages from this interaction soon after. As it happened, it was just a couple minutes after this exchange that Mike adopted a menacing tone and rough manner to accuse Rob of hoarding a popular toy figure.[5]

By creating the Mean Team and appointing himself as its boss, Mike positioned himself to punish anyone who challenged or betrayed him. However, Mike still worried that his peers might try to leave him, and in his efforts to protect himself from being abandoned, he worked hard to maintain an image of dominance and control. Even when no one challenged him, Mike seemed compelled to prove himself, for example by demonstrating that he was strong, tough, superior, and therefore deserving of admiration, respect, and his position of leadership.

Thus, the hierarchical structure and competition-based dynamics of the Mean Team (that Mike created to keep his peers in line) made it necessary for him as well to keep up his guard, so to speak, and continue his masculine posturing in order to retain his power and privilege. Unfortunately, Mike's adoption of this masculine guise could also obscure his more personable qualities and hinder his ability to relate to others. As a framework for the boys' interactions, the Mean Team therefore could make it difficult not only for the other boys but also for Mike to be authentic and at ease in relationships.

A Microcosm of Boyhood Culture

In reinforcing the boys-versus-girls dynamic that had emerged in this class and formalizing the existing hierarchy among these boys, the Mean Team was essentially a microcosm of the boys' peer group culture and structure and, as such, influenced how these boys came to view themselves and interact with their peers within this setting. Although Rob casually dismissed the Mean Team as "a very silly game," the Mean Team became a central context in which the boys developed an understanding of the norms and values of their particular peer group (e.g., what it means to be a boy in this class), and became motivated to conduct themselves accordingly. The boys' membership in and participation on the Mean Team could have implications not only for the boys' beliefs about how it was possible for them, as boys, to engage with and relate to others, but also for the boys' actual behaviors, self-expression, and relational styles. So long as Mike—along with the archetype of masculinity that he tried to project and tended to reinforce— prevailed, the boys' attempts to seek other viable options and change their circumstances remained difficult if not futile.

It could be argued that Mike's presence in this class and his creation of the Mean Team exacerbated the pressures these boys may have felt to adapt to conventional norms of masculinity. Perhaps there would have been less pressure on the boys to act like "boys," without the influences of Mike and his Mean Team. However, the boys-versus-girls dynamic[6] and the hierarchy among the boys were not unique to this class.[7] Likewise, the boys' interest in guns, the division between boys and girls, and the construal of boys and girls as opposites also have been observed elsewhere.[8] While Mike's behaviors could be problematic at times, Mike was not necessarily *the* problem. Mike was clearly the most bossy and domineering of these boys. However, in his absence (e.g., in interactions that did not involve Mike), other boys also could be bossy and domineering, or display and elicit from each other stereotypically masculine behaviors. Thus, what the boys were coming up against was not an individual boy (e.g., Mike) or the boys as a group (e.g., the Mean Team) but the competitive and gender-polarizing framework that Mike personified and endorsed, that the Mean Team epitomized and enforced, that prevailing norms of masculine behavior within these boys' peer group culture emphasized and perpetuated, and that these boys' interactions and relationships reflected. So long as this paradigm, which centered on hierarchy and competition, served as the primary context for the boys' interactions, their behaviors and styles of relating were more likely to be defensive than cooperative and their involvement with each other would continue to limit (rather than enhance) their options as individuals.

Although the Mean Team was specific to this class, the descriptions of how these boys viewed and participated in this boys' club underscore the importance of context in influencing all boys' experiences of and responses to their gender socialization. And through illustrating how Mike's adaptation to conventions of masculinity (e.g., those that emphasize toughness, stoicism, and self-sufficiency) could make it difficult for others to be open and honest with him and for him to be open and honest with others, Mike's example reveals how the behaviors and relational styles promoted by mainstream masculinity are not conducive to forming the close relationships that boys seek and that Mike tried (and failed) to bring about by force. Whereas Tony's case study shows how a boy's deviance from masculine norms could result in his lower social status and undermine his ability to establish close, meaningful connections with others, Mike's case study shows how a boy's alignment with masculine norms—despite potentially contributing to his higher social status—could similarly involve and/or result in disconnections within his relationships. Although Mike's strategy for engaging and relating to others was very different from Tony's, they ultimately led to the same outcome as both boys sought connections and resisted disconnections yet could end up feeling alone.

5

Boys' Awareness, Agency, and Adaptation

For boys, early childhood is a time when pressures to accommodate to masculine norms often intensify as they begin to spend more time at school and with peers. Focusing on boys at this age, this study highlights the tension between boys' relational capabilities—including their attunement and responsiveness to other people—and their adaptation to prevailing norms of masculinity in their school and peer group cultures. On the one hand, we can see and hear how emotionally and socially intelligent these four- and five-year-old boys are: how astutely they pick up other people's emotions, how open and honest they can be in expressing themselves, and how capable they are in navigating the human social world. In contrast to common stereotypes about boys—for example, those that depict boys as being less capable than girls when it comes to understanding emotions, communicating their thoughts, feelings, and desires, and negotiating relationships—these boys could be attentive, articulate, authentic, and direct in their interactions with one another and with me. On the other hand, we also witness a shift in these boys' relational presence, including ways in which they behaved and engaged with others, through which they appeared to become inattentive, inarticulate, inauthentic, and indirect.

The shift that I observed in the boys' relational presence was not imposed on these boys; it did not happen *to* them. Likewise, the boys' adaptation to norms of masculine behavior was neither automatic nor inevitable. Rather, as active participants in their gender socialization, the boys made thoughtful and deliberate decisions about how they conducted and represented themselves within their relationships, in light of their perceptions of group and cultural norms of masculinity.

The shift in the boys' relational presence appeared to coincide with the process of becoming "boys," wherein the Mean Team played a central role in establishing and enforcing a notion of masculinity that is defined in opposition to girls and by extension to human qualities that our culture genders "feminine." Although there were individual differences in the boys' interest and investment in the Mean Team, this boys' club and the conventions of masculinity that it represented and reinforced became a part of the boys' social landscape through which they all had to navigate. In theory, the boys could choose whether to join the Mean Team and, if so, how they would participate. However, they could not really ignore or avoid it altogether. So long as the boys wished to identify with and relate to the other boys in class, the Mean Team—as a vehicle for the boys' gender socialization—would have implications for their self-expression and presence in relationships, and could thereby influence their ability to establish the kinds of close, meaningful connections of which they had shown themselves to be capable and which they continued to seek throughout their pre-Kindergarten and Kindergarten years. Thus, it was primarily through and within their interpersonal relationships that messages about masculinity and pressures to conform to masculine norms were introduced, reinforced, incorporated, and perpetuated in ways that became personally meaningful and directly consequential to these boys.

Navigating Social Influences

As illustrated by the Mean Team and its impact on the boys' behaviors and interactions, the boys' peers (especially other boys) were becoming increasingly influential and important at this age. Peer influences could even override adult influences, as when the boys continued to make and play with toy guns despite the teachers' ban, and when Tony learned to deny his interest in dolls not when his stepdad forbade him to play with dolls but when he realized that his interest in dolls could hinder his ability to be one of the boys and with the boys. Nevertheless, parents and teachers continued to have an important role in shaping how these boys viewed and conducted themselves. In the same way that these four- and five-year-old boys were attuned to the norms and dynamics of their peer group, they were also aware of adults' assumptions about what boys are like and expectations for how boys should be. And when these included negative assumptions and lower expectations, the boys picked up on that, too.

In general, adults may convey their ideas about boys and masculinity explicitly, as when they tell boys, "Boys don't cry," or in subtler ways, as when they make off-hand comments to other adults when boys are within earshot. For instance, when Mike's mom introduces herself to Carol and me during our first visit to class, she expresses her enthusiasm for our study and immediately confesses that whereas she and her daughter "understand each other at a fundamental level," her son is "like a puzzle" to her. Mike's mom was not the only one to express such sentiments. Within and beyond my study, mothers from various social, economic, and educational backgrounds have suggested to me that boys are somehow foreign to them, sometimes while their sons were standing next to them. While these mothers may in fact experience their sons to be different from their daughters and/or from themselves, such remarks also reflect the tendency in our culture to emphasize gender differences, often to the point of viewing boys and girls as being so different that they are incomprehensible to one another. The assumption that boys and girls are polar opposites has become so commonplace that many adults are not inclined to hide these biases, much less question their validity. It is interesting to consider, however, how we might think twice about making similar remarks based, for instance, on race instead of sex.

In addition to suggesting that boys are enigmatic, adults (men as well as women) also tend to view boys as problematic or less appealing than girls. During my fifteenth visit, Lucia directs my attention to differences in the girls' and the boys' arrivals to class. On this morning, Gabriella is the first to arrive. Upon entering the room, she walks over to one of the tables in the work area, where the teachers have laid out a stack of wooden boards riddled with holes, a colorful assortment of pegs that fit into the holes, and several rubber bands. Gabriella picks up one of the boards and begins to make a "birthday cake" by inserting the colored sticks into holes on her board. Nicole arrives next, joins Gabriella at the table, and uses the sticks and rubber bands to spell her name on one of the boards. Finally, Tatiana arrives and engages Gabriella and Nicole in conversation as she joins them at the table. As the girls talk cheerfully amongst themselves, Lucia comes to stand next to me and points out how nicely, calmly, and quietly the girls arrive at class, adding for emphasis, "especially compared to when *they* [*the boys*] come in." And on my nineteenth visit, as Lucia and I watch the boys run around together during recess, Lucia comments on the boys' "pack mentality" and how they tend to move around and do things as a group.

Although these remarks may describe some of the boys' qualities—or qualities in some of the boys—they mainly serve to reinforce a narrow and stereotypical depiction of boys' capabilities and to reify conventional notions of masculinity. It is true that the boys could be boisterous at times, but there were also times when the boys played nicely, calmly, and quietly, which the adults seemed less likely to notice or comment on. Similarly, there were times when the girls moved around and did things as a group (e.g., when they were chasing or being chased by the boys), but no one compared the girls to wild animals. As social psychologists have observed, we tend to notice and focus on those things that confirm our own assumptions and expectations (e.g., when boys behave like "boys"), whereas things that challenge our preconceived notions are easier for us to overlook or dismiss as exceptions.[1]

Adapting to Expectations

Through observing and interacting with adults, these boys were learning that adults tend to view boys as troublesome and to respond to them accordingly. So, in order to avoid getting in trouble, the boys became especially careful to modify any misconduct when adults were around. For instance, the boys knew to hide or disguise their physical aggression, even when they were just pretending. For example, during recess on my nineteenth visit, all of the boys—except for Dan, who appears to be fighting on the girls' side today—gather in the "forest" to plan their next attack against the girls. When Jen notices the boys sneaking around, she calls out to them in a concerned voice, "Boys?" In response, Mike assures her, "We're going to huddle." The boys then talk quietly amongst themselves until Jen turns her attention elsewhere, at which point the boys suddenly emerge from their hiding place and run to attack the girls. When the boys enter the area where the girls (and Dan) are playing, Dan "captures" Rob by throwing his arms around Rob's torso. Min-Haeng comes to Rob's aid, helps Rob to escape from Dan's hold, and then pretends to fight with Dan as the two boys throw punches and kicks towards each other while standing just beyond each other's reach. When Jen approaches, Dan and Min-Haeng instantly stop their play fighting and engage each other in a chummy manner (e.g., by smiling at Jen and patting each other on the back). After Jen seems reassured by the boys' friendly gestures and leaves, Dan and Min-Haeng immediately separate and return to their respective teams.

The boys also learned to cover up and correct for their social aggression, such as their attempts to exclude others. During my eighth visit, I join Min-Haeng, Mike, and Dan in the work area where they are drawing in blank booklets. It soon becomes apparent that Dan is the odd man out, so to speak, as Min-Haeng and Mike team up and scheme to exclude him from their interaction. When I ask the boys about their drawings, Min-Haeng offers to show me his notebook, which contains more of his drawings, and he goes to his cubby to retrieve it. As Min-Haeng flips through his notebook and explains each drawing to me, he notices Dan looking on with interest and suddenly decides that he doesn't want Dan to look at his drawings. Min-Haeng tells Dan not to look and, when he suspects that Dan is still looking, quickly flips through the remaining pages, shuts his notebook, and takes it back to his cubby. Min-Haeng then returns to the table and continues to draw in his booklet. However, Min-Haeng soon becomes concerned that Dan is watching him draw and again tells Dan not to look. Min-Haeng also instructs Mike to make sure that Dan doesn't look. Although Dan looks hurt by this, Min-Haeng and Mike do not seem to notice. As Mike begins to explain to Min-Haeng how he will stand guard, he sees that I am watching, stops mid-sentence, smiles slyly at me, and says to Min-Haeng in a singsong tone, "Never mind." Picking up on Mike's cue, Min-Haeng hastily explains to me that he's just asking Mike a question and then leans over and whispers his next instructions in Mike's ear. Despite Min-Haeng's attempt to be discreet, I can hear him instructing Mike to tell him if Dan is looking. The boys' sudden need to be surreptitious suggests that they know they are misbehaving. Still, they are more inclined to hide what they are doing than to stop. When I ask more questions about their drawings, Mike and Min-Haeng continue to respond openly and hesitate only when they suspect that Dan is listening.

Sometimes, the boys seemed compelled to assert their innocence, even when they weren't misbehaving. For instance, during my ninth visit, when there is some tension in the block corner as Rob, Mike, and Dan debate which game they should play and Lucia comes and asks

(in a neutral tone) the boys what they are doing, Rob seems to anticipate her concern (e.g., that the boys are causing trouble or up to no
good) and immediately assures her of their good intentions and behavior: "We're good guys." The boys also had begun to incorporate adults'
conceptions (and misconceptions) into their own views—of boys as a
group and of themselves as individuals. For instance, during our meeting on my eighteenth visit, when I ask Mike about expectations for
boys, he responds by imparting a negative view.

> JUDY: Is there a way that boys are supposed to act, Mikey?
> MIKE: They're supposed to act good, and sometimes little boys are . . . (*he
> presses his lips together and makes a spitting noise*).
> JUDY: What does that mean?
> MIKE: That means hurt. They hurt.
> JUDY: They hurt?
> MIKE: They hurt everybody.

As he distinguishes between how boys are expected to be ("They're supposed to act good") and how boys are ("They hurt everybody"), Mike
uses the third party pronoun ("They") to describe a group to which he
belongs ("boys"). At some level, Mike may wish to distance himself from
boys who do not "act good." Yet, as his aggressive behaviors have led
to parent-teacher meetings and his enrollment in a behavior management program, Mike also knows that he sometimes falls short of adults'
expectations. Perhaps for this reason Mike often seemed to operate from
the assumption that most adults either thought badly of him already or
were prepared to think badly of him. Assuming that he was constantly
under suspicion, Mike was especially self-conscious around adults and
took special care to appear well behaved. All the same, this conception
of boys (and of himself) as troublesome seemed to be one of the central
images in relation to which Mike was constructing his own sense of self
and developing his understanding of how other people viewed him.

Fortunately, the boys could also incorporate adults' positive views
into their self-concept. During my twentieth visit, when Jen suggests
that Mike and Rob are nice, the boys initially respond by trying to prove
her wrong (because they had just asserted that boys are bad and girls
are nice). However, after Jen repeatedly insists that they are nice and

continues to point out their nice behaviors, Mike and Rob eventually yield to her view and seem encouraged to behave in a more friendly and cooperative manner in the moments thereafter. After their conversation with Jen, Mike and Rob head to the block corner, where they play calmly and quietly together as they wait for recess. Absorbed in their play, they are surprised when they notice that everyone else has lined up to go outside. As they hurry to join the others, Mike apologizes sweetly and sincerely to Lucia, "Sorry we're late." Consistent with theories regarding self-fulfilling prophecies,[2] adults' positive assumptions and high expectations could potentially lead boys to internalize or try to emulate a better image of themselves, just as adults' negative assumptions and low expectations could taint boys' views of their own potential and possibilities.

Social and Relational Motives

As the literature and discourse on boys has suggested, these boys' accommodation to group and cultural norms of behavior appeared to be partly motivated by a social desire for approval and acceptance in general. However, these boys also appeared to be driven by a relational desire to connect personally and meaningfully with significant adults and peers in their lives. Thus, in addition to a social component, there is also a relational component in boys' socialization and development that has been seldom acknowledged. Beyond a need to prove their masculinity and establish their masculine identities, these boys wanted to be able to engage with and relate to the other boys in their class, with whom they interacted daily and who were beginning, at this age, to comprise an important part of their world. These boys also were not merely conforming to abstract notions of boyhood and ideals of masculinity. Rather, they were adapting in particular to norms of masculine behavior that were prevalent within and specific to their school and peer group culture.

   Although the social and relational components are linked, they are nevertheless distinct. The social component is more outwardly focused and centers on the need to perform for and prove oneself to others (e.g., the world at large), for instance by projecting a particular image and maintaining certain appearances. With adults, this typically involved the boys' conducting themselves in ways that are considered proper and desirable for boys, in order to show that they're "good boys." With peers, this typically involved the boys' emphasizing their "masculine" qualities and downplaying their "feminine" ones, in order to show that they're boys, and not girls. That is, the social component highlights the process by which boys learn to fit gendered roles and display gender-appropriate attitudes and behaviors.

The relational component is more inwardly focused and centers on the need or wish to feel understood and valued by specific others (e.g., to be in relationship). The relational component manifests on a more personal level in the sense that the desire for close, meaningful connections with others (and resistance against becoming disconnected from others) comes from within the individual and taps into the range of emotions and experiences that are a part of boys' day-to-day interactions—including the boys' hurt, anger, jealousy, and sadness as well as their joy and pleasure in being with each other. Whereas the social component has more to do with socialization and how boys make meaning of and respond to cultural messages about masculinity and societal pressures to conform, the relational component has more to do with development (e.g., of emotional capacities and relational skills) and how boys learn (e.g., about themselves and their relationships) through being involved with one another as they play, explore, and imagine together. My study suggests that it was primarily this relational component that motivated these boys to align with norms of masculine behavior (e.g., act like stereotypical "boys"), even when their interests and preferences lay elsewhere. In this sense, the shift that I observed in these boys' relational presence could reflect a privileging of the social over the relational, as the boys learned through their gender socialization to display behaviors and adopt relational styles that could gain them social approval but at the cost of undermining their chances of being truly known and accepted.

A Case Study: Rob

Given their relational capabilities and motivation, one could say that the boys in my study were well equipped and well positioned to develop and maintain the kinds of close relationships and meaningful connections that they sought. Yet, as social psychologists have long emphasized, our outcomes—including our behaviors and styles of relating to others—reflect our social situations as well as our personal dispositions, capacities, and desires.[3] In order to understand the choices that these boys were making as they negotiated their identities and relationships, it is therefore necessary to consider not only their abilities and goals but also their boyhood contexts—including their family, school, and peer group cultures—and how these could enhance or constrain their possibilities. Rob's case study illustrates how boys' views of and approaches to their relationships could be influenced by their changing circumstances (e.g., at home and at school), at this age when they are figuring out whether, and if so how, it is possible for them to be with others and also be true to their selves.

Doing Together and Being Together

It was mainly through my interactions with Rob that I learned (usually through trial and error) what I could expect from the boys and also what they expected of me. For instance, on my sixth visit, Rob shows me that he is able and willing to engage me, but only if I am genuinely interested in being with him. On this day, the kids are making mobiles that reflect a sea theme. The teachers have prepared patterns of various types of fish for the kids to trace and cut out. Rob decides to draw his own sea creatures for his mobile and, after retrieving some construction paper, sits alone at one of the tables and begins to draw. When I sit down across from him (in one of my first attempts to approach and engage any of the boys individually), Rob notices me but doesn't make eye contact or talk to me. As I do not wish to disturb him, I watch quietly as he concentrates on his task. Moments later, Jen walks by and Rob voluntarily informs her that he is drawing a fish with feet. Given Rob's apparent desire to talk about his work, I ask him about his next drawing, which he immediately says is a baby fish. As he works on his third drawing, I venture a guess and ask whether he is drawing a shark. Rob nods and, as he works on his fourth drawing, he invites me to guess what it is.

As I study the large triangular figure with "o" and "u" shaped markings, I become nervous as I realize that I have no idea what it might be. I stare intensely at the drawing and look at it from different angles. I ask Rob if it is part of a stingray, but he asks, "What's a stingray?" I ask if it is a part of a whale's tail, and Rob replies gently, "No." Although Rob seems unperturbed, I begin to worry that he might feel insulted or hurt by my incorrect guesses. So, I ask him to tell me what it is. I am instantly aware of my mistake as Rob frowns, lowers his gaze, and says in a disappointed tone, "I don't want to tell." Eager to make amends, I try asking for clues, which Rob doesn't seem to mind. When I ask if the object he's drawing is a part of something, Rob abandons his downcast expression and replies softly, "Yes." I then ask if the markings on the object are scales and Rob replies patiently, "No." Finally, as though satisfied by my efforts, Rob reveals that the object is in fact an octopus's arm, or tentacle.

I had initially assumed that Rob was mainly interested in having his drawing recognized, and therefore the "success" of our interaction depended on my ability to guess the right answer. Focused on demonstrating that I could see what he was trying to show me, I worried when I couldn't figure it out. However, Rob didn't mind when I guessed incorrectly, and he was disappointed only when I gave up and asked him to tell me the answer. In contrast to studies that describe boys' relationships as focused on "doing together" and girls' as focused on "being together,"[4] Rob's responses suggest that he is at least as interested in my ability and willingness to be with him (e.g., remain engaged in our interaction) as he is in my ability to do this task with him (e.g., guess his drawing correctly).

In this and other examples, Rob's patience with and interest in engaging me helped me to understand that I could make errors in our interactions without necessarily jeopardizing our relationship. As a result, I became less concerned about always doing and saying the right things and better able to see and hear what Rob and the other boys were showing and telling me. I also saw how, in their relationships, the boys valued and took pleasure not only in doing things together but also in simply being together. And as I felt more comfortable and confident in our interactions, the boys became more certain of my presence and less hesitant to engage me.

Engaging Openly and Honestly

Although Rob tended to be mild-mannered and reserved, as compared to the other boys, his connection to his self and his capacity and desire to connect with others were evident in his ability to remain grounded in his thoughts and feelings and to be upfront and direct when he did choose to share his observations and opinions. For instance, during my seventh visit, Rob kindly corrects me when I overstate my intentions. As I am sitting with Rob in the block corner, Gabriella—who overheard me discussing my study with one of the parents earlier on—comes over and asks me brightly, "Why are you here? What are you doing here?" When I explain to Gabriella that my reason for visiting this class is "to see what all of you do every day," Rob remarks, "But you're not here every day. Only Tuesdays," and reveals that, just as I have been observing him, he has been observing me.

Also, during my eighteenth visit (when I meet with him individually for the second time), Rob responds thoughtfully and sensibly to my inquiries. When I ask him what might be a good question for me to ask the boys, he asks me in return, "Well, what do you want to learn?" When I bring out my pen and notepad, he wants to know, "What are you writing down?" So, I tell him, "I'm writing down that I'm meeting with Rob, so I can remember that I met with you." And when he notices my tape recorder, he feels free to inquire about it.

> ROB: Is that a tape recorder? Are you tape recording what we're saying?
> JUDY (*NODDING*): Um-hm.
> ROB: Why?
> JUDY: So that I can remember what you said. So I don't have to write it down.
>   Does it make you nervous, the tape recorder? Does it bother you?
> ROB (*PLAINLY*): No.
> JUDY: Have you seen a tape recorder before?
> ROB: Yes, I have. . . . My aunt has one.

As I explain my goal to learn about the boys in his class, Rob listens carefully and lets me know when I misrepresent them.

> JUDY: That's why I tape record and take notes. I'm trying to find out what it's like for you to be a boy. I'm a girl, so I don't know what it's like to be a boy. That's why I ask all these questions, to find out what it's like to be a five-year-old boy. And you and your buddies are the only ones who can teach me because I don't know any other five-year-old boys.
> ROB (*GENTLY*): I know, but some people in our classroom aren't five.

In addition to being curious about my intentions, Rob is also curious about me and seems intrigued when I mention that I also go to school. For example, Rob wants to know if I get homework, and based on my response (yes), he asks if I am a second grader (probably based on his

knowledge that his older brother, who is in second grade, gets homework). Although I explain that I am in graduate school, Rob seems satisfied and even comforted by the fact that, despite my older age, he can
identify with me as a student.

Offering Assistance

As Rob came to understand my intentions (and agreed that it's a good
idea for me to learn about the boys and their experiences), he was supportive of my efforts and became an important ally in my study. In addition to showing me how I could engage the boys and what I could ask
of them, Rob helped to facilitate my access to the boys' activities and
interactions. During recess on my nineteenth visit, as Rob and Mike are
playing under a tree, I wander over and crouch a few feet away so that
I can observe them without interrupting. When Rob notices me watching, he invites me to join them: "Judy, you want to see the arrowheads
we found?" When I move closer to the boys, Rob explains that they are
searching for arrowheads. He then offers to show me his discoveries
and encourages Mike to do the same.

Rob also tried to help me stay on task when I seemed to stray from
my goals or to contradict myself. For instance, during my nineteenth
visit, Rob reminds me of my objective when, in response to Gabriella's
request, I consider meeting with the girls. As I am sitting with Rob at
one of the tables in the work area, Gabriella approaches and (having
noticed that I have been meeting only with the boys) asks when it's
going to be the girls' turn to meet with me. While I think about how
to respond to Gabriella's question, Rob gently reminds me, "You're
studying the boys, you know," and asks why I would want to talk with
girls if I am studying the boys. When I suggest that it might be interesting to learn what the girls think about the boys, Rob—recalling the
explanation that I provided during my previous visit ("I'm a girl, so I
don't know what it's like to be a boy")—points out, "But you're a girl,
so you know about yourself [and what girls think]." I explain that different people can have different views and tell Rob, for example, that
the things he tells me are sometimes different from what Jake or Mike
tells me. However, Rob seems skeptical of my impromptu excuses and
remains unconvinced. Finally, after thinking about it for a moment,

Rob concludes that "It would be cool if a boy could study about a girl, 'cause then he could study about Gabriella." Rob's tone throughout this exchange is not accusatory but matter-of-fact; he simply says what he is thinking as he considers my reasoning. His willingness to be so forthcoming shows that he is comfortable enough in our relationship to disagree with me and to challenge me directly. His ability to offer a persuasive argument indicates that he has been paying close attention to the things I tell him and thinking carefully and critically about them. When Gabriella eventually gives up and glumly retreats to the house area, I explain to Rob that I don't want anyone to feel left out. As Rob also notices Gabriella's disappointment, he accepts this excuse and no longer questions me when I decide to meet with her.

At times, Rob was even protective of me. For instance, during my twenty-fourth visit, Rob comes to my defense when Min-Haeng engages me too aggressively. On this occasion, Rob, Min-Haeng, and I are meeting in the school library, which we have all to ourselves. When we enter the library, Rob sits down on the couch and I sit in an armchair facing him. Min-Haeng, who seems antsy and a little hyper today, wanders around the room briefly and then sneaks behind me and surprises me by lifting the back of my shirt. As my startled expression sends Min-Haeng into a giggle fit, Rob immediately steps in and orders Min-Haeng to stop. Min-Haeng settles down momentarily but then decides he wants to see my belly button and proceeds to harass me about it. When Min-Haeng refuses to take no for an answer, Rob comes to my aid again by offering to show Min-Haeng his belly button. Although Min-Haeng seems unsatisfied, he gives up on trying to see my belly button and instead gets behind me on the armchair and climbs onto my back. Despite my protests, Min-Haeng refuses to get off, so Rob warns him sternly, "Min-Haeng, if she says, 'Don't,' don't do it," and sees to it that Min-Haeng complies.

Although I am somewhat exasperated by Min-Haeng's mischievous behavior, I decide to play along when Min-Haeng climbs onto my chair, sits behind me, and whispers, "Don't tell Rob. I'm a chair." When I elicit Rob's cooperation by telling him, "Min-Haeng seems to have disappeared," and asking, "Where do think Min-Haeng is?" Rob humors me by replying in a sarcastic tone, "I don't know. Maybe he went to the other side of the earth?" Even though my attitude towards Min-Haeng changed suddenly (from being annoyed by his antics to cooperating with his scheme), Rob's responses throughout this interaction are admirable (e.g., when he tries to help me), spot on (e.g., when he detects the new levity in my tone and indulgently follows my lead), and indicative of how his attunement to people's feelings and his perceptiveness of people's intentions enabled him to adjust effortlessly to the kinds of subtle fluctuations that commonly occur in everyday interactions.

Anticipating and Resisting Disconnections

Whereas Rob had demonstrated the ability to be attentive and straightforward in his interactions with adults as well as peers, he began to find it necessary to be more strategic in his efforts to get what he needed and wanted in his relationships. Namely, as his relationships at home and at school were changing, Rob had to reconsider his assumptions about what he could expect from and how he could be with others.

At home, Rob was adjusting to having a new baby brother, which had certain implications for his relationship with his mom. During the first half of the school year, Rob had tended to be less affectionate with his mom than he was with his dad, at least while at school. Nevertheless, Rob had seemed confident and secure in his interactions with his mom. On my fifth visit, Rob arrives at school with his mom but enters the classroom unaccompanied and, as usual, heads straight for the classroom set of Playmobil toys. When Rob's mom enters the room a few moments later carrying Rob's baby brother, Rob continues to focus on the Playmobil toys and does not seem to notice his mom's arrival. As Rob plays on his own, his mom walks over to where he is sitting on the floor, checks on him briefly while she remains standing (and holding the baby), tells him, "O.K., have fun," and then goes to talk with one of the teachers. Just as his mom does not offer to join him, Rob does not ask her to do so. He also does not look for his mom or seek her attention while she is in the room. As Rob's mom prepares to leave, she mentions to Rob that she will be around at school this morning and says that she will pop her head in from time to time, which she does. As with Rob's dad, her departures did not appear to be an issue at this time and seemed to transpire without any complications.

However, the dynamic of Rob's interactions with his mom began to change during the second half of the school year, as her time and attention became more limited. On a few occasions when Rob arrived at school with his mom, she explained to him that she could not stay because she also had to check on his older brother or because she had to attend a baby group with his younger brother. Even when she did stay, Rob knew that she could not focus completely on their interaction because she also had to take care of his baby brother. As Rob began to feel less certain of his mom's availability to him, he began to ask, and even beg, his mom to stay and play with him on days when she brought him to school. During my seventh visit, as Rob plays alone on the floor, his mom comes to tell him that she is going to visit someone and will come back later to say good-bye. Rather than simply letting her go, as he did previously (just a couple weeks ago), Rob remarks that she has not spent any time with him and implies that he would like her to stay. Rob's mom responds to his request by agreeing to sit with him "for one minute." While holding the baby, she then takes a seat and watches as Rob narrates his play. When the minute is up, Rob's mom asks Rob to give her and the baby each a kiss, which he does gently, before she gets up and leaves.

The tension in Rob's interactions with his mom appeared to increase in the weeks that followed. Specifically, Rob began clinging to his mom and trying to prolong their interaction while Rob's mom tried to expedite her departure without being unfair to Rob. Whereas their time together (earlier in the school year) had seemed easy and trouble-free, their interactions now necessitated explicit negotiations, and even then, they did not always reach an agreement that satisfied them both. During my twelfth visit, Rob's mom tells him that she is leaving for a meeting but makes a "deal" with him and says she will come to visit afterwards, if he promises not to "hang on" when it's time to say good-bye. As he considers her offer, Rob remarks that she has not spent a lot of time with him. This time, however, Rob's mom cannot stay and instead asks Rob to give her and the baby each a hug as she prepares to leave. Rob complies with her request but then follows her as she heads to the door and protests her departure by whining and then demanding, "Don't go!" Although Rob sounds upset, his face does not look as distressed as his voice sounds. He also smiles when he manages to detain his mom by tugging on her jacket, which suggests that his protests are partly for show. To help facilitate their separation, Jen comes and gently peels Rob's hand from his mom's jacket, takes Rob in her arms, and distracts him by asking him to help her answer "the question of the week," which is posted at the other side of the room. As Rob allows Jen to soothe him, his mom heads out the door.

Feeling Uncertain

Although Rob continued to seek his mom's company and his mom continued to be bound by her many responsibilities, their time together could vary depending on Rob's need and his mom's schedule on a given day. Knowing that his mom's availability was unpredictable and sometimes negotiable, Rob was both anxious and hopeful as he tried to keep her with him for as long as possible. For instance, as soon as they arrive at class on my nineteenth visit, Rob immediately asks his mom if she is going to stay. Rob's mom tells him that she can stay for a little while but prepares him for her departure by asking, "What would you like to do before I go?" When Rob responds in his baby voice, "Me want you to draw a cowboy," Rob's mom sits down while holding the baby and draws a cowboy for him. As he watches her intently and contentedly, Rob reminds his mom of details he wants her to include in the drawing ("You need to draw the gun in his hand," "You didn't color it in"), and she cooperates patiently with his instructions. At one point, Rob suddenly remembers his mom's impending departure and pleads with her, "Don't go." When she responds by smiling and reassuring him, "Not quite yet," Rob relaxes enough to notice when his baby brother grabs at the Playmobil catalog (which Rob had set down on the table) and causes the page to turn. Rob remarks excitedly, "Oh! He's turning the page!" and his mom agrees, "Yeah, he's getting to be a big boy." Rob then gets up, walks over to the house area, and fetches a plush toy that he offers to the baby: "[He] can have this." At this moment, Rob seems as confident and secure as he did earlier in the year (before he began to worry about his mom's availability to him). However, when his mom finally announces, "I'm going to say good-bye now," Rob immediately whines and protests, "No, I don't want you to. No, Mom," and follows her to the door. When his mom asks for a big hug, Rob complies with her request while continuing to protest her departure. Again, Jen comes to intervene and tries to distract Rob by asking him what his job is today. Although Rob seems to understand Jen's intentions, he allows her to divert his attention anyway as his mom takes her leave.

Rob's concern about separations, which I had mainly observed in his interactions with his mom, also became apparent in his interactions with his dad, even though his dad (who did not have the baby with him on days when he accompanied Rob to class) was still available and attentive during their time together. Throughout the school year, Rob and his dad continued their routine of settling in together at the start of the school day. The closeness of their relationship—including how comfortable and in sync they were with each other—appeared to help Rob feel grounded and ready to face the school day. However, in contrast to their easy separations earlier in the year, Rob began to struggle with his dad's departures as the year progressed. For instance, during my twentieth visit, Rob immediately protests when his dad prepares to leave. On this morning, Rob and his dad are using colored sticks and rubber bands to make designs on a wooden board riddled with holes. As Rob's dad sits on a chair with his legs open at a 90-degree angle, Rob stands casually poised between his dad's knees. Rob seems to have a specific design in mind and, with his dad watching attentively, narrates his actions as he carefully places the sticks in the board and applies the rubber bands to carry out his plan. After several minutes have passed, Rob's dad puts his hands on his knees, sighs, and says, "O.K.," to signal that it's time for him to leave. In response, Rob protests, "No," and tries to delay his dad's departure by putting his arm around his dad's neck, leaning his body against his dad's torso, positioning himself so that he looks as though he's sitting in dad's lap, and thereby preventing his dad from getting up. Although Rob succeeds in restricting his dad's movement momentarily, his dad eventually manages to rise to his feet and walks to the door with Rob trailing behind him, tugging first at his dad's fingers and then at his dad's shirttail, all the time asking him to stay. As Rob's dad nears the door, Jen intervenes by grabbing Rob gently around the waist, hugging him from behind, and then turning him towards her. As his dad slips away, Rob begins to cry. Jen soothes him and engages him in conversation in an effort to distract him. After a minute or so, Rob allows himself to be comforted and eventually stops crying. Although Rob's feelings of sadness are real, he learns to move on.

Engaging Strategically

In addition to adjusting to changes in his family relationships at home, Rob was also adapting to changes in his peer relationships at school, particularly as the Mean Team became a more prominent (and restrictive) influence on the boys' behaviors and interactions. Given the Mean Team's emphasis on hierarchy and competition, all of the boys had become especially sensitive and resistant to being bossed around by their peers. If a boy wanted to solicit his peers' cooperation, he therefore had to be careful to avoid appearing bossy; only Mike could get away with that. One way that the boys downplayed their assertiveness was by expressing their opinions and preferences in a less direct, or indirect, manner. As a result, the boys' meanings and intentions, which had been clear and upfront, became cleverly disguised and self-protectively hidden.

Despite being relatively soft-spoken, Rob had tended to be forthright in communicating his thoughts and feelings. For instance, during my third visit, when Min-Haeng picks up a sword that Rob has constructed and lays it down next to his own construction, Rob looks concerned but maintains his composure as he calmly informs Min-Haeng, "That's my sword." When Min-Haeng mumbles what seems to be an explanation, Rob looks confused and asks hopefully, "You're saving it for me?" to which Min-Haeng replies, "Yeah." Rob also had been able to confront his peers without seeming defensive or causing offense. During my ninth visit, when Jake leaves the game that he and Rob had started and goes to join Mike and Dan, Rob expresses his concern straight out: "Then I won't have anyone [to play with]." Rob's tone is neither whiny nor angry. He simply alerts his peers to this fact, in case they have not noticed. Rob could even give orders and issue warnings to his peers in a way that came across as helpful rather than bossy, as when Tony and Min-Haeng use a plastic bottle filled with water to engage in a tug-of-war during my nineteenth visit and Rob convinces them to stop by interjecting firmly, "You're gonna pull [the cap] off, guys. Don't pull on it."

However, as the Mean Team's influence became more pervasive and its rules for engagement began to affect his sense of agency and choice, Rob found it increasingly difficult to be so direct and plainspoken in his interactions. By the end of his pre-Kindergarten year, Rob wasn't sure whether he wanted to continue being a part of this boys' club where he felt he had little say in matters, but he worried about what might happen if he didn't comply with Mike's orders and conform to group norms. For instance, one day during circle time, Rob seems conflicted when he wants to participate in a teacher-led activity that involves singing and dancing, which the other boys have decided to boycott. All of the kids are given the option not to participate in this activity, but it is only the boys (led by Mike) who decide to sit this one out. As the girls joyfully sing and dance in the middle of the circle, the boys remain seated along the circle's border, with their arms crossed and wearing expressions of indifference to suggest they are too cool for this activity. Caught between his desire to join in this activity and his concern about the consequences of distinguishing himself (e.g., by acting differently), Rob eventually compromises by participating briefly and nonchalantly in the activity before sitting down with the other boys.

Given Rob's need and desire to avoid appearing defiant or demanding, he learned to be more deliberate, strategic, and nuanced within his peer interactions. For instance, during a meeting with Mike, Jake, and Rob during my fifteenth visit, Rob tries repeatedly (but circuitously) to acquire for himself a toy that Mike was the first to claim. As Rob is keen to avoid conflict, especially with Mike, he does not express his preference outright. Instead, Rob tries—in an act of false benevolence—to entice Mike to swap with him: "I'll trade. [Blue Prince is] better." Although Mike makes it clear that he is not interested—"No. I don't want to trade [Dark Knight]"—Rob continues to suggest his preference, for example by telling me (when he knows Mike is listening), "I want to be the Dark Knight that Mikey is, but that's O.K." When Mike sees through Rob's not-so-subtle tactics and responds defensively, "No, I'm being [Dark Knight]," Rob immediately assures him, "I know." Although Rob's indirect approach could be self-protective (because it allowed him to deny his ulterior motives, if necessary), it also felt less honest (as he tried nevertheless to get his way).

Another way that Rob became more circumspect in his self-expression was by using a baby voice to communicate his wishes. Just as the boys used masculine posturing to project an image of toughness and dominance, they used baby voices to project an image of vulnerability and subordination. In both cases, the boys exaggerated qualities that they believed can help them to influence their peers and to elicit their peers' compliance more effectively. For instance, during my twelfth visit, when Mike and Min-Haeng are looking at a comic book together and they fail to acknowledge Rob's initial attempts to engage them, Rob changes to using his baby voice, saying, "I like [the little guy]. He's cute," which prompts Mike and Min-Haeng to respond in a more supportive manner: "Yeah." As all of the boys were sensitive and resistant to being bossed around, the boys' baby voices were less likely than their masculine posturing to elicit a defensive response and could therefore help to prevent or mediate conflicts. During my twenty-first visit, Rob uses his baby voice to signal his subordination, even (or particularly) as he takes on the leadership role in an interaction with Mike. As Rob and Mike use wooden blocks to reconstruct a project that has been knocked down, Rob initially uses his regular voice to ask, "Can you help me, Mikey?" However, when Mike uses his baby voice to admit his ignorance, "No. Me don't know how it goes," Rob also changes to using his baby voice to instruct Mike, "This is how it goes. I have this at the top . . . " From his own observations and experiences, Rob knows that Mike is unaccustomed to and uncomfortable with being at a disadvantage in his peer interactions. So, when Rob suddenly finds himself in a position to tell Mike what to do, Rob immediately downplays his advantage by using a baby voice and thereby protects himself against accusations of wrongdoing, should Mike decide (as he often does) that being told what to do (i.e., being in a subordinate position) does not suit him.

Adhering to Scripts

In his efforts to influence Mike and the other boys without causing offense, Rob also began to rely on predetermined scripts, or preconceived notions about how things ought to be, which could allow him to assert (without appearing to serve) himself. As Rob, Jake, and Mike assemble accessories for their Playmobil characters during my fifteenth visit, Rob informs Jake, "You put the chair on backwards." When Jake denies that he made a mistake, Rob insists, "[You] did. Look at the box," and refers Jake to a photo on the toys' packaging so that Jake can see for himself what the "right" way is. Similarly, on my twenty-fourth visit, when Min-Haeng ignores Rob's instructions, Rob directs Min-Haeng's attention to the Playmobil catalog to show him what accessories belong to whom, who goes where, and who can do what.

> ROB: [Blue Prince is] the king.
>
> MIN-HAENG: But the pirate gets trapped, O.K.?
>
> ROB: I know. But he needs his sword. The pirate needs his sword.
>
> MIN-HAENG: This [other] guy helps.
>
> ROB: No, [the pirate] needs [his sword] . . . Look at [the catalog], Min-Haeng, this is the, the pirate's supposed to have this sword . . . No, that guy goes in the back. (*Min-Haeng complies.*) O.K. Yeah. [This guy] rides it, not [that guy].
>
> MIN-HAENG: Does the black knight . . .
>
> ROB: Look at [the catalog].
>
> MIN-HAENG (*ENLIGHTENED*): Oh!

Rob's decision to follow the examples depicted on the toys' packaging and in the Playmobil catalog was consistent with his personal preference for order and predictability. However, whereas Rob had tended during the first half of the school year to keep his opinions to himself or to offer them modestly to others, later on, he seemed to derive a new-found confidence from having evidence to support his claims, especially within his peer interactions, wherein the structure and dynamics of the Mean Team could make it difficult for individual boys (other than Mike) to influence others.

Moreover, Rob's adherence to predetermined scripts seemed to instill in him a sense of self-righteousness such that he felt compelled and entitled to impose his views on others. For instance, during my fourteenth visit, as Rob, Dan, and Jake are constructing a play scenario, Rob checks the Playmobil catalog and boldly declares, "We *need* to get this guy in jail . . . This guy *has* to go to jail." Likewise, on the following visit, when Jake uses various Playmobil parts to construct his own creation, Rob casually intervenes to provide guidance: "This goes like this, Jake. I'll show ya how the whole thing goes." When Jake (who has something different in mind) disagrees—"No, that doesn't go there"—Rob replies firmly, "It does. I know it does," as though there could be only one correct answer. And when Rob struggles to attach a particular accessory to his toy figure and I suggest that he may have mismatched the two pieces, Rob immediately dismisses that possibility on the grounds that he consulted a legitimate source (the photo on the toy's packaging) and therefore knows how it is supposed to be.

Rob's conviction—that he knew how things ought to be and that it was important for things to be that way—was reflected in his tone and in his words as he authoritatively issued commands ("That doesn't go there," "He's supposed to have this,") and used language that implies necessity ("I need"), obligation ("you have to"), and responsibility ("we should") to urge his peers to align with the scripts and thereby do as he said. As Rob's suggestions became demands, Rob even had the audacity to correct Mike. For instance, during my fifteenth visit, when Mike (probably judging from the color of the character's attire) declares, "This guy's the black knight," Rob interjects firmly, "No, he's Dark Knight." Although Mike clarifies his proposal and explains, "No, he's *a* black knight," Rob does not consider Mike's explanation—that the character's name is Dark Knight and he is a black knight—and instead insists, "But I know he is because [the catalog says it]. He's Dark Knight."

Whereas personal opinions and preferences could be difficult to defend—particularly with the other boys, who had opinions and preferences of their own—Rob's use of predetermined scripts enabled him to introduce an alternate authority to which all of the boys, including Mike and himself, were subject. Furthermore, because Rob did not create the scripts, he could call for the boys' compliance without appearing to gain personally at the other boys' expense. As a result, Rob could now have some say in how the boys' play proceeded. However, it was mainly when the boys were playing with the Playmobil that Rob was able to use predetermined scripts to influence his peers. When the boys engaged in other activities, scripts that deviated from the Mean Team's rules and conditions—and, by implication, from prevailing norms of masculine behavior within his peer group culture—were not as readily available.

Despite having found a few effective strategies for coping with and adapting to his peer group culture, Rob nevertheless seemed dissatisfied with its restrictiveness, and he began to look for a way out. Whereas he had initially chosen to participate on the Mean Team and align with group norms because he wanted to or because he viewed the advantages as outweighing the disadvantages, Rob eventually felt more constrained than empowered by his involvement in this boys' club. By the end of his pre-Kindergarten year, Rob was not as easily convinced that the options provided by the Mean Team (e.g., for how the boys' play and interactions could proceed) were his best or only options. Rob still wanted the sense of inclusion and belonging that resulted from group membership, but he also wanted to make his own decisions, at least occasionally. Forced to choose between being a part of the group and being autonomous,[5] Rob ultimately chose the latter, ended up alone, and in this sense aligned himself with masculine norms that emphasize independence, autonomy, and self-sufficiency.

* * *

Rob's case study highlights boys' agency and awareness as they determine how it is possible for them, as boys, to express themselves and engage in their relationships. It also shows how boys are motivated to adapt to masculine norms not only by a social desire to prove masculinity and gain approval in a general sense but also by a relational desire to identify personally with and relate meaningfully to specific individuals. Moreover, Rob's example demonstrates how boys' contexts, especially their peer group cultures, can influence boys' perceptions of what they can expect in their relationships and their beliefs about whether (and to what extent) they can create other options for themselves. Like the other boys in this class, Rob was drawn by opportunities to connect with others and inclined to avoid disconnections from other people and from his self. However, as Rob tried to figure out how he could preserve his relationships and also preserve his sense of integrity, he learned and gradually came to accept that it might not be possible to have it both ways. So long as Rob remained under the influence of the Mean Team and the conventions of masculinity that this boys' club embodied, he would have to choose one or the other.

6

Parents' Perspectives on Boys' Predicament

In addition to conducting observations of and interviews with these four- and five-year-old boys, Carol and I also met with the boys' fathers[1] and mothers,[2] separately. During these meetings, which took place on weeknights in the school's library, the parents generously shared with us their thoughts and feelings about what they were observing in their sons at this age. Since Carol had initiated these meetings with the fathers (and the mothers then asked if we would meet with them as well), she took the lead both in raising questions ("What do you see in your sons that leads you to say, "I hope he never loses that?"), and also in responding to the parents. This freed me to observe and listen during these meetings, just as I had done with the boys during my visits to their class.

This chapter presents some of the parents' questions and concerns in regards to raising young boys, and also their goals in helping their sons to deal with the pressures and challenges that they were encountering, particularly in their peer relationships at school. While there was some overlap in the topics discussed by each group, the fathers' and mothers' views are presented separately—organized more or less by theme—and include summaries of what each group discussed collectively, as well as quotations from individuals. Although these parents' views cannot be generalized to all fathers and mothers, the issues that they discussed are likely to be familiar to many parents, and the insights that they shared may shed light on our own observations and experiences of the boys in our lives, as well as the challenges we face with them.

Fathers

Midway through the boys' pre-Kindergarten year, Carol and I asked to meet with the fathers as group because we had been so struck by the closeness and tenderness that we observed between the boys and their fathers, and we were interested to learn how the fathers viewed and experienced their relationships with their sons. At the end of our first meeting, the fathers expressed an interest in continuing to meet with us, so we scheduled more meetings. The fathers seemed to approach these meetings with an awareness of Carol's expertise in the fields of psychology and human development, and they used these opportunities to think through their experiences on an intellectual as well as an intuitive level.[3]

What the Fathers Cherished and Wished to Preserve

In these meetings where we asked the fathers to reflect on their experiences as fathers and also on their own experiences as boys, the fathers spoke first and foremost about qualities—including the boys' "spunk," openness, and attunement—that they valued and wished to preserve in their sons.

In describing the boys' "spunk," the fathers referred to their sons' "exuberance," "high energy," "spirit," "gleam," "pizzazz," "vibrancy," and "vivaciousness." The fathers were careful to point out that these qualities were somewhat different from the rowdy and rambunctious energy that is typically associated with boys being "boys." Rather, the boys' "spunk" had more to do with the boys' ability to be "out there," "imaginative," "joyful," and "friendly"—qualities that made the boys "charming" and "endearing." To offer an example, Mike's dad recounted an incident that occurred during a school assembly:

> [Mike] got up on stage, picked up the microphone, and started off saying, "Well, I dunno, I'm a little, I was *going* to sing 'Hound Dog' but I'm a little nervous here so I don't know if I can do it." And then, you know, there were a few giggles and silence. And I of course was sitting there thinking,

"What's wrong with him—that he would want to embarrass himself in front of the entire community?" And then he did it. He got up, he sang, he did a little dance. . . . That's the kind of spunk. Or that he's so friendly to people, strangers, imaginative in every play that they do. There's this sort of joy about it and if he can keep that, he would be a very happy person.

As Mike's dad described, Mike's "spunk" included his ability to express himself openly and wholeheartedly, and seemed to reflect his comfort with himself and his trust in other people (to be supportive and not laugh at him).

Although Mike's dad viewed Mike's "spunk" as a positive thing, he also knew that this openness could get boys into trouble (because it tends not to be socially valued, especially in boys) and is therefore at risk as boys learn to behave and be "good." Mike's dad wished to preserve Mike's ability to be "out there" in this way, but he also worried that Mike's "spunk," if allowed to persist, could make Mike vulnerable to criticism and rejection. As Mike's dad explained,

I think it's pretty tricky because of the energy level. . . . He's out there. He needs to really be out there. . . . It's always tricky to figure out how much you want to clamp down on him. . . . He was getting in all sorts of trouble here at school—punching kids in the face and getting in fights— and even just getting, I think, too wound up. And . . . you say, "That's unacceptable behavior, that you're running around jumping just because you can't stop jumping." . . . And I always think about it, there's spunk there. There's this way that he's very spunky. And I hate for that to be squeezed out of him, as I believe that it was squeezed out of me, you know. You get sort of socialized into being a "good" boy. . . . So, how can you somehow convince him, "You can still be the 'good' boy, but it's O.K. if at times . . . you want to be out there." . . . Drawing these boundaries and being clear about them has been a real challenge. . . . At the same time, [so has] trying to . . . let him really go wild. And I find it tricky to figure out the balance with a high-energy kid, especially at the end of the day when you're tired, you know, what do you do? Where you don't want to resort to repression or put him in front of the T.V., you want to somehow engage, but you're exhausted and there's an element of energy that you just can't deal with. It's really difficult.

Mike's dad remembered having that "spunk" ("I was exactly like that"), and losing it.

> I think I just got in trouble so much in school. . . . I mean I would be good, you know. I was good enough in school that I could get good grades. But every now and then . . . there'd be a parent-teacher conference where, you know, "This kid is out of control. There's too much energy here," or something like that. And then I just became good and decided to study hard and blend into the crowd. . . . That was it. . . . It's sad. . . . I really don't want that to happen to [my son]. You know, there's a definition of what it means to be a "good" boy . . . just make sure that you don't cause trouble and, you know, teachers [will] like you or something like that. . . . You get socialized into being a "good" boy, [but you lose] that spunk . . . [of] just being able to let go and enjoy and be wild and stuff like that.

Although Mike's dad understood the need for boys to learn what is considered appropriate behavior and to know how to adapt to societal expectations, he hoped that Mike could also find a way to preserve the "spunk," so that Mike could be both "good" and "out there."

Another quality that the fathers delighted and took pride in was the boys' ability to be "so open right now," in terms of what they could "put out there" and also what they could "take in," "physically, intellectually, and emotionally." The fathers were impressed by the boys' ability to "feel their feelings fully" and "let their feelings happen." The fathers marveled at the boys' ability to be "comfortable," "honest," "upfront," and "expressive" in their relationships. The fathers were amazed by the boys' willingness to "try and fail," and how they could make mistakes "without shame or embarrassment." The fathers seemed almost envious of how "uninhibited" the boys could be, that they could "let things come right out," and that they were not hesitant about "saying what they feel" and telling others what was on their minds.

Jake's dad talked about being proud of Jake's eagerness to explore everything and how he hoped that Jake could continue to be so open and enthusiastic, which he linked to Jake's high level of energy and considered to be "at risk," particularly in classroom settings that emphasize sitting still and learning to think about things in a specific way.

[Jake's] thinking is very uncategorized. . . . When he sees something, . . . it'll make him think about something totally different that has some quality that it shares, . . . he'll think about things and say things and make connections that are just very wide open. . . . At home we try to keep that going, but in a school setting it's easy for that kind of quality to be sort of squished down, . . . and I'd hate to see that go. And partially that's a function of his energy level. You know, there's this sort of ability to get some input and then he's thinking so fast and hard, and it's like, "Ooh!" everything's, "test, test, test, boom, boom, boom," that he checks out all the edges of everything. . . . So, for Jake, . . . the world is really a much more interactive place. . . . Everything is there to be touched, to test, to smell, to mess around with, just experienced. We [adults] don't do that so much anymore. . . . And it's always a blast to go cruising around with him 'cause it's, like, so, sort of eye opening. This very afternoon, we were shoveling horse manure into the garden. Oh boy, did he like that! Just the concept of it: horse manure. And he put on his big boots. He was jumping around in it, taking it and smelling it, messing with it. I'm not gonna do that, you know? But that's sort of, that ability to *not* care that you're not supposed to put your hands to horse manure, to not care that we're just supposed to be shoveling this thing and doing it—it's like, "No, this is here to experience. Let's check . . . see what it's really like." And that's what happens with everything. Of course, it's a pain in the ass when you're like trying to, you know, get everybody's clothes on in the morning to get out to school and he wants to fully experience the process of running around the house with his shirt over his face. Well, . . . that's the kind of stuff where I run into that trouble of, like, "O.K., where do I gotta stop this? Where do I wanna just let it go?"

While Jake's dad admired Jake's "ability to not care" about doing the proper thing all the time, he anticipated that boys' ability to "just go with" their instincts and interests would soon become difficult to maintain as boys come up against societal expectations to act and be a certain way. Determined to try to prevent Jake and Jake's brother from feeling limited in this way, "like they have to be in a single voice," Jake's dad explained,

That's something I very strongly resonate with, that issue of . . . being able to use your expressive abilities, . . . how you have to be *careful*. . . . A lot of people can't handle this kind of thing . . . you know, using a lot of tonality and dynamics in [your] voice and in [your] presentation. . . . There are all these voices the kids have. And they want all of them. . . . If you can get fired up about something, you feel great. . . . That's something that we [adults] don't do anymore either . . . you know, [for adults] it's hard to be really, really excited about something.

Based on their own experiences, the fathers knew that it would become difficult for boys to remain open and to maintain the fervor with which they approached new experiences. Nevertheless, the fathers hoped to help the boys retain these qualities so that even as the boys learned to adapt to societal expectations, they could still get "fired up" and "excited" about things; they could still "be in the moment" and have fun.

As they described what the boys were "taking in," the fathers also mentioned the boys' attunement and perceptiveness. The fathers said they were astonished by what the boys could notice and comment on, and how the boys would "pick up [on] everything, even if they pretend that they don't pick it up." When Carol asked the fathers how well their sons could read them, Mike's dad replied, "Very well. Too well," and said that Mike could sometimes be "too clued in to reading people's facial expressions [and] tone of voice." Although Mike's dad appeared to complain that Mike was "just too in tune sometimes" to interpersonal dynamics (because it meant that he had to be careful about the example that he was setting), he also expressed an underlying sense of awe and wonder at Mike's ability to read emotions and relationships with accuracy and at a deep level of understanding.

In combination, the boys' spunk, openness, and attunement enabled them to be and to feel emotionally close to other people. As Jake's dad described:

It's always something I've worked hard to encourage. . . . It's something for me that I feel very strongly about. And I try to help [my sons] to go ahead and feel comfortable getting close and getting quiet and hearing and talking on [a] very personal level. Those are things we do together. And that's actually one of the cool things about kids—you can do that. Like with Jake, we can sit there and have these great conversations and be really physical and have this very sweet time, so un-self-consciously. . . . [For example,] he was taking a bath and I'm sitting there talking to him and he's sorta playing, fooling around with bubbles and just hanging out, very calm and comfortable and very relaxed. . . . And he was telling me some stories about his buddies and how much he likes his buddies and then he was asking me about my buddies . . . just like, "So, what's friendship about?" you know, "What's it mean to you?" kind of thing. . . . He was just talking and I was talking. We were playing, you know. There was nothing to accomplish. . . . It's not about anything in particular. . . . There's nothing else going on.

The fathers observed this kind of connection in boys' friendships as well. As Rob's dad remarked,

> They're so delighted to have a playmate, you know, a friend. Like Rob will always say, "Well, that's my Mikey." . . . It's just so sweet, the sort of excitement they feel and the warmth they feel, even if it doesn't translate into always getting along together. I think they're delighted to have that connection.

The fathers were aware that the boys' interactions were not always harmonious ("it doesn't translate into always getting along together"), and they wondered how the intensity and variability of the boys' feelings, which could "seem unstable" or perplexing to adults, impacted the boys' relationships. As Mike's dad described,

> They get so close. . . . I'll see our sons playing . . . then the next day [I'll] hear [Mike say], like, "Yeah, I punched him in the face," or something . . . [and] I'm like, "Wait, you had a wonderful play date yesterday. Why?" And I don't know, it's this guy thing . . . it's just hard to keep that closeness.

Whereas Mike's dad assumed that the need to be "constantly negotiating" put a strain on the boys' friendships ("it's just hard to keep that closeness"), Jake's dad suggested that maybe the boys' closeness enabled the boys to have "that kind of volatility [in] the relationships," and to experience and express a broad range of feelings with each other:

> [Jake] could be really happy and have a great time with somebody and then, like, have it change and be really angry with someone, and then have it change again and be really happy again. . . . And that was more

a matter of actually being comfortable with somebody—that he felt free enough to go ahead and let that happen.

The fathers discussed with Carol the possibility that the boys' intense and fluctuating feelings were a part of the relationship, and that the closeness of the boys' relationships enabled them to "move to different places" emotionally in the process of being together.

> CAROL: So, then the question is, can that go on? Can that [intensity and range of emotions] be just this sort of ongoing [thing]? . . . Or is there a sense that we need to stop it so that we're one way or the other way or, do you know what I'm saying?
> JAKE'S DAD: Do you mean, is it something where you sort of pick one [way] and harden into it?
> CAROL: Yeah, and call that relationship.
> JAKE'S DAD: As opposed to remaining fluid.
> CAROL: Right. And it seemed to me to sort of stay in an ongoing relationship is to stay in that fluidity.

Although the fathers could appreciate the advantages of remaining emotionally "fluid," as opposed to becoming "rigid" or "static," they also knew that the kind of closeness and connection that enables this fluidity is hard to maintain, because the qualities that enable boys to be close with and connected to others are hard to maintain.

What the Fathers Worried About

As the fathers deliberated about what was making it difficult for the boys to maintain the qualities that allowed them to be "lively, vibrant, brilliant, and real" in their relationships, they suggested that part of it had to do with the boys' becoming increasingly aware of cultural norms of masculinity and societal expectations for boys and men. In part, the fathers were remembering their own experiences of coming up against externally defined standards and ideals and learning to adapt. As Mike's dad described:

> It's almost like I have to like re-program myself [in order to be close to people]. . . . I think I got myself programmed . . . by learning how to be

good. . . . I've been measuring myself constantly in this external way. And I don't want [my kids] to repeat this. I really *don't* want them to repeat this.

The fathers knew something about the world in which boys and men must live, and they foresaw the shift in boys' relational presence that can occur as boys adapt to that world. They also knew "what's at stake" for boys as they negotiate the process of becoming "good" boys. They remembered "dealing with issues of masculinity," how the "gendered rules come down," trying to work through questions with no easy answers, and the feelings of "vulnerability," "powerlessness," "loneliness," and "loss" that they experienced throughout that process. At the same time, they hoped that things could be different for their sons.

However, the fathers were already observing this process in their sons. For instance, Mike's dad found that Mike was already learning to modify his behaviors as he transitioned from private and public settings.

I find it so interesting that Mikey, you know, he has this dog he carries around, Bobo. . . . And he loves Bobo. . . . And takes Bobo in the car. And then as we get to the stairs of the school, he says, "Here Dad, can you hold him?" and he doesn't want to be . . . seen in public with this stuffed animal. Now, how did he learn that at five . . . that he had to kind of, you know, project a certain image?

In particular, the fathers found that the boys were coming up against gendered norms and expectations that encourage boys to hide their sensitivity and softness. Referring to the notion that boys "are at risk if they look too vulnerable," Rob's dad explained,

I think there are certain situations in the world [where] you sort of feel like you'd be better off if you were much tougher, rougher. And I think that does have an effect. . . . I think there is an expectation that you grow up with, "Well, as a man you should not do this and this and this and this." Those are expectations that are out there, that you'll respond to, just like you respond to cues about what's appropriate.

Rob's dad suggested that, regardless of how individual boys feel about the expectations that exist for boys and men, they must deal with those expectations. Moreover, they often feel compelled to meet those expectations, for instance by "catering to what's expected and elicited from them" and "doing things they're supposed to do."

> We sort of internalize, "Oh yeah, we should be able to do whatever is asked of us." And if we have other feelings, we don't pay attention to them. If we have feelings of vulnerability, . . . it's like [they don't count]. . . . The only thing to do is to go ahead. . . . And then if it doesn't work out, um, you know, you take the blame or you don't look for excuses.

Dan's dad added that in the event that boys and men find themselves unable to meet gendered expectations, it was imperative to "Pretend that you can do it. Bluff your way. If you can't do it, you bluff your way through it."

In discussing what is at stake as the boys figure out how to respond to restrictive norms and expectations (e.g., regarding how boys ought to act and be), the fathers considered with Carol whether boys' sensitivity is a liability or strength. They also wondered what becomes of boys' sensitivity as they encounter messages that devalue this quality in boys.

> ROB'S DAD: I can see [Rob] sort of tentatively stepping up to the world, but he has so much sort of hidden within. . . . I think he's very careful. . . . I think for him, trusting that it's O.K. to be out in the world is more sort of the issue. . . . When he's at home, and with [his older brother], and when he's comfortable with his friends, . . . I can see a real joy in sort of just being silly. . . . He can sort of relax a little bit. . . . I hope that . . . he finds the world trustworthy enough that he can sort of . . . want to come out. . . . 'Cause I do think he does have a tendency to hide a lot of his sensitivity and stuff. . . . I think it was the same way when I was growing up, that I was very sensitive to what the expectations were. . . . And that's not always a good thing.
> CAROL: But that's a very double-edged thing because if you're sensitive—let's just say to what's going on around you—then you can read the world. And if you are reading the world and what you're picking up—let's just say in other people's responses and feelings and thoughts—[is] that you shouldn't be doing a bunch of stuff that maybe you want to do, then you can kind of stop reading the world and do [what you want] anyway . . . [or you can keep

reading the world and] stop doing it [and adapt to what's expected instead]. . . . So, I mean, what I'm trying to say is that's a sort of a lose-lose dilemma."

JAKE'S DAD: And [in] reading the world, . . . [there's] then this mediation between doing what it is the world is expecting of you and doing what it is you would really like to do. And for some kids probably, it doesn't really become an issue because they mesh very cleanly. But with most kids, it doesn't, so it's an issue.

Although Rob's dad did not seem to know at that time about the Mean Team (and how it could constrain the boys' behaviors and styles of relating to each other), he saw that Rob was careful about what he revealed and that Rob was trying to figure out how he could be with others. Rob's dad detected Rob's uncertainty and concern about how others would respond to him, and he hoped that Rob would find the world to be welcoming, safe, and trustworthy. However, Rob's dad worried that Rob's sensitivity to expectations (and to pressures to meet those expectations) could hinder Rob's ability to feel comfortable enough in general to be uninhibited (e.g., as he was at home and with friends). In response, Carol pointed out the dilemma for boys in having to choose between doing what other people expect of them and doing what they want (which, incidentally, Rob experienced and articulated), and how choosing one over the other could lead only to dissatisfaction. Likewise, Jake's dad suggested that this process of reconciling other people's expectations (e.g., how they ought to be) and their own desires (e.g., how they want to be) is a struggle for most kids and raises the question of what boys (and parents) can do about it.

On one hand, the fathers understood the boys' need to regulate their self-expression in order to adapt to societal expectations, and that such self-regulation often had more to do with protecting themselves from disapproval and rejection than with gaining approval and acceptance. The fathers noticed that as the boys were learning that there is a "right" way for them to be, they were becoming more anxious about and eager to avoid doing the wrong thing. Through their own experiences, the fathers knew that in situations where boys feel they are being judged, it is not safe for boys to be "out there," because it leaves them "too exposed," as well as vulnerable to "being sort of slapped down." To give an example, Jake's dad explained that for "very high-energy kids, it's very easy to go ahead and say . . . the things [they're] thinking and feeling because . . . that's their energy level, things come out." However, the boys' openness can make it easier for other people to criticize them or to say, "That's an inappropriate thing," or "Don't do that." As a result, the boys learn that they "have to be careful" about what they reveal, and that aligning with accepted norms and expectations can help to shield them from scrutiny by ensuring that they don't stand out.

On the other hand, the fathers worried that the boys' adaptation to group and cultural norms of masculinity—including notions about how to be good, appropriate, well-behaved, socially acceptable boys—was resulting in a "narrowing range" of what the boys could experience and express. As Jake's dad described, "For the boys, it's like the ability to experiment with your identity gets more and more sorta mushed down and pretty soon these expectations are heavy on you." Mike's dad similarly described how boys' adoption of stereotypically masculine behaviors could limit their options for how to engage with and relate to other people.

I think that different boys learn different styles [of relating]. . . . Mikey's way of contact is to . . . get a lot of attention by being loud or getting people to chase him or something like that. But then when he wants to switch gears, he can't because other people won't . . . follow the cue. . . . [Mikey] gets himself into situations [where] he'll be running around and chasing and stuff like that, and then suddenly there'll be people chasing [him] and he's afraid. . . . I guess I worry that with these kinds of more active boys, that it's almost like a shield, all this activity. . . . [The boys] have this other feeling, but it's the stuff that . . . only gets expressed when they're, you know, in the back of the car feeling totally safe, or in some sort of quiet moment. . . . I think it's very easy for those types to get reinforced. I mean with Mikey I just see, go to the playground and people will say, you know, "Mikey, you want to chase me?" Or he'll just be screaming and just really loud and it's just a whole role. Whereas if I'm with him, you know, . . . just doing our little things, he's incredibly quiet.

The fathers suggested that in being expected to accommodate to other people's expectations and subsequently learning to "tone down" their emotions and "regulate" their behaviors accordingly, there was the risk the boys would lose their vibrancy and versatility and get "locked into" enacting unidimensional and stereotypical roles that leave little room for the full range of their feelings, qualities, and capabilities.

The fathers also noted how the boys' increasing awareness of societal expectations (and of the implications of not meeting other people's expectations) was leading the boys to become guarded in their social interactions and relationships. As Rob's dad described, "Growing up, I think it does change. . . . There's a certain guardedness. . . . Part of it, I suppose, is inevitable. . . . The world can be an indifferent place and . . . I think those [expressive and sensitive] qualities can get easily lost as you grow up." Mike's dad also pointed out that

> You're not in many settings, I think, in your adult life as a man where you do open yourself up. . . . I think that . . . makes it really, really hard for guys to keep that softness going, have these kinds of relationships. . . . I think for boys it's kind of the softer more sensitive part— it seems it's not just the spunk part, you know—[that] gets channeled, at best. . . . Because these boys in this classroom, they're very sensitive, they're emotional, they seem to like each other very much. There's this soft side . . . but somehow they can't show this. I feel like they have to hide it and they've learned *so* fast how to hide it, except for these moments, you know, with my kids it's usually in the car . . . or at nighttime after reading to them. [I'm] sort of lying with them a little bit, and then [they ask] these incredible questions and it opens up. . . . But it's a thing that [Mike] would hide . . . because *here* [at school], he'll be like, . . . "You're embarrassing me," and you know, stuff like that. In this other moment, there'll be this softness. And he has it for Daniel, he has it for Robby, and it's interesting how they, like, [have] these different sides.

Again, the fathers could understand why the boys were becoming more shielded ("the world can be an indifferent place"), but they also recognized the subsequent losses that could result from this adaptation. As the fathers reflected on how the boys were learning to manage their emotions and stifle the expression of feelings and qualities that are deemed inappropriate or bad, they commented on how it was ironic and unfortunate that "in trying to make a good impression," the boys began to "cover up" their innermost qualities, because "Actually, that's what's most appealing" about the boys.

What seemed to concern the fathers the most was that in learning to be appropriate and good, not only were the boys becoming less spontaneous and more "stoic," "controlled," and "calculated" in their self-expression, but also they would eventually "shut down" and "contain" their most vibrant qualities—qualities that enable them to be comfortable and happy with themselves and to develop close connections with other people. For instance, the fathers observed that the boys' voices were becoming more "monotone" as they began to "edit" and "censor" themselves. The fathers also observed that the boys were becoming "desensitized" and "tuning out," whereas they had been emotionally perceptive and socially insightful. The fathers worried that this process wherein the boys were suppressing their sensitivity and concealing their vulnerabilities might be permanent and irreversible. As Rob's dad remarked, "I think there [are] so many situations where you'd have to turn it off, so the question becomes: Can you turn it back on again?" Similarly, Mike's dad added,

> My sense is that boys learn how to, they have to, you do have to shut it down. . . . And you shut it down because, in the public world, you have to be something else. . . . And then I think it becomes very hard, especially when you get good at [shutting it down], [to turn it] back on when you want. And I would hate to see that being repeated, although I think I'm already seeing it.

The fathers knew that this practice of "putting up a front" and "learning to detach" was "a way for [the boys] to interact" that was "relatively easy," "readily available," and "serves as a shield." Nevertheless, the fathers were sad to see the boys retreat from being "out there" and close themselves off—because they valued their sons' spunk, openness, and attunement and also because they knew that "being guarded" in this way is "not conducive to connecting and relating" to others. As the fathers explained, when you "can't let down your guard," it becomes "hard to develop and maintain closeness" and you become vulnerable to other problems.

To offer an example of times when boys are compelled to overcome or set aside their sensitive feelings in order to meet societal expectations, the fathers mentioned the struggles that sometimes occur when parents drop off their kids at the start of each school day. Along with their sons, the fathers were learning how best to handle these necessary separations. As Mike's dad remarked to Rob's dad:

> I'm always curious about Rob because Rob and you, it seems so tender in the morning when you guys are sort of sitting there. . . . You're drawing together and chatting. Although the other day, . . . maybe I had just missed you but . . . [Rob] was crying afterwards and there was something very touching about that. But I know that, . . . like, it's not good that he has a hard time with transitions and eventually it won't be good if he cries when a parent [leaves], but there was something nice.

Although the fathers understood that these separations "should be easy," they also found themselves "wanting to stay close," enjoying the feeling of "needing and being needed" by each other, and being sad when it came time to separate. When Rob's dad considered how he could help Rob not to feel sad about the transition, Carol offered a different take on the situation: "In the circle of this conversation, it occurs to me to ask a question that I don't think I would have thought of before. . . . What's wrong with crying when you leave? I mean, what's wrong with having a moment of intense sadness at that moment? It doesn't immobilize Rob for the whole day." Rather than viewing Rob's sadness as a "failure" or a "problem with transitions," Carol suggested that this was an appropriate response when tenderness and closeness must come to the end— because the sadness was genuine, felt in the moment, and part of the range of normal human emotions. Carol proposed that instead of asking why Rob was sad, we might ask why the fathers were not sad or, if they were sad, why they didn't show it more. Carol also raised the question of whether there is a loss when boys stop feeling sad about separations.

The fathers agreed with Carol's point but could not see a way around the dilemma that boys face. While the fathers appreciated and wanted to encourage their sons' sensitivity and softness, they also knew that boys who revealed such qualities risked being ridiculed and rejected. As Mike's dad recounted, "Boys are taught not to cry . . . it's [considered] a softness. . . . It became a matter of principle. You just didn't do it." Although he added "I don't want that for [my son]," Mike's dad also wondered whether it was possible to help the boys remain "open" without "sacrificing their safety."

> How can we help preserve our sons' vulnerability without putting them at risk for teasing and being beaten up. . . . [On one hand,] we're trying to also express [our sensitivities] and stuff. On the other hand, there is this concern, which is you don't want to put them in a situation where, you know, out in the "real world" they will get trampled.

The fathers could see how boys "get squeezed in the middle" between the need (or desire) to become how boys are expected to be and the desire (or need) to be other things, too. As Rob's dad described, "There's definitely a value on being able to adjust to social situations." However, he observed that Rob "is still also trying to maintain his hold on [his] feelings." And so the fathers tentatively concluded that rather than choosing (or because it may not be possible to choose) between one's external and internal worlds, so to speak, the issue becomes a matter of figuring out which aspects of our selves can stay "out there" in public and which aspects need to become private.

What the Fathers Wanted for Their Sons

For these fathers, being with their sons and observing their sons' experiences at this age, with their peers, and in school led them to recall how they have navigated through their world and their relationships, and what they have given up along the way. Sometimes, this process took the fathers back to places they did not want to go. The fathers remarked on how "kids notice things," and "bring to light" things about people and relationships that "adults may notice, but act like we don't." The fathers noted how "kids cut through adults' layers of control," which allow adults to maintain a certain distance and thereby keep things more manageable. They also observed that in contrast, "kids don't yet have many layers," so their honesty is more apparent. The fathers talked about how there is a simplicity and immediacy to the ways in which kids are present and how, in turn, "kids elicit [adults'] presence." They "get at the heart of you." They "want the real thing." In fact, "it's the only thing they'll respond to." The fathers explained that being with kids meant that "adults have to face it, own up to their feelings and experiences," and how this "can be intense for parents." The fathers described how "Adults' gut responses can get buried" over the course of their socialization and in the process of growing up, "but the knowledge is there," and "kids unravel what's been carefully tucked away."

Despite any uneasiness they may have experienced, these fathers were willing to look back and dig deep, so to speak, in hopes of helping their sons to find better options (as compared to what the fathers felt had been available to them). The fathers suggested that early childhood is an important time for boys in that they are "in the midst" of "learning how it is permissible to express themselves and be with others," and "looking for a way" to engage in relationships that feels comfortable and true to them. As Jake's dad expressed, "I feel as though Jake . . . is at risk kind of, no, that's kind of a strong word . . . but that now is the time that's, like, important for him." The fathers felt that the ways in which adults respond to boys during this critical period could influence how boys make sense of the "pressures and challenges" that they encounter and how they decide "what to do with feelings" in their everyday interactions and relationships.

In thinking about how they could support their sons, the fathers expressed their wish to "join" their sons by "meeting [them] where they're at," "going there with them," "having fun," "hanging out," "sharing," "doing their thing," and "getting to know each other." The fathers knew that being emotionally intimate and available in this way "is exhausting" and "requires patience, energy, and focus," and indicated that one of the biggest challenges for them was learning to "listen without judging." For instance, Jake's dad described a time when

> Jake was talking about women . . . and I was about to go (*in a scolding tone*), "Now Jake," [but] I was [thinking to myself], "Wait. Don't. Let him play it out. Let's try and learn something here." And so I asked him about it and we talked and I was really trying hard not to be judgmental about what it was he was saying. And, uh, it was very effective. It was good. I learned that . . . there were things . . . that he had heard . . . and he didn't quite understand. And so it was useful to talk about. It was very nice.

The fathers found this practice of "reflecting before responding" to their sons' behaviors to be helpful in their efforts to "sympathize and understand" their sons' perspectives and "not to repress, squelch, or discourage" their sons' individuality and spirit. Rob's dad also talked about becoming more aware of his reactions to his sons' behaviors.

> I've been more conscious, sort of conscious of my interactions . . . certainly around discipline things, . . . you know, what makes me come down harder, what do I react more strongly to. . . . I guess the question of how you respond to boys' excess energy and stuff, you know. Being a boy [or man] doesn't make you immune [to] . . . being bothered by the hysteria of it all. . . . When do I feel most bothered by it? Or when do I feel most productive when I interact with them?

Despite having been boys themselves, the fathers did not always know how to handle boys' "excess energy." However, the fathers felt that "with awareness" (e.g., of what pleases or upsets them and why), they could "become more available and receptive" to their sons.

As they considered what lay ahead for their sons, particularly in terms of societal expectations that could constrain or stifle the boys' self-expression, the fathers emphasized the importance of helping boys to "strike a balance" between adapting to expectations (e.g., being "good") and maintaining the ability to express themselves openly and fully (e.g., being "out there"). The fathers' hope was that they could help prepare their sons to be "in the world" while also "preserving boys' range of voices and emotions." To this end, the fathers focused on helping the boys to develop and maintain close relationships in which they could "confide in others," "talk to someone," and feel "acknowledged," "recognized," and "validated." The fathers suggested that boys need "relationships where they feel safe and O.K.," where there is "someone to meet them half way," "someone willing to join them," "so they can read the world in a way that makes sense to them." The fathers emphasized that such relationships were crucial in enabling boys to make choices around remaining open, as opposed to "shutting down." Among the fathers' greatest concerns was that their sons might become "afraid to tell somebody," or feel like they "could never tell anybody," how they are feeling, which could leave them feeling helpless and alone.

With the goal of helping boys develop and maintain the kinds of close relationships that would protect them from (too much) loss and loneliness, the fathers sought to enable their sons to "feel comfortable and confident about who they are," as well as entitled to their vulnerable feelings, so that they could ask for help when they needed it. In reflecting on his own experiences, Jake's dad explained:

> As a kid, it was more that I didn't feel comfortable. . . . It wasn't so much that I was unsupported . . . but that I just was not strong enough . . . [to] say, "Geez, I feel really bad about this." . . . And I want to provide [my sons] with . . . enough emotional strength to go ahead and have those feelings and express them and to get the help they need in dealing with things. . . . "I really didn't feel comfortable doing this. I'm just not going to do it." I'd love for [my sons] to be able to say that.

The fathers also spoke about giving boys "language to express their observations and experiences" as part of teaching boys how to "get along, interact, and relate" with other people.

In their desire to enable their sons to experience a range of feelings and preserve their ability to be "true to themselves," the fathers sought to model this through their own behaviors but wondered what exactly this would or should look like. As the fathers discussed how to do this, Carol asked the fathers to consider, for instance, whether it's O.K. for boys to see men's sadness and anger. Carol acknowledged that it was not always easy to stay with one's feelings—particularly strong or complicated feelings—because we learn to become simplistic for the sake of order, manageability, comfort, predictability, and fitting in, and we know that there are negative consequences for those who fail to simplify and fit in. Carol suggested that as boys (and girls) often learn how to deal with strong feelings by watching how men (and women) deal with strong feelings, the fathers' examples could provide their sons with a sense of how these feelings can play out and be bearable. Carol clarified, however, that she was not suggesting that adults "just do everything for the kids' [sake]." Jake's dad agreed that "It's more a matter of just going ahead and being real. . . . It's like you gotta show [all these feelings] to them so that when they get old, they get that. . . . 'You can think about [it], you can feel it.'"

In addition to modeling a range of feelings, Jake's dad felt it was also important to model mistakes, or try to provide "positive models for screwing things up and it being O.K."

> I used to be bugged a little bit about that stuff . . . thinking, "Oh my God, [my sons are] reading this stuff, they're sucking in all of my anxieties about things." And I've come around a little bit to sort of think that, well, it's an opportunity to talk about my anxieties as a way of—to some extent it helps me—but also as a way for [my sons] to understand that you can have anxieties about things and it's not the end of the world. It's like, "You can be wrong or you can change your mind about what you did." . . . Like, "I got very angry. Getting angry is a problem. That happens to you, right? You get angry. . . . Let's talk about how that feels."

Furthermore, Jake's dad emphasized the importance of modeling resistance— "showing boys how to change or get out of unhappy situations" and teaching them to consider "If they're not where they want to be, how can they do it differently," so that they don't feel that they just have to accept it and stay in it. As Jake's dad described, "There's something about being able to handle your world and being able to sort of, while being pushed around, not be pushed around." The fathers knew that in order to illuminate a broader set of options and alternatives, they needed to learn to let things be "messy, out of control, complex, undecided," to create "space for all of it to happen," and to "just go with it." Although they admitted that this could be a struggle, as they could feel themselves "craving control," especially around intense feelings or "points of anxiety," the fathers strived to offer and to model for their sons a definition of masculinity and success that would enable boys to retain their vitality and humanity (and thereby their close connections with other people) as they negotiated the expectations and pressures that are a part of life and being in the world.

Mothers

When the mothers objected (partly in jest) to being left out of our meetings with the fathers, Carol and I offered to meet with them as well. In these meetings, the mothers seemed to relate to Carol primarily as another mother (of sons), and they shared their stories and observations with her as they might with any other mother in the context of a social gathering or a play date.

What the Mothers Experienced with Their Sons

When Carol asked the mothers about their experiences with their sons, the mothers began by talking about the challenges of trying to understand their sons. For instance, Rob's mom said that

> Sometimes I find that, with Rob, if I think there is something on his mind, . . . [he] can be kind of incoherent in what he [says]. . . . [I'm] trying to figure out, you know, like what is he really saying or is something bothering him, . . . I find it challenging. . . . If I have a concern or something I want to elicit from him, it's tough.

Some of the mothers commented in particular on how boys could be "harder for moms to figure out," whereas girls were found or presumed to be easier (especially for moms) to understand. For instance, Mike's mom—the only mother in this group who has a daughter as well as a son—explained:

> I have a girl who I can just read. I just *know* her. And my son, I don't, it's harder to figure, you know? . . . [My daughter] feels so familiar to me. She responds to things in a way I would respond. . . . Mike responds in a way that I need to compute. I need to figure out. . . . When Mike's upset about something, for example, he won't tell you. He'll, like, if his sister says, "You can't come in my room now," he'll go and he'll make trouble and he'll kind of tweak me and make trouble about something, but it's totally separate from the fact that he's upset that he can't go in his sister's room. So, he'll say, you know, he'll just pick a fight almost, (*mimicking Mike, using a cranky tone*) "I want to watch a video." (*authoritatively*) "Mike, you know you don't watch videos on weeknights." (*grumpily*) "But I want to." And I'll say, (*comprehending*) "Oh,"—and it finally got through to me—I'll say, (*gently*) "Mikey, are you really upset because . . . [your sister] was mean to you, because you can't go in her room?" (*complaining/explaining*) "Well, yeah, she should," and he'll go right into it. But it's

making that connection. And I was kind of spoiled, you know, with [my daughter] it was just so easy.

Although the mothers suggested that it was harder for them to connect with boys than with girls, they also spoke fondly of the boys' "loyalty" and "protectiveness." For instance, Jake's mom talked about Jake getting "into this whole fantasy that he was protecting me. He was like, 'I'm your knight, Mom.' . . . And he'd walk with me in the house and it was like, 'I'm your knight. I'm going to protect you.'" On a similar note, Min-Haeng's mom said that Min-Haeng "is very fierce on my behalf. . . . If he perceives threats [against] me, he gets very angry."

Like the fathers, the mothers also noticed and appreciated the boys' attentiveness and responsiveness, which pleased but sometimes surprised them. They readily recounted anecdotes about their sons "paying close attention to Mom" and "being very aware," "concerned," and "tuned in to how things affect Mom." For instance, Jake's mom told us:

> You know, this morning Jake said, "Mom, your voice sounds kind of happy and it also sounds like you're kind of worried about something." And I said, "Well, I'm happy that it is a beautiful day today but, you're right, I'm worried because I know it's going to be a really busy day for me." So he said, "Well, have a nice day, Mom." So I wish, you know, just this, you know, nobody pays attention to me like that. Jake is just, like, clued in. It's like, "Mom, why did you kind of use that kind of angry voice with me?" . . . He's constantly decoding me.

Mike's mom agreed: "Yeah. And it's almost half conscious for me that I'm feeling tense or stressed or distracted, and Mike will say, 'Mom, why are you sounding angry?' or 'Why are you, are you tired, Mom?'" So, even if the mothers believed that they could understand and identify with girls more easily, they found that "the boys can read us as well," and that the boys were "clearly picking up . . . a lot of the emotional stuff."

In describing their relationships with their sons, the mothers emphasized the intensity and distinctiveness of these connections. For instance, Mike's mom described her love for Mike as being "Very intense. It felt a little different than daughter love. . . . It's this mother-boy thing. . . . There is this compelling-ness about boys. . . . And it's different from [my love for] my daughter. It's different." Also, Min-Haeng's mom spoke about Min-Haeng's ability to be "in the moment" and how this in turn created for her a unique space in which she could do the same.

> I think that's what I really appreciate about this age. And, in my case with Min-Haeng, it's like he still can be completely whatever he is in the moment. And that's what he allows me [to be]. . . . It's a different kind of intimacy, that sense of different intensity. . . . That's what I allow myself to be with him, . . . be completely whatever it is that I'm feeling in the moment, in relation to him, whatever it is that he hooks in me or he generates in me. . . . I think I am more aware of, sort of more than ever before, like being intensely angry, . . . and yet also, with him, having the most intense love, just sort of "no holds barred" kind of love. . . . So I appreciate that about him and what I can be with him and hopefully I am also allowing him to be that way, too.

As Min-Haeng's mom speculated that what enables boys this age to be "in the moment" is that they don't yet "have to be self-conscious" or worry about "external values" and "how they're perceived," she also implied that the boys might not always feel so unencumbered by other people's perceptions and expectations of them.

What the Mothers Saw Boys Coming up Against

Just as the fathers foresaw how pressures for boys to adapt to gendered norms and expectations could undermine the boys' ability to be open and "out there," so the mothers sensed that something was coming that threatened to change their sons and also their relationships with their sons. For instance, the mothers described how in transitioning from preschool and daycare to elementary school, their sons were feeling vulnerable, confused, and anxious as they tried to figure out how to engage with and relate to their peers in this new world of big kids and of expectations for "big boys." Mike's mom described how Mike had adopted a tough guy act to deal with and cover up his fears and vulnerabilities.

> Mike, as you all know, he came into pre-K saying he's going to be a bully. And he's very frightened of school and very frightened of big kids. . . . And

he just happens to be the oldest and the largest [boy] in the class. . . . And he's always been the youngest in pre-school, before [this school]. He was always the baby. And so now, all of a sudden, it's like, "Whoa, I've got some serious power here." And it took him months to work on that. I think now he's settled down a bit, but he's a very intense kid.

As the mothers brought up the boys' interest in guns, Mike's mom explained how for Mike, this too was linked to his wish to feel safe within his changing and expanding world: "Mike wanted to have the guns because then no one would hurt him. . . . And now he is a spaceman because, so he can manage space and the aliens won't get him. . . . For him, it's all about being in charge." Although like the fathers and the other mothers, Mike's mom does not mention the Mean Team (possibly because the boys had managed thus far to keep their boys' club a secret from their parents as well as their teachers), Mike's creation of and leadership position within this boys' club (which shielded him from being betrayed or abandoned) reflect exactly the goals that his mom describes: to appear tough and in control when he in fact felt vulnerable and powerless.

On the topic of how the boys were responding to their peer group culture, Jake's mom found that Jake had been perplexed by and concerned about the dynamics of his peer interactions in this class, which seemed more complicated and esoteric than anything he had experienced previously. However, she also felt that things had gotten better over the course of the school year.

> Well, what was fascinating was, getting into the beginning of the year was like joining a tribe for Jake—that there were so many rules and there were very careful alliances, and people he was supposed to be with, and for certain amounts of time, and conditions. . . . He would come home and he would be very worried that he had broken the rules of the tribe, which was interesting because the year before when he was at the daycare, he didn't worry about that; they were just kind of like this pack of puppies. And so for [Jake], it was this very intense social scene with all these rules and, you know, it's like, "Well, did I do something wrong?" You know, "Why is this so difficult?" "Why is this relationship with this one little buddy so difficult?" You know, "Is this my fault?" and "Have

I done something?" and "What are the rules here?" . . . And what I've seen [recently] is, especially in that part, [Jake] kind of saying, "Yeah, it's not under my control. He's having a bad day. Not my problem," you know, and letting [go] of that and not feeling as though he's always got to have it [figured out]. It's like, you know, "Some people just have bad days sometimes," or "I don't feel like that. You guys can go off and do that. I'm going to come in and do something else."

While the "tribe" and the "very intense social scene with all these rules" that Jake's mom described sound very much like the Mean Team, Jake's mom had also observed similar expectations and dynamics among boys in other contexts:

> And I've seen that in the neighborhood as well. There is a whole pack of kids that kind of runs around. And kind of seeing [Jake] feel like, "O.K., I can do what I wanna do." . . . There is one boy across the street who is kind of quiet and is usually kind of the focus of a lot of antagonism. And it's been really interesting watching Jake dealing with that over the year because in the beginning he was kind of like, "Well, what are the rules? Do I have to be mean to Peter because these kids are being mean to Peter?" . . . And now it's kind of like [Jake saying], "If you are going to be mean to Peter, get out of my yard." And that's been really interesting in terms of [Jake] saying, "No, the pack doesn't rule," and that there are things that are more impor- tant. . . . It's kind of a blossoming of self, which I see.

Although Jake had struggled to make sense of the rules for engagement within his peer group culture (e.g., at school, in his neighborhood), his parents helped him to see that when faced with pressures to go along with the group, he did have a choice and did not have to give in. With his parents' guidance, Jake was learning that he could resist pressures to conform, if that was what he wanted.

When Min-Haeng's mom asked about the "rules of the tribe" and whether Jake "now knows that he doesn't have to toe the line all the time," Jake's mom replied:

> Yeah, [Jake knows] that there is some freedom, that on some of the stuff, he can [resist]. And I think a lot of it was, we would talk about stuff and

we would talk about what was bothering him and ways of dealing with it and—I must admit I'm kind of an individualist—[I'm] like, "Well, if you don't like it, don't do it." You know and hearing it from me and probably from [his older brother] as well—I don't know what kind of conversations [Jake's dad] and [Jake] have had about it—saying, "It's O.K.," and kind of talking about some of these situations. . . . You know, he would come home and he would say, "Why was so-and-so so mad at me today?" It's like, "Well, maybe they are upset because of something else that's going on that isn't school." So it's been an interesting kind of discussion and talking about it. He doesn't tell me as much anymore.

Jake's mom (and dad) gave him the language, permission, and support to follow his instincts, rather than go along with the group ("if you don't like it, don't do it"). However, within his peer group context, where Mike's domineering behaviors were often directed specifically at him and his desire to remain on the Mean Team made him susceptible to its rules, it was not always easy or practical for Jake to do his own thing. In fact, it was during my twenty-second visit—which took place ten days after his mom shared this observation with us—that Jake told me about how he hid his friendships with girls in order to avoid being fired from the boys' Mean Team. Thus, in this setting where conformity was emphasized and deviance punished, Jake had to find other ways to cope with the constraints of his peer group culture and dynamics. For instance, Jake figured out that he could align his behaviors with group norms (e.g., by hiding his friendships with girls) while maintaining his beliefs (e.g., that it was possible for boys to be friends with girls) and continuing (albeit in secret) to be friends with the girls. In this sense, Jake could resist cultural conventions of masculinity even as he adapted to them.

After listening to Jake's mom describe how Jake had found a place for himself among his peers where he could feel comfortable and entitled to make his own decisions, Dan's mom indicated that Dan was also struggling to understand the dynamics of his peer interactions and to engage with his same-sex peers, but that unlike Jake, Dan had not found a way to lessen his confusion or mediate his anxiety. If anything, things had gotten worse.

[Dan's] description is that nobody will play with him and that he is lonely and scared and, if anybody plays with him, it is to beat him up. . . . Now, that doesn't work for me in my mind of . . . this little guy who can talk to all sorts of people, and play all sorts of games. So I haven't a clue. I think he is really vulnerable and that he feels about himself that he is very vulnerable and in some ways, a magnet for attack. And so, when that happens [and he gets attacked], it sort of confirms his original sort of description of himself. But I don't see him as . . . being this little pathetic person. . . . I sort of think of [what Dan tells me] as stories that have hints of truth in them, as opposed to big, long descriptions. So, you know, . . . he is a real puzzle for me. I really don't know. I've seen lots of changes in terms of academics or in terms of who he wants to talk about playing with, but the actual playing with people and being in school, I just sort of see it as sort of crumbling away. So, he wails and howls and won't get dressed in the morning. He refuses to go to school. He refuses to not be attached to my body. I don't see this as a little person who is sort of feeling stronger over the months. . . . So, I don't know. He seems a puzzle to me. He's hurting a lot. That I know.

Responding to this account, Jake's mom shared a similar story:

> We had a period with Jake where, "Nobody ever plays with me at recess. I'm getting beat up at recess," not wanting to come in to school, stomach aches keeping him awake at night and stuff. And we talked to the teachers a couple of times saying, "This level of stress is real. It's not happening at home." But their comments were that, "This is not something we can do anything about."

Jake's mom regarded Jake's refusal to go to school as being linked to his concern about "the rules"—not just of the school but of the boys' peer group culture—and she interpreted Jake's meaning as being "I don't want to go to school. . . . I don't want to keep getting put into this situation where I don't know the rules." When Carol asked her, "What is it, the thing about the rules?" Jake's mom explained:

> For the kids, I think that part of it is being so perceptive of the relationships between people and worrying that they are doing something that is going to hurt somebody, or it's not going to be the right thing to do, or things like that. Jake would worry so much about doing something that would make somebody feel bad. He's very empathic. He would come

home and say, "So-and-so is really unhappy and I don't know why." It was like this sense of "What is it that made this person feel so bad? Is it something I did? I don't know what I [could] have done." So, it's not really rules as in, "Don't step outside of the box," or "Always walk on the right-hand side of the wall." It's kind of like, "How do you say things? How do you do things? Who works with you? What are the social patterns?" And I think that [the boys] expect to be able to pick up on those. They expect the pattern to come out. And sometimes it's not a clear pattern. . . . And the rules were things that [the boys] had to participate in. They weren't given a choice. But it's like being asked to take part in a square dance when you don't where the music is coming from, and you don't know what the steps are, and you are kind of swirled up in it. You don't want to step wrong 'cause you will mess everybody else up.

When Carol observed that, "the concern about being wrong or not getting it right" seemed to have a kind of "intensity for boys . . . and for men," perhaps starting at this age, Jake's mom agreed:

Yeah, I mean there was a lot of peer pressure among the kids in the beginning of the year. A *lot* of peer pressure. . . . Oh, "We don't like girls," or "We are all going to make guns," or "We are all going to do this." And, you know, phrases. And I'd be sitting in the middle of [the classroom during morning drop-off] and it's like, "Oh, that's where that phrase [that I heard Jake say] came from," you know, and it was a kind of a convergence in the way of saying things.

However, Jake's mom also saw evidence of the boys' resistance to peer pressure and felt that towards the end of the school year the boys seemed less compelled to go along with the group.

In the beginning, the boys would go over to the boy corner [*the block corner*] and they would build stuff. What I have seen recently is forays out of it. That, you know, there may be a critical mass of them in the corner but one of them, like Min-Haeng, will be doing something at this table and Rob will be drawing pictures and it'll kind of, they'll kind of move apart. They don't have to gang together for comfort quite as much. It's O.K. for them to mingle with [girls].

As the mothers discussed the boys' peer interactions and how carefully the boys must navigate the rules, expectations, and dynamics, Rob's mom casually remarked that "it makes you realize how much work it is for them just to do what looks [to adults] like fun."

What the Mothers Wanted for Their Sons

The rules for engagement that these boys were encountering in their peer group culture were in many ways an introduction to or initiation into the exciting but sometimes scary world of "boys" and men. While the boys seemed eager to enter that world, they also approached it with some degree of caution and trepidation. As Jake's mom described,

> There was this issue of, you know, Jake says, "I really, really want to do this," and it's like, "Well, do you really?" 'Cause, you know, there's this incredible balance between "I want to do something exciting," and "Hold me back, hold me back!" and this sense of, "If I'm doing something silly, Mom, stop me now." And it's like, "Well, O.K., you said you wanted to do it."

Although the boys wanted to be "big boys" or "real boys" and be out in the world, they also wanted to stay close to their moms and craved the comfort and security of that relationship. As Rob's mom commented, "With Rob, I see a strong wish to still be kept safe and cuddled." Mike's mom agreed, "Oh, Mike, too, . . . is happiest when he's close." Jake's mom added, "What I get is, 'I want you to stay home with me all week.'" Thus, the boys exhibited two age-appropriate desires: the desire to move forward and explore what lies ahead, and the desire to retreat to a familiar and trustworthy haven, where they could find a respite from whatever challenges or threats came their way and also gather strength to face them.

The mothers' wishes were similarly divided. Of course, the mothers wanted their sons to be able to participate and be successful in the world of "boys" and men, but they also hoped their sons could remain close with them. While the boys had not yet come to regard these two things as being mutually exclusive, the mothers seemed to anticipate that it would become increasingly difficult for the boys to do both and that the initiation into "boyhood" or "manhood" would ultimately involve or result in their sons' separations from them. As Mike's mom described:

I treasure these moments with Mike. I mean, in terms of the close-ness. . . . I know also at a certain point he's gonna really want to distance himself. . . . I remember how my brother was with my mother, really pushing her away. She adored him. He was the youngest. I was the old-est. He didn't want her around when he was ten, eleven, twelve.

Jake's mom agreed that there's "this sense that boys become indepen-dent. . . . And boys separate themselves and go off and do their own thing. And they do that exact separation thing; they push their mothers away." As they faced this alleged impending separation that is linked to the boys' emerging masculinity, the mothers wondered how long and in what ways they could "stay connected" with their sons.

When Carol asked the mothers what they think it means to "stay connected," Mike's mom indicated that she felt anxious about discon-nections precisely because she was uncertain as to what kinds of con-nection are possible between mothers and their grown sons.

Well, that's the quest. That, to me, is the quandary [figuring out what it means to stay connected]. Like, how to do that, with all the coding and all the acting out. . . . That's kind of my goal as his parent . . . to stay con-nected. And I don't know what it [will involve], you know, I think it's gonna have lots of variations on the theme [of staying connected]. But the fear is disconnection. That's my fear.

On the topic of staying connected (and fearing disconnection), Rob's mom described her desire to remain physically and emotionally close to her sons and to preserve in her sons the sensitivity and vulnerabil-ity that enable such closeness. Referring to an image of Rob holding a stuffed bunny in one hand and a Lego gun in the other, Rob's mom remarked,

It just sticks with me, 'cause to me it's just, I just want to hold [my sons] close, hold that bunny stage close. I think it is all about the fear of becoming disconnected from them as they get older. . . . I think partly it's hard for me to believe that, you know, that [my sons are] going to really pull apart [from me] and that that's O.K. I mean, I think [the mothers at this meeting] all . . . sort of have the idea that we are going to be different, that we can be close to our sons. . . . But how [do we] negotiate that, you know, with all the necessary distances or the distances that get thrown up because of my temperament, their temperament, the stuff I bring from my upbringing, ideas about what needs to be squashed.

As Min-Haeng's mom pointed out, these mothers wanted their sons to "know how to sort of go through in this life, you know, be a social being." However, they also worried about how that process of becoming socialized was affecting their sons, particularly in terms of the boys' ability to stay connected to their mothers and to maintain their ability to develop close relationships with others.

Like the fathers, the mothers also spoke about what seemed to be at risk as the boys adapted to expectations and pressures to be "boys" and men. For instance, Mike's mom recounted how Mike's dad, Steve, responded to Mike's recent struggles at school.

This year when Mike's had such a hard time, Steve remembered that he used to get really rough and really active as a young boy. And he didn't remember that until he experienced Mike being that way, "I was like that." And it feels so different from now, 'cause [Steve] is *so* not like that. . . . And that is Steve's worse fear. He doesn't want Mike to get squashed like he was. . . . Steve's parents [were] . . . really into acting a certain way. So there was a lot of what I would call repression. And, you know, Mike has such a joie de vivre, just such a spirit. And Steve says, "I must have been like that," you know? And it's hard for Steve to be spirited, to feel spirited. So that's very important to us, but it's a fine [line], it's a slippery slope that spirit, you know? . . . 'Cause [the boys] get in trouble, and the teachers get tired, and, you know, you're called in a lot to "special" meetings.

Although the mothers knew that the boys' "joie de vivre" and "spirit" could sometimes get the boys into trouble, they also valued these qualities and wondered how they might preserve them. As Rob's mom described, "I think there is a pride in boys' 'boy-ness,' too, that I, as a mom, have. . . . That's that compelling aspect [in boys]. . . . There's a certain pride in the way they are too loud, too noisy, too exhausting, too 'boy.'" On a similar note, Jake's mom explained that she felt "proud of my kids' exuberance . . . what my kids are able to do in terms of physical competence and in terms of fantasy play and in terms of being able to express a lot of things." At the same time, she knew that other people's responses could be "very different from mine," and acknowledged how culture shapes people's "sense of what is a well-behaved child."

* * *

In many ways, these fathers and mothers told a familiar story of how the process of growing up and entering the world of "boys" and men can constrain boys' self-expression and hinder their relationships. As I had observed in my study, these parents recognized the boys' desire to connect with others and noticed how the boys were adapting to group norms in their efforts to identify with and relate to each other. The parents also saw how in learning to behave and engage others in ways that are considered "appropriate" and "acceptable" for boys (and men), their sons were finding it necessary to subdue the very qualities that enabled them to connect and be close in their relationships. Yet the parents were unwilling to accept this outcome as inevitable, and so they sought to discover how they could help to sustain their sons' exuberance, openness, and sensitivity without putting them at risk for ridicule and rejection. Conversely, they also sought strategies for helping boys to be socially competent and successful without squelching their humanity.

Although these parents each had their own ideas about how best to support their sons, they seemed to agree on the importance of fostering in boys the sense that they are valued and joined (e.g., by their parents, teachers, and peers) and that they can trust their own instincts as they navigate through their boyhood contexts. In other words, boys' connections—to other people and to their selves—can enable them to think and act of their own volition and to resist overly restrictive norms and expectations when they are faced with pressures to conform. As Jake's mom pointed out, these parents' views, concerns, and goals reflect their culture to some extent, including their middle-class backgrounds and their American upbringings. However, the notion that our interpersonal and intrapersonal connections are necessary to the health and success not only of individuals but also of societies has been acknowledged and emphasized in other cultures as well.

Conclusion

This exploratory study contributes to our understanding of boys and boys' development by examining their experiences of gender socialization at a critical moment of transition when they are under pressure, possibly for the first time, to cover up their relational capabilities and thus shield parts of their humanity. What was remarkable about these boys at this age was that they were in the midst of becoming "boys." In focusing on early childhood (the time before boys' behavioral and learning problems generally set in), my study highlights a period when boys can be open and honest in their relationships but are gradually becoming more guarded and selective about how they express themselves and engage others. By documenting the shift in boys' relational presence during this period in boys' development, my study sheds light on what may be the first—and possibly the most important in the sense that it sets the stage for what follows—in a series of transformations (and losses) associated with boys' socialization and development, and suggests that early childhood may therefore be an obvious time for intervention.

Beyond considering the content of the messages boys receive (e.g., about what makes a boy a "real boy") and the sources of pressure in boys' lives at this age, my study focuses on boys' perspectives to explore how boys themselves make meaning of and respond to messages about masculinity and pressures to conform, and how their choices can influence the ways in which they come to view and feel about themselves—as individuals and as a group—and about their relationships. By presenting the experiences of young boys in their own voices and the world they inhabit as seen through their eyes, my study offers insight into what's going on for boys during this time when they are beginning their formal schooling, encountering gendered expectations that may exceed or differ from what is expected of them at home, and figuring out how they can fit in and get along with their peers. We see, for example, how the boys think about their peer group culture—as epitomized by the Mean Team—and about whether to align with prevailing norms of masculinity in order to identify with and relate to their peers. We also see how the boys' adaptation to group and cultural norms, although intended to enable their connections to others, can ironically involve or result in disconnections from others and from their selves. By emphasizing the boys' perceptions of the obstacles they face and of what their viable options are, this work provides the grounds for thinking about how parents, educators, practitioners, and researchers can respond most effectively to what is often described as a "boy crisis" (i.e., the high incidence of behavioral and learning problems among boys), especially during the transition from early to middle childhood.

In highlighting boys' relational capabilities, the findings from my study counter prevalent stereotypes that depict boys as being emotionally impaired (e.g., out of touch with people's feelings, including their own) and relationally incompetent (e.g., oblivious or unresponsive to interpersonal cues). In most of the literature and discourse on boys and boys' development, their relational capabilities have been underrepresented. When boys' relational capabilities have been addressed in the past, it has been mainly in terms of boys' deficiencies and struggles, particularly in comparison to girls. A couple of reasons why boys' relational capabilities have not been more widely acknowledged are that: 1) we do not expect to see boys' relational capabilities and therefore we do not tend to notice or look for them, 2) boys' relational capabilities are not always apparent, especially in older boys (and men). In cultures and societies where sensitivity to emotions and reliance on relationships are stereotypically associated with femininity, we expect girls and women (not boys and men) to be emotional and to place value on relationships. As these cultures and societies also tend to dichotomize masculinity and femininity, boys often learn to conceal their capacity and desire for close, meaningful connections with other people, which may be viewed as undermining masculinity and regarded as a weakness or liability for boys. As a result, we may be prone to overlook, underestimate, devalue, or discourage in boys and men relational qualities and skills that, despite being more readily acknowledged in girls and women, are in fact *human* strengths.

Over the past fifty years, ideals of femininity and norms of feminine behavior have evolved such that we can now imagine women fulfilling roles and occupying professions that have been traditionally dominated by men. As a result, it has become acceptable and even admirable in many Western cultures and societies for girls and women to display "masculine" qualities (e.g., prioritizing work and being ambitious, competitive, and self-sufficient), and to participate in realms that traditionally have been exclusive to and dominated by boys and men, such as sports and careers that require professional degrees. However, despite these advances for girls and women, there can still be a lot at stake (e.g., status, respect) for boys and men who display "feminine" qualities (e.g., prioritizing relationships and being nurturing, cooperative, and interdependent with others) or who otherwise fail to exhibit "masculine" qualities (e.g., by pursuing interests and occupations that are stereotypically associated with femininity or considered "women's work,"[1] such as childcare and careers in education). While we have been encouraged in recent decades to challenge our assumptions about girls' capabilities and expand our expectations regarding what girls can do and be, the ways in which we view and respond to boys continue to be heavily influenced by conventions of masculinity, including those that have been shown to be outdated or harmful to boys' and men's well-being.[2] So long as the expression of tender feelings and the wish for close relationships involve revealing vulnerability and are linked to femininity, we can expect that boys will continue learning to project a cool indifference (e.g., as evidenced by the claim, "I don't care") that can simultaneously protect their vulnerability from risky exposure and affirm their masculinity.

It is worth reiterating that it was through focusing on boys during early childhood and developing comfortable and trusting relationships with them that I was able to observe and experience the boys' relational capabilities. As Min-Haeng's mom suggested, the younger boys do not yet have to worry (or have just begun to worry) about society's expectations and how they are perceived, and this frees them to share themselves in ways that older boys (and men) have learned can be unsafe.

Expanding Our Understanding of Boys' Nature

The cardinal discovery of my research is that what is often perceived and described as natural to boys is in fact not a manifestation of their nature but an adaptation to cultures that require boys to be emotionally stoic, aggressive, and competitive, if they are to be perceived and accepted as "real boys" (i.e., masculine not feminine). My study indicates that boys have certain relational capabilities that are a part of their human nature and essential to their health and happiness but are at odds with and become less apparent as boys adapt to dominant norms of masculinity. The examples presented in this book illustrate this adaption among boys, its costs, and also boys' resistance to losing aspects of their humanity.

In broadening our views of boys' emotional and relational capacities, this work is part of a more general reconsideration in academic studies of what constitutes human nature and what are the components of our humanity. For example, the primatologist Frans de Waal calls for "a complete overhaul of assumptions about human nature," noting that these assumptions have been skewed by the emphasis on competition and aggression.[3] More specifically, feminist researchers have revealed human development to be a relational process (i.e., occurring primarily through and within relationships) and emphasize the centrality and importance of relationships in the lives and experiences of boys and men[4] as well as girls and women.[5] This emerging new picture of human nature and human development challenges us to re-evaluate the goals and implications of our socialization, and maybe redefine our notions of success.

As for thinking about boys and boys' development in particular, my findings regarding their relational capabilities serve as a reminder that there is more to boys than being "boys," and that boys are not limited to stereotypes that emphasize, for instance, their alleged detachment, disinterest, and deficiency in dealing with relationships. At some level, we may have known (or suspected) this already, as many of us can recall moments when the boys in our lives (e.g., brothers, friends, sons) have shown themselves to crave closeness and to be gentle, caring, sensitive, and considerate. We may have tended to view these examples (or these boys) as exceptions. However, empirical studies indicate that such examples are not deviations from the norm but evidence of a fuller range of what boys want and what boys are capable of knowing and doing in their relationships. We now know that boys (as well as girls) can possess abilities that exceed the narrow and confining roles assigned to them by traditional conceptions of gender. Therefore, in encouraging boys' relational capabilities, we are not teaching boys anything new or asking them to be something they are not (e.g., girls), but helping boys to stay with (or return to) what they know and to develop qualities and skills that they already possess.

Focusing on Boys' Agency and Resistance

Thus far, efforts to support boys' healthy development have focused on trying to change the content and contexts of boys' gender socialization, for instance by deconstructing, redefining, and expanding upon cultural messages about masculinity and by trying to identify and counteract societal pressures to conform to masculine norms that can manifest in boys' everyday lives. However, not all cultural messages about masculinity are inherently problematic. Although certain portrayals of masculinity—such as those emphasizing violence and aggression as pathways to manhood—are obviously troublesome, qualities such as autonomy and self-sufficiency, which are also associated with masculinity, can be admirable and valuable in certain situations. Likewise, not all societal pressures to conform are a negative influence on boys. It is also through their socialization that boys learn to behave appropriately in everyday scenarios and to get along with others. Rather, cultural messages and societal pressures become problematic and can have a negative impact when individuals consequently feel compelled to censor, distort, or misrepresent themselves in order to accommodate to externally imposed standards and ideals that ultimately inhibit their connections to their selves and to others.[6]

It is certainly important and worthwhile to reconsider and, to the best of our ability, update and correct for messages about masculinity that have been found to be detrimental to boys' psychological and physical health and social well-being. However, it is not enough simply to replace one list with another, for instance by steering boys towards an alternate image of masculinity that we believe, for now, to be an improvement. While we should continue in our efforts to identify and offset societal pressures that have been shown to constrain boys' self-expression and hinder boys' relationships, we must also recognize that it is a huge and heroic task to bring about change at the level of society and culture, and that such progress can be slow. Alongside our efforts to change society and culture in general, we can also make a significant impact by supporting individual boys—and that is where family members, teachers, mentors, and other adults who are a part of boys' everyday lives can be particularly effective. My study shows that boys can be perceptive and insightful about their emotional and social worlds and instrumental in determining how messages and pressures associated with their gender socialization can influence their options and their sense of having options. To support boys in ways that are practical and relevant to their lives, we should therefore start by listening to boys and trying to understand their experiences from their perspectives. Boys as young as four and five years old know and can tell us what they need and how we can help, if they feel that we are really interested in what they have to say.

My study of boys at early childhood indicates that the process of becoming "boys"—namely by aligning with prevailing norms of masculinity—is neither automatic nor inevitable. Consistent with Lyn Mikel Brown and Carol Gilligan's findings with adolescent girls[7] and Niobe Way's findings with adolescent boys,[8] notions of agency and resistance are also central in this work with younger boys. That is, the boys in my study similarly showed themselves to be active participants in their learning and development, and demonstrated the ability to resist as well as adapt to gendered norms of behavior within their peer group culture.

Based on the research with adolescent girls, Gilligan distinguished among three meanings of resistance: 1) healthy resistance, as to disease (e.g., fighting off infection), 2) political resistance, as to external constraints on one's liberty (e.g., speaking truth to power, forming underground societies), and 3) psychological resistance, as to the return of repressed knowledge (e.g., in a psychoanalytic sense, refusing to know what one knows).[9] In tracing girls' development, Gilligan identified "a trajectory of resistance whereby a healthy resistance to losses that are psychologically costly turns into a political resistance, which then can become a psychological resistance and manifest, for instance, in signs of dissociation, depression, and eating disorders, as girls make moves that are in one sense adaptive but in another detrimental."[10]

In these terms, the boys' resistance during early childhood appeared to be healthy and political, as these boys had only recently begun to question (and were still struggling to cover up) those parts of their selves that are deemed inappropriate for boys. The extent of each boy's resistance (e.g., against pressures to conform to group and cultural norms) reflected among other things his unique personality and temperament, his social status among his peers, and his access to support (e.g., for his resistance) at home and at school. It should be noted, however, that these boys were not necessarily opposed to displaying "masculine" behaviors. The main issue for these boys was not whether they wanted to act tough or be mean, for example, although their agreement (or disagreement) with particular conventions of masculinity could certainly affect their levels of resistance. The boys also were not merely repelled by pressures to conform. While the boys did not like to be bossed around, they sometimes did not mind doing what other people expected or asked of them, especially if it was what they wanted to do anyway or if they perceived their compliance to serve a worthwhile cause (e.g., preserving group harmony, strengthening bonds of friendship). Rather, the boys' resistance was primarily against silencing their selves, so to speak, and surrendering their sense of agency, and mainly surfaced when other people's expectations obstructed their ability to speak up and decide for themselves how they wanted to act or be.

Considering Social Gains and Relational Costs

Despite the boys' resistance against constraints on their self-expression, most (if not all) of the boys nonetheless learned to accommodate their behaviors (if not their beliefs) to group and cultural norms of masculinity. The boys' adaptation to masculine norms was largely motivated by their desire to identify with and relate to the other boys. Regardless of their actual interests and personal preferences, boys who wished to fit in (e.g., be one of the boys) and be accepted (e.g., be with the boys) learned to conform to, or at least not deviate too much from, culturally prescribed and socially imposed standards for acceptable and desirable behavior for boys. Within cultures of boyhood that emphasize hierarchy, competition, and conformity, a boy's ability to align with conventions of masculinity could be viewed as socially adaptive and even advantageous.

Nevertheless, there was an unavoidable sense of loss as these boys—in their efforts to gain approval from the other boys and to protect themselves against rejection—became more guarded and selective regarding what they revealed about themselves and to whom. Whereas these boys had demonstrated a remarkable ability to be fully present and genuinely engaged in their relationships, they began to nuance their behaviors and modify their styles of relating in ways that could feel contrived and made their relational capabilities more difficult to detect. Although the boys were capable of being open and forthcoming in expressing their thoughts and opinions, they began to shield the qualities that had marked their full presence and genuine engagement in relationships. And as these boys became savvy about how they expressed themselves and strategic about how they related to others, their posturing and pretense gradually detracted from and overshadowed their presence, such that they began to appear disengaged, disinterested, or even defensive in their interactions. That is, they began to look more like stereotypical "boys," or how boys are often said to be.

Moreover, although all of the boys in my study sought to establish and maintain connections and avoid disconnections in their relationships, their adaptation to masculine norms seemed to undermine their efforts.[11] As we saw in Mike's example, the boys' masculine posturing (e.g., projecting an image of toughness, stoicism, and self-sufficiency) could make them seem less approachable. As we saw in Tony's example, the boys could—in their focus on maintaining certain appearances and trying to impress others—neglect to be attentive and responsive in their relationships. As a result, it became more difficult for the boys to engage with and relate to others (and for others to engage with and relate to them) in meaningful ways. As we saw in Rob's example, the boys' conformity to group norms could also lead to frustration when it prevented them from making their own decisions and when the boys subsequently felt compelled to choose between preserving their connections to others (e.g., relationships) and preserving their connections to self (e.g., sense of integrity and individual agency).[12] And as we saw in Jake's example, even the boys' resistance against constraints on their self-expression could hinder their relationships, particularly within contexts where a boy's insistence on being open, honest, and outspoken in his relationships was more likely to be regarded as a threat than as a boon to the status quo. In sum, these boys' examples illustrate how presence depends on relationships and relationships depend on presence, and how the shift in these boys' relational presence—towards appearing indifferent, inaccessible, individualistic, and insincere—could therefore decrease the boys' chances of developing the kinds of close relationships that they sought and that have been linked to psychological health.[13]

Fortunately, this transformation wherein the boys were becoming "boys" was neither complete nor irreversible. It was not that these boys were present and then not present, nor that they were in relationship and then out of relationship; these boys continued to be both present and in relationship. Despite becoming obscured as the boys shifted from presence to pretense via posturing in their behaviors and interactions, the boys' relational capabilities remained intact and were not lost. For example, in a study that I conducted to explore adolescent boys' experiences of gender socialization, I saw many of the same qualities that impressed me about the younger boys, such as the capacity for thoughtful self-reflection and deep interpersonal understanding.[14] Although the adolescent boys were even more adept than the younger boys at adjusting their attitudes, behaviors, and relational styles to align with masculine norms (and could therefore appear emotionally reserved or detached), they were nonetheless capable of being fully present and genuinely engaged in their relationships, and could be very perceptive and articulate in describing their experiences. Despite learning to put up a front, so to speak, and deny their "feminine" desire for close relationships, the adolescent boys continued, albeit with greater caution, to seek closeness within their relationships.[15]

Similarly, studies of adolescent sexuality and adolescent friendships—on which I collaborated with Deborah Tolman and Niobe Way, respectively— reveal discrepancies (and tensions) that can exist between prevailing norms of masculinity and the realities of boys' capabilities and instincts. Tolman's research indicates, for example, that boys seek emotional as well as physical intimacy in their romantic and sexual relationships, even though they feel expected, as boys, to focus and place greater value on physical intimacy.[16] Likewise, Way's research emphasizes that boys' need and wish for emotional closeness in their same-sex friendships persists, even as they realize that their chances of establishing and sustaining such connections are decreasing. Together, these studies highlight boys' relational strengths (and vulnerabilities) and provide evidence that, despite becoming less apparent during early childhood, the capacity and desire for emotionally close relationships that researchers observed in boys at infancy carry forth through adolescence, at least.[17]

Furthermore, Way's findings reveal patterns in boys' resistance during adolescence that correspond to my observations of boys' resistance during early childhood, and thus suggest a possible developmental trajectory. My research shows how—along with their relational capabilities—boys at early childhood initially display a healthy resistance against constraints on their self-expression but soon learn—for the sake of identifying with and relating to their same-sex peers—to align with group and cultural norms of masculinity. Way suggests that, as a result of this accommodation, boys during middle childhood often resemble gender stereotypes in the sense that they may seem oblivious and/ or indifferent within their social interactions and relationships. Way observes, however, that boys' healthy resistance to conventions of masculinity and evidence of boys' emotional attunement resurface at early adolescence, around the onset of puberty when changes in their bodies awaken feelings of vulnerability and prompt boys to seek solace within their close friendships.[18] Way concludes that, as close relationships become less available in late adolescence and adulthood[19] and pressures to adhere to masculine norms of behavior increase, boys' (and men's) vulnerability once again goes underground.

Supporting Boys' Healthy Development

My study shows how, beginning at early childhood, boys learn to project an image of masculinity that is very familiar but may misrepresent them. This image is familiar because it centers on conventions of masculinity that, despite being archaic, continue to be valued and celebrated in boys and men today. In order to project this popularized image of masculinity, the boys learned for example to act tough, adopt a competitive or distrustful attitude, and denounce femininity. Moreover, as the boys came to view overt expressions of affection, care, and concern as feminine (and therefore a threat to their masculinity), they began to cover up their relational capabilities, including their capacity and desire for closeness and intimacy, and to shift their relational presence. However, this image of masculinity that boys learn to project also misrepresents boys because, despite learning to conceal qualities and behaviors that are deemed feminine, the boys did not necessarily lose these qualities (as popular discourse on boys suggests); nor did they feel less inclined towards these behaviors. Rather, boys' socialization towards cultural constructions of masculinity that are defined in opposition to femininity seems mainly to force a split between what boys know (e.g., about themselves, their relationships, and their world) and what boys show. In the process of becoming "boys," these boys essentially were learning to dissociate their outward behaviors from their innermost thoughts, feelings, and desires. Whereas these boys had demonstrated the ability to say what they meant and mean what they said, they came to understand through the course of their socialization that they could separate their behaviors from their beliefs. And if their behaviors did not need to reflect their beliefs, then it became possible for the boys' words and actions to mean less, or to become meaningless.

These findings remind us that, in our efforts to support boys' healthy development, the goal is not solely nor even necessarily to change boys' behaviors, unless boys risk endangering themselves or others. There are reasons, even good ones, why boys act the ways they do. Although boys may adopt certain "strategies of disconnection"[20] that can hinder the close relationships they seek, these strategies are likely to remain in place so long as boys perceive them to be useful for adapting to their boyhood culture and coping with its challenges and constraints, or until they perceive equally viable and effective alternatives to be available to them. Rather, it may be more practical and productive to help raise boys' awareness and foster boys' critical reflection so that they can make more informed decisions about how they want to be and act. While boys may learn through their socialization to regulate their self-expression and modify their behaviors and relational styles according to prevailing norms of masculinity, they can preserve their sense of integrity by remaining mindful of their compromises and by continuing to realize (even if they do not always express) a full range of thoughts, feelings, and desires. If boys can maintain their connections to their own perceptions, experiences, and opinions, then their adaptation to masculine norms need not preclude their resistance nor imply their surrender.

The greater risk for boys in coming up against pressures to conform is not that they will compromise themselves, for instance by aligning their behaviors with masculine norms, but that they will *over*-compromise themselves by losing sight of what they know, what they want, and how they experience themselves to be. Although there is a tendency in our culture and society to regard compromise as negative (e.g., because it implies weakness and defeat), compromise is often a necessary and inevitable part of our everyday interactions. We must compromise because we cannot always have things our way. We learn to compromise because doing so enables us to get along with other people and have relationships with them. Over-compromise, however, happens when we become so focused on and accustomed to trying to be what other people expect of us that we automatically override or forfeit our own desires and will. What distinguishes compromise from over-compromise is our ability to remain aware of and conscientious about our choices, particularly our sacrifices. Over-compromise is dangerous because it undermines our connections to our selves (e.g., our self-awareness), which can in turn hinder our ability to connect with others (e.g., in future as well as current relationships). Conversely, when we can retain our beliefs—even as we accommodate our behaviors to other people's expectations or wishes—we prevent compromise from becoming over-compromise and improve our chances of establishing healthy and satisfying relationships.

In turn, our connections to others can strengthen our connections to our selves. Research on resilience has shown that the single best protector against both psychological and social risk is having access to at least one close, confiding relationship in which one feels truly known, accepted, and valued.[21] Characterized by intimacy and mutuality, such relationships are a potential source for understanding, validation, and care, and are linked to social adjustment and competence for boys as well as girls.[22] Through developing trusting and respectful relationships with the boys in our lives, we can help boys to value and acknowledge their relational capabilities, which they may otherwise learn to discount or overlook. We can also offer and model for them definitions of maturity, masculinity, health, and success that will enable them to remain grounded in their self-knowledge (e.g., as they encounter societal pressures to conform to group and cultural norms), and to form relationships that will sustain rather than constrain them. We must also remember that, while we may wish to protect boys from harmful influences and hurt feelings, it is not possible to do so completely or consistently. There is a Native American proverb that suggests: Serenity is not freedom from the storm but peace within the storm. We cannot shield boys from gendered expectations and socialization pressures that can limit their options and restrict their movement. However, we can teach and enable boys to weather the storm, so to speak, by helping them to identify sources of strength in their selves, draw support from protective relationships, and thereby navigate confidently and proficiently through the obstacles and challenges that they are likely to encounter in schools and beyond.

ACKNOWLEDGMENTS

I wish to express my heartfelt thanks and appreciation to:

Carol Gilligan—my extraordinary teacher, mentor, and friend—who provided unwavering support, generously offered her time and brilliant insights, and instilled in me the faith and confidence I needed to see this project through to fruition. I cannot thank her enough for all that she has taught, given to, and shared with me. I have the utmost respect for her tremendous intellect and endless admiration for her courage. I will always be in awe of her ability to see straight to the heart of things, and I am deeply grateful for her love.

The boys who participated in my studies for allowing me into their world and teaching me what they knew; the boys' parents for welcoming Carol and me into their lives; and the teachers and administrators—especially Ginny Kahn and Richard Perry—at the "Friends School" for inviting us to be a part of their wonderful community.

Niobe Way for her helpful editorial suggestions and big-sisterly advice, which provided me with some direction when I could not see the way forward.

Michael Kimmel for his amazing leadership, benevolent spirit, and enduring influence.

Marcelo and Carola Suárez-Orozco, Renée Spencer, Sarah Shaw, and Tatiana Bertsch for their wisdom and warmth during the course of this study and beyond.

Jennifer Hammer, Constance Grady, and Dorothea Halliday at New York University Press for patiently and graciously guiding me through the publication process. Also, the anonymous reviewers and copyeditor of my manuscript for their thoughtful comments and recommendations.

Allyson Pimentel and Michelle Porche for kindly reading multiple rough drafts and providing much-appreciated feedback and encouragement over the years.

My teachers—including Frances Sexauer, Jean Parks, Mike Hartman, Ann Busenkell, Richard E. Snow, and Ray McDermott—for believing in my abilities and nurturing my strengths.

My family and friends—especially John and May Chu, Kathy Teng, Eddie Chu, Rich and Jeanne Jacobson, Wendy Wu, Elizabeth Beatty, and Therese Madden—whose integrity, magnanimity, and humility inspire me daily.

Matthew and Xander—my angels—who enable me to stay focused on and grounded in the things that matter most.

NOTES

NOTES TO THE FOREWORD

1. Donald Moss, *Thirteen Ways of Looking at a Man* (New York: Routledge, 2012), 140.

2. Ibid., 141.

3. Carol Gilligan, *The Birth of Pleasure: A New Map of Love* (New York: Vintage, 2003), 67–74.

4. Carol Gilligan, *Joining the Resistance* (Cambridge, UK: Polity Press, 2011), 8.

5. Niobe Way, *Deep Secrets: Boys' Friendships and the Crisis of Connection* (Cambridge: Harvard University Press, 2011).

6. Moss, *Thirteen Ways of Looking at a Man.*

7. Anne Frank, *The Diary of Anne Frank: The Revised Critical Edition,* prepared by the Netherlands Institute for War Documentation, translated by Arnold J. Pomerans and B. M. Mooyaart-Doubleday and Susan Massotty (New York: Doubleday, 2003), 719.

NOTES TO THE INTRODUCTION

1. Carol Gilligan, *The Birth of Pleasure: A New Map of Love* (New York: Vintage Books, 2002).

2. Judy Yi-Chung Chu, "Learning What Boys Know: An Observational and Interview Study with Six Four-Year-Old Boys" (Ed.D. diss., Harvard Graduate School of Education, 2000).

3. Lev S. Vygotsky, *Mind in Society* (Cambridge: Harvard University Press, 1978).

4. Erik Erikson, *Childhood and Society* (New York: W. W. Norton and Company, 1950).

5. Carol Gilligan, Lyn M. Brown, and Annie G. Rogers, "Psyche Embedded: A Place for Body, Relationships and Culture in Personality Theory," in *Studying Persons and Lives,* eds. A. I. Rabin, R. A. Zucker, R. Emmons, and S. Frank (New York: Springer, 1990), 86–94.

6. Carol Gilligan, "Centrality of Relationship in Human Development: A Puzzle, Some Evidence, and a Theory," in *Development and Vulnerability in Close Relationships,* eds. G. Noam and K. Fischer (Hillside, NJ: Erlbaum, 1996), 237–61.

7. Lyn M. Brown and Carol Gilligan, "Listening for Self and Relational Voice: A Responsive/Resisting Reader's Guide" (paper presented at the annual meeting for the American Psychological Association, Boston, MA, 1990); Carol Gilligan, Renee Spencer, Katherine M. Weinberg, and Tatiana Bertsch, "On the Listening Guide: A Voice-Centered, Relational Method," in *Qualitative Research in Psychology: Expanding Perspectives in Methodology and Design*, eds. P. M. Camic, J. E. Rhodes, and L. Yardley (Washington, DC: American Psychological Association Press, 2003).

8. Pseudonyms are used for the school, teachers, and students.

9. This study was part of the "Strengthening Healthy Resistance and Courage in Girls" project and is described in Carol Gilligan, Annie G. Rogers, and Normi Noel, "Cartography of a Lost Time: Women, Girls, and Relationships" (paper presented at the Lilly Endowment Conference on Youth and Caring, Miami, FL, 1992).

10. These researchers included Lyn M. Brown, Nona P. Lyons, Annie G. Rogers, Amy M. Sullivan, Mark Tappan, Jill M. Taylor, Deborah L. Tolman, and Janie V. Ward.

11. Lyn M. Brown and Carol Gilligan, *Meeting at the Crossroads: Women's Psychology and Girls' Development* (Cambridge: Harvard University Press, 1992); Carol Gilligan, *In a Different Voice: Psychological Theory and Women's Development* (Cambridge: Harvard University Press, 1982); Carol Gilligan, Nona P. Lyons, and Trudy J. Hanmer, eds., *Making Connections: The Relational Worlds of Adolescent Girls at Emma Willard School* (Cambridge: Harvard University Press, 1990); Carol Gilligan, Annie G. Rogers, and Deborah L. Tolman, eds. *Women, Girls, and Psychotherapy: Reframing Resistance* (New York: Harrington Park Press, 1991); Jill M. Taylor, Carol Gilligan, and Amy M. Sullivan, *Between Voice and Silence: Women, Girls, Race, and Relationships* (Cambridge: Harvard University Press, 1995).

12. Carol Gilligan, "Joining the Resistance: Psychology, Politics, Girls, and Women." *Michigan Quarterly Review* 24, no. 4 (1990): 501–36. Presented as the Tanner Lecture on Human Values, University of Michigan, March 16, 1990, and reprinted in *The Female Body*, ed. Laurence Goldstein (Ann Arbor, MI: University of Michigan Press, 1991); Gilligan, *Joining the Resistance.*

13. Carol Gilligan, personal communication, January 3, 2013.

14. Ibid.

15. Ibid.

16. Judy Y. Chu, "A Relational Perspective on Boys' Identity Development," in *Adolescent Boys: Exploring Diverse Cultures of Boyhood*, eds. N. Way and J. Y. Chu (New York: New York University Press, 2004), 78–104.

17. Daniel N. Stern, *The Interpersonal World of the Infant: A View from Psychoanalysis and Developmental Psychology* (London: Karnac, 1985).

18. Colwyn Trevarthan, "The Concept and Foundations of Infant Intersubjectivity," in *Intersubjective Communication and Emotion in Early Ontogeny,* ed. S. Braten. (Cambridge: Cambridge University Press, 1998), 1–14; Edward Z. Tronick,

"Emotions and Emotional Communication in Infants," *American Psychologist* 44, no. 2 (1989): 112–19.

19. Katherine M. Weinberg and Edward Z. Tronick, "Infant Affective Reactions to the Resumption of Maternal Interaction after the Still-Face," *Child Development* 67, no. 3 (1996): 905–14.

20. Victor J. Seidler, "Rejection, Vulnerability, and Friendship," in *Men's Friendships: Research on Men and Masculinities*, ed. P. Nardi (Newbury Park, CA: Sage Publications, Inc., 1992), 15–34.

21. Judith Jordan, Alexandra G. Kaplan, Jean Baker Miller, Irene Stiver, and Janet L. Surrey, *Women's Growth in Connection: Writings from the Stone Center* (New York: The Guilford Press, 1991).

22. Way, *Deep Secrets.*

23. Stuart Miller, *Men and Friendship* (Los Angeles, CA: Jeremy P. Tarcher, Inc., 1992).

24. Carol Gilligan, *In a Different Voice.*

25. The best known of these books include: William S. Pollack, *Real Boys: Rescuing Our Sons from the Myths of Boyhood* (New York: Random House, 1998); Daniel Kindlon and Michael Thompson, *Raising Cain: Protecting the Emotional Life of Boys* (New York: Ballantine Books, 1999); Michael Gurian, *The Wonder of Boys: What Parents, Mentors, and Educators Can Do to Shape boys into Exceptional Men* (New York: Putnam, 1996).

26. Jean Piaget, *The Construction of Reality in the Child* (New York: Basic Books, 1954).

27. See Way, *Deep Secrets*, for a more comprehensive review of recent studies (and their limitations) of boys (43–53) and masculinity (58–67).

28. See Way, *Deep Secrets*, for an excellent account of studies of resistance in girls (67–70) and in boys (70–74).

29. Carlos E. Santos, Niobe Way, and Diane Hughes, "Linking Masculinity and Education among Middle-School Students" (paper presented at the Society of Research on Child Development, March 2011).

30. Carlos E. Santos, *The Missing Story: Resistance to Ideals of Masculinity in the Friendships of Middle School Boys* (Ph.D. diss., New York University, 2010).

31. Jean Anyon, "Intersections of Gender and Class: Accommodation and Resistance by Working-Class and Affluent Females to Contradictory Sex-Role Ideologies," *Journal of Education* 166, no. 1 (1984): 25–48; Lyn M. Brown and Carol Gilligan, *Meeting at the Crossroads*; Janie V. Ward, "Raising Resisters: The Role of Truth Telling in the Psychological Development of African American Girls," in *Urban Girls: Resisting Stereotypes, Creating Identities*, eds. B. J. Leadbeater and N. Way (New York: New York University Press, 1996), 85–99.

32. A small but growing body of research that indicates boys' resistance to gender and racial stereotypes includes: Gary Barker, *Dying to Be Men* (New York: Routledge, 2005); Gilberto Conchas and Pedro Noguera, "Understanding the Exceptions: How Small Schools Support the Achievement of Academically Successful Black Boys," in *Adolescent Boys: Exploring Diverse Cultures of Boyhood*, eds. N. Way and J. Y. Chu (New York: New York University Press, 2004),

317–38; Stephen Frosh, *Young Masculinities* (England: Palgrave Macmillan, 2001); Michael Reichert and Sharon Ravich, "Defying Normative Male Identities: The Transgressive Possibilities of Jewish Boyhood," *Youth and Society* 20 (2009), 1–26; Deborah L. Tolman, Renée Spencer, Tricia Harmon, Myra Rosen-Reynoso, and Meg Striepe, "Getting Close, Staying Cool: Early Adolescent Boys' Experiences with Romantic Relationships," in *Adolescent Boys: Exploring Diverse Cultures of Boyhood*, eds. N. Way and J. Y. Chu (New York: New York University Press, 2004), 235–55.

33. Carol Gilligan, "Remembering Iphigenia: Voice, Resonance, and the Talking Cure," in *The Inner World in the Outer World: Psychoanalytic Perspectives*, ed. E. Shapiro (New Haven: Yale University Press, 1997), 143–68. Carol Gilligan, *Joining the Resistance.*

34. Jean Piaget, *The Construction of Reality in the Child* (New York: Basic Books, 1954).

35. Lawrence Kohlberg, "Moral Stages of Moralization: The Cognitive-Developmental Approach," in *Moral Development and Behavior: Theory, Research, and Social Issues*, ed. T. Lickona (New York: Holt, Rinehart, and Winston, 1976).

36. Erik Erikson, "Life cycle," in *International Encyclopedia of the Social Sciences*, vol. 9, ed. D. L. Sillis (New York: Crowell, Collier, 1968), 298.

37. Sigmund Freud, "Family Romances," in *The Freud Reader*, trans. P. Gay (New York: W.W. Norton and Company, 1908/1989), 297–300.

38. Eleanor E. Maccoby, "Gender and Relationships: A Developmental Account," *American Psychologist* 45, no. 4 (1990): 513–20.

39. Michael Rutter and Norman Garmezy, *Stress, Coping, and Development in Children* (Baltimore: Johns Hopkins University Press, 1983).

40. L. A. Sroufe, "Ritalin Gone Wrong," *New York Times*, January 28, 2012.

41. Heinz Kohut, *The Analysis of the Self* (New York: International Universities Press, 1971).

NOTES TO CHAPTER 1

1. The overarching narrative of this book is written in the past tense. The examples are written in the present tense.

NOTES TO CHAPTER 2

1. Judy Y. Chu and Niobe Way, "Presence in Relationship: A New Construct for Understanding Adolescent Friendships and Psychological Health," *THYMOS: Journal of Boyhood Studies* 3, no. 1 (2009): 50–73.

NOTES TO CHAPTER 3

1. Margaret Mead, *Male and Female: A Study of the Sexes in a Changing World* (New York: Morrow Quill, 1949).

2. Michael Kimmel, *Guyland: The Perilous World Where Boys Become Men* (New York: HarperCollins Publisher, 2008).

3. Sandra L. Bem, "Enculturation and Self-Construction: The Gendered Personality," in *The Lenses of Gender* (New Haven, Yale University Press, 1993), 138–59.

4. Studies of family functioning show that even with dual-earner, equivalent employment heterosexual couples, childcare and housework still falls primarily on the woman. See Dana Vannoy-Hiller and William W. Philliber, eds., *Equal Partners: Successful Women in Marriage* (Newbury Park, CA: Sage Publications, 1989), 46.

5. Freud, "Family Romances," 297–300.

6. Lucia is referring to the title of Vivian G. Paley's book, *"You Can't Say, 'You Can't Play,'"* (Cambridge, MA: Harvard University Press, 1993). She gives me a knowing smile as she says this because she knows I am familiar with this title.

7. The boys use "Black Knight" and "Dark Knight" interchangeably.

8. As cited in Allyson M. Pimentel, "Supporting Boys' Resilience: A Dialogue with Researchers, Practitioners, and the Media" (report from a meeting for the Ms. Foundation for Women, New York, NY, November 2003).

NOTES TO CHAPTER 4

1. The boys use "Nice Team" and "Good Team" interchangeably to refer to the girls' team.

2. A fuller description of this example appears in chapter 5.

3. Mike's mom said that when Mike learned that Min-Haeng would be attending a different school the following year, Mike asked to switch schools as well so that he could be with Min-Haeng. When Mike's mom explained that there would be other ways for them to be together, Mike cried and became "inconsolable." Incidentally, the woman who helped to transcribe my data misheard Mike's mom as saying that Mike cried and became "out of control," which exemplifies the tendency among adults to interpret boys' behaviors through a stereotyped lens (e.g., assuming that a boy would deal with sad feelings by acting out in anger).

4. Baby catching became a popular theme in the boys' play after Rob's baby brother was born and (like all newborns) made things a bit more challenging at home.

5. A fuller description of this interaction appears in chapter 2.

6. Vivian G. Paley, *Boys and Girls: Superheroes in the Doll Corner* (Chicago, The University of Chicago Press, 1984); Barrie Thorne, "Boys and Girls Together . . . But Mostly Apart: Gender Arrangements in Elementary School," in *Men's Lives*, eds. M. S. Kimmel and M. A. Messner (Boston: Allyn and Bacon, 1998), 87–100.

7. Raewyn W. Connell, "Teaching the Boys," *Teacher's College Review* 98, no. 2 (Winter 1996): 206–35. Barrie Thorne, *Gender Play: Girls and Boys in School* (New Jersey, Rutgers University Press, 1993).

8. Ruth G. Goodenough, "Small Group Culture," in *Jossey-Bass Reader on Gender in Education* (Jossey-Bass Education Series, 2002), 217.

NOTES TO CHAPTER 5

1. Charles G. Lord, Lee Ross, and Mark R. Lepper, "Biased Assimilation and Attitude Polarization: The Effects of Prior Theories on Subsequently Considered Evidence," *Journal of Personality and Social Psychology* 37, no. 11 (1979) 2098–2109.

2. Robert Rosenthal and Lenore Jacobson, *Pygmalion in the Classroom: Teacher Expectation and Pupils' Intellectual Development*, expanded ed. (New York: Irvington, 1992).

3. Lee Ross and Richard E. Nisbett, *The Person and the Situation: Perspectives of Social Psychology*, 2nd ed. (Great Britain: Pinter and Martin Ltd., 2011).

4. Deborah Belle, "Gender Differences in Children's Social Networks and Supports," in *Children's Social Networks and Social Supports*, ed. D. Belle (Oxford, England: John Wiley and Sons, 1989), 173–85.

5. This is similar to the dilemma that girls faced at adolescence, as described by Carol Gilligan and her colleagues from the Harvard Project on Women's Psychology and Girls' Development.

NOTES TO CHAPTER 6

1. The four meetings with the fathers took place in February, April, May, and July of the boys' pre-Kindergarten year. Jake's father attended all four meetings; Mike's, Rob's, and Dan's fathers each attended three of the meetings; Min-Haeng's father attended one meeting; and Tony's stepfather did not attend any of the meetings.

2. The two meetings with the mothers took place in April and May of the boys' pre-Kindergarten year. Jake's, Rob's, Min-Haeng's, and Dan's mothers attended both of the meetings, and Mike's mother attended one of the meetings.

3. Of the fathers who attended these meetings, only Mike's dad had a daughter; the others only had sons. Therefore, comparisons between daughters and sons are not made.

NOTES TO THE CONCLUSION

1. Michael S. Kimmel, *The Gendered Society* (New York: Oxford University Press, 2008).

2. Michael A. Messner, "Barbie Girls Versus Sea Monsters: Children Constructing Gender," *Gender and Society* 14, no. 6 (2000) 765–84.

3. Frans de Waal, *The Age of Empathy* (New York: Three Rivers Press, 2010).

4. Chu, "A Relational Perspective"; Way, *Deep Secrets*.

5. Carol Gilligan, *Joining the Resistance*.

6. Joseph H. Pleck, "The Gender Role Strain Paradigm: An Update," in *A New Psychology of Men*, eds. R. F. Levant and W. S. Pollack (New York: Basic Books, 1995) 11–32.

7. Lyn M. Brown and Carol Gilligan, *Meeting at the Crossroads*; Gilligan, "Remembering Iphigenia."

8. Way, *Deep Secrets*.

9. Gilligan, "Joining the Resistance." Carol Gilligan, personal communication, January 3, 2013.

10. Carol Gilligan, personal communication, January 3, 2013.

11. Pleck, "The Gender Role Strain Paradigm."

12. In studies of adolescent girls, Gilligan observed this choice between self and relationships to be a "choice-less choice," or a lose-lose situation, because either way the individual ends up feeling alone.

13. Harry S. Sullivan, *The Interpersonal Theory of Psychiatry* (New York: W. W. Norton and Company, 1953).

14. My study of adolescent boys was conducted prior to my study of boys at early childhood. See Chu, "A Relational Perspective on Boys' Identity Development," in *Adolescent Boys: Exploring Diverse Cultures of Boyhood*, eds. N. Way and J. Y. Chu (New York: New York University Press, 2004), 78–104.

15. Judy Y. Chu, "Adolescent Boys' Friendships and Peer Group Culture," in *Exploring Close Friendships among Adolescents,* volume eds. N. Way and J. Hamm, in *New Directions for Child and Adolescent Development,* series ed. W. Damon (2005), 7–22.

16. Tolman, Spencer, Harmon, Rosen-Reynoso, and Striepe, "Getting Close, Staying Cool," 235–255.

17. Chu, "Adolescent Boys' Friendships and Peer Group Culture."

18. Way, *Deep Secrets*.

19. Stuart Miller, *Men and Friendship.*

20. Jean B. Miller and Irene Stiver, "Movement in Therapy: Honoring the "Strategies of Disconnection" (work in progress at Wellesley Centers for Research on Women, Wellesley, MA, 1994).

21. Michael D. Resnick et al., "Protecting Adolescents from Harm: Findings from the National Longitudinal Study on Adolescent Health," *Journal of the American Medical Association* 278, no. 10 (1997): 823–32.

22. Duane Buhrmester, "Intimacy of Friendship, Interpersonal Competence, and Adjustment during Preadolescence and Adolescence," *Child Development* 61 (1990): 1101-1111.

Judy Y. Chu is Affiliated Faculty in the Program in Human Biology at Stanford University, where she teaches a course on Boys' Psychosocial Development. She received her doctorate in Human Development and Psychology at Harvard Graduate School of Education. She is co-editor of *Adolescent Boys: Exploring Diverse Cultures of Boyhood* (NYU Press, 2004). She is also the mother of a ten-year-old boy.